UNDER SIEGE

ARTHUR AUGHEY

Under Siege

Ulster Unionism and the
Anglo-Irish Agreement

THE BLACKSTAFF PRESS
BELFAST

First published in Ireland in 1989 by
The Blackstaff Press Limited
3 Galway Park, Dundonald, Belfast BT16 0AN, Northern Ireland

First published in Great Britain in 1989 by
C. Hurst and Co. (Publishers) Ltd.
38 King Street, London WC2E 8JT

Printed in Great Britain

British Library Cataloguing in Publication Data

Aughey, Arthur
Under siege: Ulster Unionism and the Anglo-Irish Agreement.
1. Northern Ireland. Government. Treaties: Anglo-Irish Agreement
I. Title
341.4'2

ISBN 0-85640-428-4

To my Parents

PREFACE AND ACKNOWLEDGEMENTS

In the introduction to his book *Northern Ireland: The Orange State*, Michael Farrell claimed that he had allowed ''events to speak for themselves''. That is a classic example of an author trying to mislead his readers with a spurious assertion of authenticity. Of course, events can never speak for themselves. Events must be judged, assessed and interpreted, and it is absurd to believe that they can have any status apart from that effort of the intellect. Despite his protestation of dumb objectivity, Farrell went on to argue that his book was ''not an impartial book''.[1] Unaware of this contradiction, he proceeded to judge, assess and interpret the events of Northern Ireland's history in such a way as to advocate the central propositions of Irish nationalism, albeit an Irish nationalism wrapped up in a tortuous jargon inherited from Third World Marxism. Farrell is entitled to do this, but certainly not to proclaim that this is the only conceivable understanding of those events.

This book makes no claim to allow events to speak for themselves. Nor does it make any pretence to be impartial. It is designed to provoke a new debate about the state in Northern Ireland. It is an attempt to address the experiences of a particular phase of Ulster politics – at the time of writing, the most recent – from a particular perspective on the Union, a perspective that today seems to find little favour in either of the two main unionist parties. The book takes a clear stand on what has become known, unfortunately, as the ''national question'', although for unionists the question is not about nationality; it is about the state. For them it is really a political question which has nothing to do with the crypto-racism of Sinn Fein or the ethno-geographical determinism of modern constitutional nationalism. In terms of argument about the state, this book does not conceal its advocacy of full and equal citizenship within the United Kingdom. Since that political demand is distinct from considerations of nationality and ethnicity, there is not necessarily any incompatibility between it and the recognition of an extensive catholic ''ethos'' in Northern Ireland.

Under the old Stormont regime, unionists relied on the fact of power to do their talking for them. Political argument of the abstract kind was left up to those – nationalists – who were excluded from power in Northern Ireland. That inheritance of political inarticulateness, an inheritance which almost constitutes a form of apoliticism, has frustrated attempts to address adequately the current nationalist challenge to the Union. There has been a penchant on the part of unionist politicians for activist bravado coupled with a reluctance to engage in serious strategic thought.

vii

Chapter 1 is a brief essay in review of some of the positive features of the unionist political culture, features which provide the possibility for progress. It tries to redress the balance of interpretation and to indicate the weaknesses of some recent and influential theses. The lament of Saul Bellow's Moses Herzog is appropriate to unionism in current circumstances, a lament which understands the modern political character to be "inconstant, divided, vacillating, lacking the stone-like certitude . . . deprived of the firm ideas of the seventeenth century, clear, hard theorems". Unionism is like this precisely because it has an inadequate understanding of its own "inner experience".[2] Unionism does lack a full understanding of its own character, its own political inheritance, and has allowed others to define for it its assumed ideological contours. Unionist guilt, like Jewish *angst*, has had much to do with the nationalist stereotyping. Herzog knew his Hegel well. He might have appreciated the idea that the unionist Owl of Minerva can only come to flight too late. It still seems worthwhile to try to put some air beneath those wings. Like Richard Weaver in a very different ideological context, one is led to believe that the idea of the Union has suffered "not so much because of inherent defect as because of the stupidity, ineptness and intellectual sloth of those who for one reason or another were presumed to have their defense in charge".[3] The suggestions of Chapter 1 may encourage others to pursue the argument and the exploration further.

Chapter 2 examines the evolution of the Anglo-Irish Agreement in terms of a summary of the assumptions of policy which underlie it. The chapter argues that while the Agreement suited the purposes of the two signatories as conceived in London and Dublin, it did not, and could not, satisfy the conditions for an equitable agreement within Northern Ireland. Taken by many to be a great triumph of statesmanship on the part of the SDLP leader John Hume, it was really an expression of the historical failure of the SDLP in Northern Ireland. Within the framework of the general interests of the two sovereign powers, the Agreement subscribed to the SDLP's long-standing attempts to circumvent the will of the vast majority of voters in the province. It was also designed to help it to evade the electoral challenge of Sinn Fein. But the Agreement only inflamed unionist opinion and did not defeat Sinn Fein. Rather than a new beginning, it symbolised the decadence of constitutional nationalism. If unionists, as Chapter 1 suggests, need to re-evaluate their ideas, then Irish nationalism north and south of the border needs to re-consider its own doctrines. The Conclusion to this book very tentatively and hesitantly presents a possible outline of accommodation, fully aware of the limited impact intellectual speculation may have upon political passion.

Chapters 3 and 6 examine the unionist response to the Anglo-Irish

Agreement. The former looks at the immediate response and the plan of campaign up to the summer of 1987, and the latter at the development of the anti-Agreement campaign – or lack of development – from the United Kingdom General Election of June 1987 to the beginning of 1989. I have been very conscious that writing on such immediate events is the equivalent of trying to walk up or down an escalator in the opposite direction to that in which it is moving. Often it was difficult to know which tense to use in describing the topics under discussion. It is not so much a case of fearing to be proved wrong by events – whatever the particular circumstances, one has to have the courage to let one's judgments stand – but rather it is the problem of knowing which events are the most crucial, a case of second-guessing the cunning of reason. However, what will not stand up to historical scrutiny may eventually be of value as a historical curiosity. As a book which tries to understand unionism since the Agreement, it may help future historians to gauge the temper of the times.

Chapters 4 and 5 examine the cases made for devolution and integration. Not all of the arguments within unionism (a term employed in this case to describe those committed to the idea of the Union and not only to members of the unionist parties) fit neatly into either category. Nevertheless, it seemed most appropriate to organise the material in this way. Despite all the problems with terminology, the participants to the dispute conducted themselves as if those labels had, and continue to have, real meaning. Until they are abandoned, it seems only right to take them seriously. Both cases have on the whole been well argued. But if it is true that nationalism in Ulster is not committed, historically or ideologically, to devolution, then neither is unionism. Integrationists have had the better of the intellectual debate. Whether they will have the better of the practical debate – not just within the ranks of those concerned to maintain the Union but between unionism, the forces of Irish nationalism and the interests of the British government – remains to be seen.

The one significant development of the period under review is the emergence of broad and untapped reserves of political sympathy for full participation in the life of the British state. Those advocating the case for equal citizenship – the civil right of voters in Northern Ireland to be allowed to join and to vote for the major political parties, e.g. Conservative or Labour, which have the power to rule them – have had a popular impact far beyond their expectations. For a long time it was possible for the British media and politicians to ignore the (rather inconvenient) possibility that support for the Union, however it might be expressed, transcended the rigidly hostile categories of the two – and only two – communities. That is no longer possible. The idea of equal citizenship has taken on a life of its own. It has shaken off whatever lingering connections it may have had with the old identity of unionist politics, and has opened up the possibility for the development of a new political framework in Northern Ireland. It provides the opportunity of an alternative outlet for the constructive political energies of those citizens who do not want to play according to the sectarian rules which London, Dublin and the provincial parties seek to maintain. The idea of the Union which equal citizenship embraces may be dismissed, indeed has been dismissed, as pure idealism. Like Coleridge, one must argue that the import of a political ideal "has real existence, and does not the less exist in reality, because it both *is*, and *exists as*, an IDEA".[4]

Acknowledgements

This book is very much a personal statement on unionist politics and the current crisis. Nevertheless, without the advice and comment of others, without innumerable discussions and arguments, no individual effort would ever come near to fulfilment. For informal comment and suggestions I would like to thank Henry Patterson and Paul Bew. For wide-ranging and congenial conversations which helped me to firm up some ideas, my thanks are due to John Cobain, John Robinson, Harry Bunting, Donna Carton and Nuala Carton. The staff at the Linen Hall Library in Belfast were extremely courteous and helpful in allowing me access to the Library's invaluable collection of material on the current Troubles. Of course, any errors or misrepresentations and all the views expressed are mine alone. Most of the manuscript was written while I was on study leave from the University of Ulster at Jordanstown. I would like to thank the Faculty of Humanities and my Head of Department, Terry O'Keeffe, for making this possible. Thanks are also due to the Thoerl-Maglern Sport Verein and to UUJMC for helping me to take my mind off the subject. Finally, nothing at all would have been written if it had not been for the encouragement of Ines and the solicitous attention of Hasso.

NOTES

1   M. Farrell, *Northern Ireland: The Orange State* (London: Pluto Press, 2nd edn, 1980), p. 12.
2   S. Bellow, *Herzog* (London: Penguin Books 1985), p. 107.
3   R. Weaver, "Up from Liberalism", *Modern Age*, 3 (Winter 1958/9), p. 23.
4   S.T. Coleridge, *The Constitution of Church and State, According to the Idea of Each* (London: J.M. Dent Everyman Library, 1972), p. 9.

CONTENTS

GLOSSARY

Alliance Party Founded in April 1970 as a non-sectarian party seeking support from both catholics and protestants. Committed to power-sharing devolution between all parties in Northern Ireland. It gives critical support to the Anglo-Irish Agreement.

Ancient Order of Hibernians Catholic equivalent of the protestant Orange Order and dating from the early nineteenth century. A communal institution reflecting and promoting the catholicism and nationalism of its members.

British and Irish Communist Organisation Small but influential grouping of political radicals whose existence dates back to the Civil Rights marches of the late 1960s. BICO's intellectual impact since 1985 has been significant, especially in the development of the idea of equal citizenship. Now calls itself the Ingram Society.

Campaign for Equal Citizenship Pressure group formed in 1985 to promote and mobilise support for the right of citizens in Northern Ireland to join and vote for the major United Kingdom political parties.

Charter Group Small devolutionist faction of the Official Unionist Party committed to "full-blooded" regional government for Northern Ireland.

Campaign for Conservative Representation Offshoot of the Campaign for Equal Citizenship designed to exert pressure on the Conservative Party to organise in Northern Ireland.

Campaign for a Devolved Parliament Pan-unionist grouping whose aim is to work for a negotiated devolved government for Northern Ireland.

Campaign for Labour Representation Organisation campaigning to end the exclusion of Northern Ireland citizens from membership of the British Labour Party.

Democratic Unionist Party Founded in September 1971 and led by Ian Paisley, the DUP has had an uneasy relationship of cooperation and competition with the Official Unionist Party. The DUP's appeal is fundamentalist both in its protestantism and its politics.

Fianna Fail The most successful of the political parties in the Republic of Ireland and the most traditionally nationalist. The constitution drawn up by a Fianna Fail government in 1937 confirmed the catholic confessional character of the Irish state.

Fine Gael The main political competitor of Fianna Fail for the governance of the Republic. It shares most of the nationalist assumptions of its rival, and it was a Fine Gael Prime Minister, Garret Fitzgerald, who signed the Anglo-Irish Agreement.

Friends of the Union An association founded after the Agreement designed to encourage understanding of and support for the Union in Great Britain.

Forum for a New Ireland Conference in 1983 of the main parties of the Republic and the nationalist Social Democratic and Labour Party of Northern Ireland. It was designed to build up moral and political pressure to weaken the unionist position in Ulster, and to modify the rhetoric of Irish nationalism without changing its substance.

Irish Labour Party Has been the political home of some intelligent critics of the Republic's catholic-nationalist exclusiveness, most notably Conor Cruise

O'Brien. Despite its relatively small vote, the Labour Party has often played a strategic role in the state. It has formed governing coalitions with Fine Gael.

Irish National Liberation Army Small, faction-ridden Irish nationalist terror group. Purportedly "Marxist" in inspiration (Republican Socialist), it uses revolutionary language to justify sectarian murder.

Kilbrandon Report Report of independent inquiry in 1984 into the ideas outlined by the report of the New Ireland Forum.

Maryfield Site in East Belfast of the secretariat of the Anglo-Irish Conference established by the Agreement. Officials from Dublin help operate a mechanism of joint consultation on Northern Ireland affairs.

New Ulster Political Research Group Political research group of the Ulster Defence Association. In the late 1970s it advocated a negotiated independence for Northern Ireland. After the Agreement the NUPRG has tried to encourage moves towards a devolved government and a Bill of Rights.

Northern Ireland Office The central government department responsible for administration in Northern Ireland. The Secretary of State at the NIO has a seat in the Cabinet.

Official Irish Republican Army The "Official" IRA resulted from a split in the movement in 1970. The "Officials" were committed to seeking political progress in Ireland through mainly left-wing political activity. Since declaring a ceasefire in 1972, the Officials have not engaged in military activity except on occasions of republican feuding.

Official Unionist Party This is the commonly-used name for the Ulster Unionist Party. It is the largest political party in Northern Ireland, and was responsible for the government of the province from 1921 to 1972. After 1972 there were tensions and splits within the Unionist party, and the term "Official" became normal to distinguish the main body of the party from those who had separated from it. For most of its history the party had formal links with the Conservative Party.

Orange Order Protestant organisation now linked to the OUP but dating from the late eighteenth century. It takes its name from William III (Prince of Orange) whose victory over James II in 1690 ensured the protestant succession to the English throne. It is forgotten by most people in the United Kingdom that the Glorious Revolution of 1688, which is celebrated as the foundation of British liberty, is the very same Williamite Settlement to which Orangemen pay allegiance.

Progressive Democrats A new party in the Republic formed as a result of disaffection within Fianna Fail over the leadership of Charles Haughey in 1985.

Provisional Irish Republican Army The "Provos" have been responsible for waging an insurgent war against the "British presence" in Ulster since 1970. Their aim is to break the will of the British government to fulfil its commitments to Northern Ireland, and to encourage London in turn to break the will of unionists. During most of the present Troubles, the PIRA has set the agenda which others have either exploited or deplored.

Provisional Sinn Fein the political wing of the PIRA. PSF has made electoral gains in Northern Ireland since 1981, receiving between one-third and two-fifths of the catholic vote. However their support in the Republic is less than 2 per cent, weakening its claim to speak for the Irish people.

Social Democratic and Labour Party Founded in August 1970, the SDLP replaced the moribund Nationalist Party as the political voice of Ulster catholics. Originally its leadership, with figures such as Gerry Fitt and Paddy Devlin, was interested in translating the claims of the Civil Rights movement into a political programme of social and economic reform with an Irish "dimension". Since John Hume became leader, the party has become absorbed in seeking Irish and international support to achieve a united Ireland. This has helped to provide a space for the grassroots politics of Provisional Sinn Fein.

Stormont The site in East Belfast of the parliament buildings of the former government of Northern Ireland.

Task Force Common abbreviation of the Joint Unionist Task Force established by the leaders of the OUP and the DUP. Its task was to consult with unionist opinion on how to maintain support for the anti-Agreement campaign and to consider alternatives to the Agreement.

Ulster Clubs Originally formed in 1985 to oppose the re-routing of traditional Orange Order marches. After the Agreement, the Clubs saw themselves as a nucleus of local and provincial opposition to any moves toward a united Ireland. They have had little influence.

Ulster Defence Association Developed from protestant vigilante groups which had emerged spontaneously to protect their own areas at the start of the Troubles, the UDA is the largest paramilitary organisation in Northern Ireland. It has not been proscribed.

Ulster Freedom Fighters The UFF is the *nom de guerre* of militant protestants closely associated with the UDA. It has claimed responsibility for murdering a number of Sinn Fein and IRA activists.

Ulster Loyalist Democratic Party The political wing of the UDA.

Ulster Resistance Organisation with paramilitary trappings, launched in November 1986 by members of the DUP and the Ulster Clubs to take, if necessary, direct action against the Anglo-Irish Agreement.

Ulster Volunteer Force Proscribed protestant paramilitary group which, under a number of different labels (e.g. Protestant Action Force), has been responsible for murders of catholics and republicans.

Workers Party An all-Ireland party which developed from the political wing of the Official IRA. While it argues for socialist solutions to Irish divisions, it has shown a willingness to work for democratic agreement for devolved government in Northern Ireland.

1

THE CHARACTER OF UNIONISM

Unionists think of themselves as a much-misunderstood people. There is a prevalent tendency to vest responsibility for this misunderstanding, such as it is, in two distinct sources. One is the malevolent and determined conspiracy of Irish nationalism to misrepresent unionism as reaction and oppression. The other is the British government, the policy of which is perceived as being, at best, equivocal on the Union, and at worst as subscribing to the central propositions of nationalist argument. Nationalist conspiracy and British bad faith are considered the cause of the hostility to, or – what often amounts to the same thing – the irritation with the unionist case which informs British public opinion.

Whatever the truth of this belief, unionists cannot exclude themselves from culpability. Concentration upon the iniquities of others has often been an excuse for political self-indulgence. The usual consequence of political self-indulgence is political irrelevance. What is well-known as the "inarticulateness" of unionism is really only the manifestation of this inadequacy of discourse. If unionist politicians are only prepared to formulate arguments appropriate to their determinations, then it may be no wonder that others are reluctant to listen to them sympathetically. In other words, the way in which unionists have presented their own case, or failed to do so, has in no small measure contributed to their sense of isolation and ineffectiveness. This does not imply that there exist no extrinsic factors (what some would prefer to call objective conditions) which have worked, and continue to work, against unionism. However, any political engagement is essentially one of faith; not only faith in one's own values but also faith that advocacy and organisation can significantly alter "objective conditions" in one's favour.

No one doubts the unionist faith or the ability of unionist politicians to mobilise support. What have been questionable are the politically intelligible and defensible principles which have shaped such activity. It may be argued, of course, that these principles are not a matter of choice but the inescapable condition of unionism as a historical phenomenon. Such fatalism is another escape from reality and in practice has often meant that unionist politics has been reduced to its most paranoid and emotional elements. It is an error, though, to assume that these elements are the whole of unionism. The argument of this Chapter is that unionism is defensible in terms that are rational and coherent, and that its compatibility with contemporary political notions has been consistently neglected.

Is it perverse to suggest that unionist politics has much to learn from the efforts of conservative thinkers over the last two decades to engage seriously in principled debate with liberals and socialists? The most articulate and influential of conservative thinkers of this period, Roger Scruton, has admitted that as a form of argument conservatism is, in essence, "inarticulate". Nor does it have "any confidence that the words it finds will match the instinct that required them".[1] Certainly unionism shares with conservatism a traditional defensive mentality, although this does not mean that those who favour the Union are necessarily committed to those larger values generally associated with conservative politics. The lesson to be learnt is not the specifics of discourse but the willingness to reflect upon a tradition and to express its positive features in such a way that it may adequately challenge the intellectual hegemony which Irish nationalism has been able to achieve. Observers of British politics are in no doubt that the self-confident and intelligent expression of conservative thought has done much to disorient and, in some cases, demoralise radicals.

Of course, all such effort could be in vain. There is no necessary correspondence between a well-formulated and rational argument and political success, although again one must assume that those actively engaged in public life must believe that it is worth the candle. Even if politicians are just going through the motions, it might be relevant for them occasionally to reflect upon the ideal mainsprings of those motions. If they do not, then the likelihood is that others will do it for them in a way inimical to their own best interests. Generally, whatever reflection there has been on Ulster unionism, and whatever would pass as contributing to the debate at more than a parochial level, has hardly been flattering to its subject. And even if one has but little regard for the liberal notion of open and informed debate between differing ideas, such an imbalance of interpretation ought to be disturbing (one is often surprised at how easily unionist politicians are prepared to take this for granted).

The purpose of this introductory Chapter, then, is threefold. First, three popular and influential interpretations of unionism are explored and their central propositions criticised. These interpretations have attempted to define the nature of unionism respectively in terms of religion, identity and loyalty. Secondly, the understanding developed in the criticism of these theories will attempt to establish those enduring features of unionist politics which more accurately and appropriately reveal its character. And thirdly, the exploration of this character will indicate the nature and the substance of the profound unionist opposition to the Anglo-Irish Agreement.

The term "character" figures prominently in this Chapter, and therefore deserves some preliminary explanation. The German romantic Novalis believed that character is fate, and that one's path in life, if not written in the genes (that particular understanding only developed in a more modern age), could be understood by reference to one's immanent nature. There may be some truth in this as a view of the individual, but it does not accurately convey the meaning in this case. What the term "character" seeks to express in the political sense is the limited but recognisably coherent variety of a tradition of discourse. As such it has little to do with determinism, although it acknowledges that the options open to such a tradition are in some way circumscribed.[2] A tradition has a range of resources upon which to draw, and these resources, depending on conditions, may be rational or emotional, intelligent or shortsighted, united or divided. It will usually be the case that any projected activity will be founded on some confluence of all of them. The task of leadership at any given point is to draw upon those resources that seem appropriate to the task in hand. It may of course be that such is the weakness of character, that managing the conflicting pulls of interest may absorb more energy than doing anything in particular. Insofar as every character, individual and corporate, is part Jekyll and part Hyde, the balance of this Chapter, by way of academic redress, leans towards Jekyll. All analysis is to some degree recommendation and this Chapter is no exception to the rule.

Unionism as protestantism

There has recently been reconsideration of the role of religion in Ulster politics, and at the heart of it has been the criticism of two long-standing fashionable interpretations.[3] The first asserts that religion does not "really" matter at all. Protestantism and catholicism are identified as labels of extent, defining and delimiting the contending political factions. Beyond this demonstrable role as flags of convenience, of value to participants and to social scientists alike, religious beliefs themselves embody little, if any, political substance. Religion is not the cause of the divisions and violence in Northern Ireland. It is merely a manifestation of divisions which are held to be real and material and not ideal and spiritual. Variously interpreted, these divisions are to do with the interests of British imperialism or the defence of colonial privileges or the curiously distorted and sectarian class struggles within Ulster.

This interpretation has always held a superficial attraction, because there seems to be ample evidence – of a negative kind – to support it. Certainly a holy war of medieval or modern Middle-Eastern proportions has not been the experience of the last few decades. Neither "community" is set on the forcible *religious* conversion of the other, and where the formalities of worship are concerned, there is a general willingness to agree to differ. Rarely have church buildings been the objects of sectarian attack, and when this does occur the general feeling is that it is outside even the very fluid rules of political violence in Ulster. Indeed it is likely that those involved in such violence have rarely attended church as adults.

However, the apparent self-evident, common sense nature of this view might leave one feeling a little uneasy about the extent of the dismissal of the religious factor. In a society so permeated with religious imagery and sectarianism, where geographical, social, sporting and familial relationships are so intimately bound up with the terms "protestant" and "catholic"; and where recognising the signs of religious identity (upon which a whole language has developed) is an elementary stage of socialisation, it ´does seem rather sweeping to reduce religion to a mere label or manifestation. Simply to reject it as the wraith-like dance of bloodless categories is perhaps to elevate theory above truthful observation.

For instance, Geoffrey Bell, in his book *The Protestants of Ulster*, establishes to his satisfaction that religion is only used "as an easily available means of recognition". He argues that since a "renewal of the campaign for the dissolution of the monasteries" has never figured in protestant demands, then we must look elsewhere for causes. His book is thin on intelligent reflection, and he nowhere fully substantiates his claim.[4] In similar fashion Michael MacDonald argues that religion is best understood politically not as confessional preference but as a label of colonial status. For him, "the conflict that appears to be about religion is really about the vestiges of colonial privileges which Protestants retain over Catholics."[5] In the development of this simplistic thesis, MacDonald cannot answer the question (indeed he appears to be unaware of it) why the protestant plantation, of all the invasions and settlements which Ireland has experienced, should remain of crucial significance, its political consequences remaining in many different "manifestations" to the present day. He cannot acknowledge Conor Cruise O'Brien's insight that it was a "Reformation settlement in Counter-reformation territory"; or indeed that even modern Ireland might subscribe to a reversal of the key concept of that time and be understood in terms of *cuius religio, euius regio*.[6]

The second interpretation to which criticism is addressed is the opposite of the first, but in a similar way it trades in the superficiality of labels. Only this time the understanding does not look beyond religious conflict to anything of political substance. In this view the present Ulster crisis is a gross anachronism. Protestants and catholics and all their troubles represent (to adapt another phrase of Conor Cruise

O'Brien's) the seventeenth century in modern dress. For most English people in particular, the seventeenth century suggests political turmoil and intolerance, a state of affairs they no longer associate with the "genius" of the British polity. Generally, the major brunt of the distaste for the style of politics in Ulster is borne by the unionists. First there is the direct involvement in public affairs by clergymen of various denominations; and secondly the language of unionist politics is sometimes firmly in the religious idiom. Such a view of Ulster politics in general and of unionism in particular involves a secular prejudice notable in the history of political thought and which in the English-speaking world owes much to Thomas Hobbes: it is that religious fanaticism and dogma are destructive of order and tranquillity and ought to be put firmly in their place. That is a sound prejudice.

The frequent mixing of religious and political idioms by unionists tends to make what they have to say appear unworthy of rational consideration. To the modern observer unionism often presents itself as the self-justification of an exclusive sect of bigots whose guardians of the faith delight in whipping up their demented enthusiasms: it appears as nothing other than a primitive local cult given to rituals of a barbaric nature. As Sarah Nelson has noted, "bewilderment, distaste or outrage seems to have discouraged outsiders from even trying to study and understand the loyalists of Ulster."[7] One quite representative example of this approach is Martyn Harris's article in *New Society*, which dismisses the notion that English observers like himself can be accused of failing to understand unionist politics as if it were all too subtle and complicated. In his opinion, unionism is religious sectarian "simplicity itself. It is about keeping out the Taigs [Catholics]."[8] Like most misrepresentations this judgment embodies a partial truth, but what it leaves unexamined – the complex inheritance which religious thought has bequeathed to political practice – is precisely what illuminates the whole character of unionism. With a little caution and humility, Harris could not have made the foolish claim that unionism is Britain's only "flourishing totalitarian ideology" and that the only way "to outface it is in the end to break it".[9] (It is interesting how often English "liberality" and "tolerance" brings forth such draconian conclusions.) A failure of comprehension is often the key to simple-minded solutions.

For the English, who constitute 80 per cent of the United Kingdom, the interpenetration of religious and political values is an anachronism because religious division is a problem solved (how recently religious issues did divide England socially and politically is often forgotten). In some ways the thoroughgoing secularisation of English society is exceptional: fresh research on European politics has shown that "religious elements in partisan politics have shown a remarkable ability to survive, despite general trends towards secularisation and even where they have declined or disappeared, the religious factor in a number of significant cases continues to operate as a sort of hidden agenda.''[10] In Northern Ireland, religion is part of an open and a hidden agenda; open because of the confessional nature of partisanship, hidden because of some of the unexamined suppositions of political activity. Some recent and welcome re-assessment of these relationships has added vigour to what appeared to be a tired debate.

Probably the most influential and provocative fresh consideration of the particular relationship between unionism and protestantism has come from a sociologist, Steve Bruce, who has tried to reinvigorate the religio-political categories denied by the first interpretation and to save understanding from the embrace of moral outrage characteristic of the second. The central premise of his work is that ''the actions of Ulster protestants will not be understood until the importance of their religion is comprehended.''[11] Indeed he goes further and argues that the core of unionist ideology is evangelical protestantism, and that ultimately the character of unionist politics may be reduced to this essence.

It is important to follow Bruce's reasoning here. He sets out to explain and make sense of Ian Paisley's political career, and this he does with a sure feel for the inner meanings of fundamental protestantism. However, he goes beyond the particular to establish a wider claim. The potency of this evangelical fundamentalism is not just the ''only conclusion that makes sense of Ian Paisley's career''; it also enables us to make sense of unionism. Ultimately, for the Ulster unionist, the ''Northern Ireland conflict is a religious conflict.''[12] As to why this should be so, Bruce makes much of the distinction between ethnicity and nationality. Protestants form an ''ethnic'' group. Catholics are part of a distinctive ''nation''. There do not seem to be any specific criteria which distinguish these two concepts, yet Bruce's conclusion is significant. He argues that such is the strength of identity of Irish nationalism that it is no longer reducible to catholicism; it can ''dispense'' with catholicism.[13] Nationalism in Ireland, then, has moved away from its nineteenth-century dependence on the cultural power of the Church and now leads an independent existence founded on modern secular principles.

The contrast with loyalism or unionism could not be more stark. According to Bruce, ''beyond evangelical Protestantism, no secure identity is available'' for unionist politics.[14] Thus he is happy with the purely negative definition of such a political identity: ''Unionism is about avoiding becoming a subordinate minority in a Catholic state.''[15] In times of crisis, it is to the faith that unionists rally and hence to the person who appears most fervent and uncompromising in its defence. Paisleyism appears to express the true meaning of what it is to be a protestant and a unionist, with the rather dramatic conclusion that the "only coherent set of ideas which explains the past, which gives them a sense of who they are, which makes them feel justifiably superior to catholics, and which gives them the hope that they will survive, is evangelical protestantism."[16] This is a large claim, and the integrity of Bruce's scholarship requires that it be taken seriously and considered with care. At least three qualifications need to be made – retaining the valuable insights that Bruce provides but integrating them into a more adequate perspective.

First, the religious lineage of unionism can only be understood in terms of the corresponding relationship of catholicism and nationalism. It is here that Bruce's argument is weakest, for it maintains that nationalists do not need religion to anchor their sense of belonging and community because they possess a secular political ideology which provides the necessary identity. Catholics within Northern Ireland can identify with the Republic of Ireland because it expresses their sense of belonging in effective statehood. Thereby, Irish nationalism has transcended religion. But this argument can be stood on its head by being taken to mean that catholicism is so thoroughly a part of that state to which northern nationalists profess allegiance that it is perfectly redundant and certainly inexpedient for them to talk about it. Irish nationalism may have transcended catholicism, but not in the sense of leaving it behind: it has transcended it by incorporating the catholic ethos into the very fabric of its being. As Stanley Gebler Davies puts it, "Eire is not a foreign country, but it is a catholic country." [17] That is a potent enough reason why nationalists in Northern Ireland favour unity and why unionists oppose it. These are potent reasons but not the only ones and without labouring the point further, Bruce overestimates the political secularism of nationalism and undervalues its religious significance. Similarly he underestimates the secularism of unionism and severely overplays its religious particularism.

In other words the analysis suffers from the reductionist fallacy, the belief that there must be a true "core" which is revealed when all incidentals are swept away. But the character of political belief must involve and express its whole nature. To claim that evangelical protestantism is the "truth" of unionism is to caricature it. Indeed, to claim that, once their "Britishness" is removed, unionists have nothing left but their religion is rather disingenuous. If Ulster nationalists have their "Irishness" removed, then all that remains is their religion. It is an argument of infinite extension.

The second qualification is really an extension of the first. Evangelicalism, "kick the pope-ism" or whatever it is called is undoubtedly a part of protestant politics, but it is not even the whole of this tradition. It is certainly not all there is to be said about unionism. Insofar as

nationalism may assert the transcendence of catholicism, then there is
in unionism the idea which transcends protestantism. Bruce's insis-
tence that fundamentalism provides the only coherent set of ideas
around which unionism can rally *in extremis* is an exaggeration. The
character of the whole need not be determined by the coherence of a
part.

Thirdly, the political influence of protestantism is portrayed as an
exclusive one, with protestantism identifying the true élite as a
religious one. Unionism is therefore the possession of a sect, the articles
of whose faith deny catholics not only their ''national aspirations'' but
any effective role in the government of the province. Here Bruce
portrays his fascination for Paisley's Democratic Unionist Party,
which embodies the immediacy of the religious vision in politics. This
party does believe that ''political liberty is linked to the religious
heritage of the nation'',[18] and it holds this belief in a ''uniformity of
political fundamentalist attitudes shared by the party's membership''.[19] Yet, despite this clear conclusion, Bruce is ambiguous even on
the nature of Paisleyism. For instance Paisley is understood to
represent, at one and the same time, the core of unionism and a ''distinctive'' position stressing its religious dimension. Bruce also recognises – in a revealing passage – that the DUP and Paisley's Free
Presbyterian Church are ''so strongly committed to their unionism
that they are prepared to go some way towards moving some of their
evangelical principles into the area of private life and personal choice,
rather than alienate non-evangelical unionists''.[20] An admission like
this sits ill with the central theme that the political nature of unionism is
only a vehicle for the religious; or that the Britishness of unionism is
clearly subordinated to the protestant identity. Bruce's thesis does not
support the weight of interpretation placed upon it, nor does it really
get to grips with the historical and ideological interrelationship
between protestantism and unionism.

Freedom of worship and of conscience is a central tenet of protestantism. In particular there is a rejection of the exclusive spiritual
authority of the priesthood, and of the idea that salvation can be had
from good works alone or from mere outward conformity to the
demands of faith. The primitive democracy of Ulster presbyterianism
also involved a severe kind of liberty. It too had to endure the persecution of the established episcopalian church. It was only when catholicism and nationalism became indissolubly linked together in the nineteenth century that divisions within protestantism became secondary
to the combined political and religious threat of Home Rule. Denomi-
national differences were subordinated to the political defence of the
common heritage of civil and religious liberty. But what was the nature
of this liberty with which protestantism and unionism was identified?

The protestant idea of liberty has been intelligently explored by

Marianne Elliott who reveals two aspects of political consequence. First, there is a "dogmatic brand of libertarianism" suspicious of any established power, and with a disposition toward self-help as a counter-part to individual salvation. This libertarian tradition was strongly represented within presbyterianism and – as Elliott shows – fostered the political radicalism of the eighteenth century in the atmosphere of humanitarian liberalism of the Enlightenment. Secondly, there is an élitism, a sense of the superiority of the protestant faith and the material and civil benefits which accompany it. These notions of liberty were that much sharper in Ulster where a dramatic contrast existed. "Protestant ideas of liberty, therefore, have had a long history of development in relation to protestant notions of catholicism."[21] The colour and depth of protestant self-definition had to do with impress-ions of catholics; of a people in thrall to an authoritarian church, moulded in the image dictated by priestly convenience and thereby not eligible for the full and responsible citizenship which liberty demands. For protestants, the Reformation was the revolutionary key to civil emancipation. If catholics stubbornly refused to recognise it, that was not only their tragedy; it was also a persistent threat to the liberty of the Ulster settlement.[22]

Marianne Elliott's distinctions help to bring together the complex contribution of protestant ideas to the fabric of unionist politics. It is clear from her study that she believes the course of Ulster history to have fostered élitist particularism at the expense of libertarian inclu-siveness. Because of its embattled mentality and its sense of siege, the politics of unionism turned in on itself and failed to expand beyond the interests of the group. This tracing of the influence of protestant ideas in unionist politics finds echoes in the work of other scholars, not only in idealist analyses but in Marxist analyses as well. For instance Peter Gibbon, in his study of the origins of Ulster unionism, refers to two counterpoints of unionist politics from the late nineteenth century onwards: modernity-and-diversity and tradition-and-unity. The former was concerned to blend the fate of Ulster with that of the British state, the imperative of keeping the province within the mainstream of metropolitan advance. The latter was concerned to maintain the integrity of the popular protestant alliance against catholic nationa-lism; it was exclusive in its partisanship, and expressed a rigid con-servatism. In the violent and uncertain circumstances that prevailed during the establishment of the state in Northern Ireland, Gibbon remarks that "the parochial aspects of Ulster conservatism were given a renewed lease of life as a regime was created which was heavily dependent upon confessional particularism, discrimination and even oppression."[23] Or perhaps, as Elliott writes, that partition elevated élitism at the expense of the libertarian inheritance.

Thus, what unionism inherited from protestantism was the

interplay between a sectarian exclusion and a liberal comprehension, but it has to be acknowledged that the two aspects are part of one reality: Unionist politics in Northern Ireland between 1921 and 1972 was, in its character, a complex synthesis of both these elements. It exhibited a triumphalist, élitist group identity, and attempted to mould Ulster in an exclusive image. It also accommodated Ulster to the social democratic achievements of the British state. The motives for this were not just materialism and self-interest, though these were important enough; they were ideological as well. Unionist politics, for all its parochial stupidities, identified itself with the inherited if not always the current values of the British state. That is what British Ulster meant. In both regards, unionism constructed a political order and a set of socio-economic expectations very different from that in the Republic. If the former proved intolerable, not only to catholics but also to many protestants, the latter did not. Probably the enduring political achievement of fifty years of rule by the Unionist party has been to divide catholic opinion between a sentimental nationalism and an awareness of their relative wellbeing – in terms not merely of state benefits but also of individual freedoms, especially for women.

The political values of unionism bequeathed by protestant libertarianism have been interestingly developed in a pamphlet by the unionist politician and lawyer Robert McCartney. It provides a distinctive and provoking perspective and brings the character of unionism into relief. McCartney relates the liberal tradition of Ulster protestantism and the unionist politics that developed from it to significant texts in the history of Western thought. For him that tradition has as much in common with the ideas of Tom Paine, J.S. Mill and the framers of the United States Constitution as it has with Calvin, Luther, Henry Cooke* or Ian Paisley. In particular, it has to do with "reason and Enlightenment, not romance and cultural identity." From this distinction in Ireland's history flow two contrasting notions of the nature of man. In the first, "man is seen as a free spirit, naturally good, but stunted, limited and frustrated by archaic and restrictive institutions whether of church or state." According to the second vision, man is a "creature of limited freedom, only partly good and whose only salvation is within the great authoritarian frameworks of states, churches or parties."[24]

McCartney's interpretation is that the historically positive character of unionism is found in its espousal of the former of these two ideas. It is nationalism which has been the carrier of authoritarianism in Ireland in the guise of freedom and independence. And the religious

---

*A nineteenth-century Ulster Presbyterian fundamentalist.

influence in the exclusive claims of nationalism cannot be overlooked. The politics of Irish nationalism meant that the priorities of individual freedoms and liberty of conscience "were to be sacrificed for values which were regarded as being higher and which were determined by no subjective standard but by the objective requirements of Church doctrine and dogma". However, although the divisions in Ireland have deep roots in these religious visions, they can none the less be understood in quite other and secular forms. The constitutional divisions pose the alternatives in this particular way. One should either remain within a pluralist United Kingdom "with all its faults" albeit a state liberal, tolerant and diverse; or owe allegiance to a state constructed on the principle of national homogeneity and religious authority. If the summation of Irish nationalism's claim is Parnell's statement that "no man has a right to fix the boundary of the march of a nation", then, as McCartney says, "the answer of a dissenting unionist must be – that no nation has the right to set limits upon the development of the individual liberty and unique nature of man."[25] McCartney must accept not merely the United Kingdom with all its faults; he must also co-exist with protestant sectarianism, and all its woes. One will discount McCartney's vision because it is sectarian to the extent that one acknowledges the claims of Irish nationalism.

It is manifest that the doctrine of "national self-determination, despite a not entirely honourable history, is firmly rooted in the modern evolution of political thought."[26] Irish nationalists have availed themselves of the terminology and idioms of the rooted vernacular of nationalism, a doctrine which asserts a universal and comprehensive truth. This has dignified and given world historical significance to the nationalist cause in Ulster, which, if understood in other terms, would appear a squalid and murderous sectarianism. The central proposition of Irish nationalism is that loyalty to the nation is the only way to transcend sectarianism and truly reconcile the age-old conflict between protestant and catholic. What informs that proposition is the assumption that the nation is the "natural" political basis of the state. This, of course, is nonsense, unless one empties the term "nation" of any exact meaning and advances the argument that the legitimacy of the state depends upon the recognition of its authority by the people who come within its jurisdiction. For unionists these beneficent claims of Irish nationalism must be examined in the light of the particular and the specific, that is, in terms of the development of the Republic of Ireland.

In current circumstances, such an examination is to the advantage of unionism. Irish nationalism, like unionism, embodies the complex interplay of different ideological currents. For the sake of convenience, we will call them the élitist and libertarian strands. The first may be taken to represent catholic particularism, the second its claim to secular universality. Authoritative nationalism in Ireland represented by the policy of the Republic reveals a distinctive élitism. Nationalism pre-supposes a society fundamentally one and fundamentally catholic. Recent constitutional travails over divorce, contraception and abortion have shown how distinctive the Republic wishes to remain – and this at a time when there was every incentive to prove its liberality and when this appeared to be the official strategy of successive governments. It is not wrong that this should be the case; Irish solutions to Irish problems (or catholic solutions to catholic problems) represents a sound enough principle that should be respected. However, authoritative nationalism is far from the assump-tions of modern pluralism. Not only do protestants find this intoler-able, but so do many northern catholics as well. As one acute observer put it, the catholics of Northern Ireland "have no difficulty in distin-guishing between the principle of a united Ireland and the practical realities for which they would settle, short of it, or even instead of it. For protestants, there is no problem."[27]

A powerful factor in the élitism of unionist politics was the existence of devolved state institutions within which protestants were assured of dominance. Since this is no longer the case, protestants and catholics in Northern Ireland are on an equal *political* footing – so long as the principles are justice and welfare and not national irredentism. By con-fronting the claims of nationalism and positing an intelligent and justi-fiable universalisation of unionist values, McCartney has shown the way forward for unionist politics. At least he has proved that rationality is not one-sided. The task is clearly not easy, as he himself recognises: "The dilemma of liberal unionism is its support" for civil rights, liberties and equal citizenship in opposition to unionist élitism, and its rejection of Irish unity, "which would entail being governed for the foreseeable future by an authoritarian and non-pluralist state."[28] The Anglo-Irish Agreement, might, ironically, have created the conditions, within which the liberal idea of unionism would have greater force – first, as catholics are confronted with the real possibility of unity, and secondly, as protestants are confronted with the untena-bility of parochial particularism.

The politics of identity

The formalised interdependence between religious faith and political commitment, which some have perceived to be essential to the character of unionism, has partly informed another fashionable inter-pretation. A popularly-held belief is that unionism suffers from a thorough crisis of identity. This is thought to explain why, on the one hand, unionism has been unable to counter the challenge of nationalism and why, on the other, it has been incapable of adequately communicating a positive image. There are at least two crucial presuppositions of such an understanding.

First, the fundamentals of protestantism may be sufficient for unionists to understand the world and their role within it. Unionist may speak happily unto unionist but the major difficulty for them is making sense to others. As Bairner noted, modern politics entails explaining to critical opinion how unionists want to live. "Recourse to seventeenth-century politico-religious doctrine is simply inadequate."[29] In other words the protestant identity, as an assertion of political right, lacks credibility in the modern age. Unionist principles appear as the flotsam and jetsam of political thought which has foundered in history: the faster the tide of change, the more tenaciously and desperately unionists hold on to the wreckage. Fidelity to the Williamite settlement of 1689–91 cuts little ice with policy-makers concerned with the problems of the last quarter of the twentieth century. We have already observed the shortcomings of this understanding of unionism, and the point does not need to be laboured.

The second presupposition is that unionist politics is riddled with irreconcilable contradictions and inconsistencies precisely because it lacks a definite national identity. In the words of Lord Windlesham, a former Minister of State in the Northern Ireland Office, the *fons et origo* of unionism is a "fear of not belonging".[30] The historical insecurities, the siege mentality, the ideal of loyalty are all founded on a fundamental confusion about who, as a people, unionists actually are. For some, unionists are colonists who have lost the culture of their origins and yet not adapted the identity of the land in which they settled; they exist in an incoherent political limbo. For others, they are in fact Irish, but cannot see it. Or again, they are neither Irish nor British but Ulsterfolk. Thus unionists live on the island of Ireland but are unable to assimilate the natural consequences of that political "fact". They feel "British", but are not regarded as being fully so by those who live in Great Britain. There exists a germ of Ulster nationalism, but this is ultimately inadequate, for the title to the territory of Ulster is contested by Irish nationalism. From these presuppositions the conclusion reached is quite logical: it is that if the "crisis" of identity is somehow resolved, then political progress is possible. Generally the conclusion involves the breaking of the Union.

Constitutional nationalists hold that some imaginative political initiative which recognises the Irish dimension of the Northern Ireland crisis can, slowly but surely, enable unionists to embrace a nationalist identity and play their full part in a new Ireland. Academic nationalists have a faith that a thorough understanding of their own history will enable unionists to understand how they too have been used and abused by the English. A recognition of a common suffering may encourage a common identity. Militant nationalists like the IRA believe that unionists will have to be forced to be free, and that their confusions will only be resolved when the Brits agree to go. Confronted with that reality, unionists will come to terms with the Irish nation and their place within it. Some unionists have even been seduced by the cultural logic of this interpretation, and have set about formulating a distinctive Ulster identity. This has involved excursions into anti-quarianism and the celebration of the uniqueness of Ulster within the history of Ireland. Intrinsically this is a purely harmless activity, but insofar as it is used to underwrite some notion of political independence for Northern Ireland, it is nothing other than playing the nationalist game: it accepts the postulates of nationalist argument and therefore becomes a form of embryonic separatism.

At first sight there would appear to be something of a paradox in the formulation of this argument. On the one hand, we have the view that unionism has a stunted identity – limited and anachronistic, frozen in a seventeenth-century mould. All it has is the one significant legitima-ting myth of 1690 and the Battle of the Boyne. Compared to nationa-lism, argues Terence Brown, unionism's identity is "impoverished" and "bound to comprehend much less of the human condition"; it lacks the "complex, rich, emotional identity" of nationalism. Unionism is simply "emotionally exclusive".[31] (It is characteristic of such "emotional" claims that Brown nowhere cites evidence of the cultural richness of nationalism. For too long this idea has held sway without critical examination. Bord Failte kitsch and Irish-American nostalgia hardly constitute a fully adequate cultural form. However, the point is that unionism does not claim to be an entire philosophy of life but a rational political idea. To criticise it in such terms is to do so according to the assumptions of nationalism.)

On the other hand, we have the opposite view. Unionism may lack a definitive coherence, but its identity is multi-layered and variegated, with cross-cutting patterns of experience and emotional attachment. As Clifford Smyth noted, the unionist tradition is one which "embraces those of the Gaelic-speaking Irish who were converted to the Reformed Faith, Puritan settlers from England, Huguenots and the Scots Presbyterians".[32] It is an identity that associates itself with the affairs of a multinational state, expansive and outward-looking in a way that self-absorbed Irish nationalism could never be. How do the advocates of the identity crisis thesis try to resolve this apparent paradox?

The resolution of the paradox seems to be that the intense demands of unionist solidarity within Northern Ireland, especially under the

pre-1972 Stormont regime, placed a premium on the subordination of
the diversity of cultural expression. Unionism is essentially a negative
view of the world which stifles political and cultural imagination and
creativity. It has been asserted that the maintenance of domination
over catholics depended on a "sort of willing servitude" to Britain.
This servitude was in the long run debilitating. It alienated protestants
from their own essential condition and made them lean on a socio-
political crutch, the strength of which was not theirs to determine.[33]
Considerations of identity and culture were secondary to the mono-
tonous celebration of victory over the catholics. Once the British constitutional connection became threatened in the early 1970s, unionists
were made aware of the emptiness of their values. At the heart of
unionism is a vacuum. This vacuum will only be filled when unionists
come to realise their Irishness and allow a thousand cultural flowers to
bloom forth.

Whatever the particulars of analysis, there does appear to be a
common view that the crucial question a unionist must address is:
"Who am I then, and where do I belong?"[34] Thus Sarah Nelson, and
as she goes on to argue, it is essential for unionists to consider "[what]
does it mean to be British, or Irish, or Ulster and are the answers
acceptable to us?"[35] Indeed the "identity" question has become something of a journalistic cliché, which may be stated and allowed to stand
on its own as a significant revelation of the mind of loyalist Ulster. For
instance, a *New Society* report on the popular culture of protestant
marching bands and their camp-followers made the issue of identity
central to its (somewhat cloudy) thesis. Much was made of the
apparent confusion of the young people about what their marching and
their music signified, compared with the resurgence of cultural
nationalism in Ulster. "By comparison with this assertiveness, the
protestants' cultural and ethnic identity" seemed to lack coherence
and confidence. The problem is that it is difficult being "British" in
Ireland. To stress his point, the author quotes the following response of
one of the bandsmen to his question on identity:

Well, I'd like to call myself British, a British person like. But you look deep into
it like, I'm Irish . . . because Northern *Ireland* like. You don't hear the English
going round and saying, "I'm British". They'd turn round and say "I'm
English" . . . like the Scottish . . . I'd like to classify myself as a British
person – if anybody asks me my nationality I'd turn around an' say,
"British" . . . I hate calling myself Irish, myself like . . . but it's a thing you
have to face up to. It's the truth, you look at yourself, you're living on one
island.[36]

The interpretation put upon this response by the questioner is the one
which advocates of the identity thesis would find congenial: namely

that herein lies a profound tragedy and crisis. The incoherence of language, the manifest struggle to come to terms with the roots of belonging, the inability to communicate – this illustrates the unionist confusion and is the source of Ireland's discontent.

Yet despite the tortuous expression and crudity of grammar, these comments may be understood otherwise to embody, suitably inter-preted, a profound modern political wisdom – a wisdom which the identity–advocates ignore or are simply unable to recognise. For the confusion, such as it is, appears not to lie in the stumbling formulations of unionism but in the narrow perversity of the whole idea of the politics of identity. It is an interpretation which cannot stand on the shifting sands of its foundation. The muddled thinking of this approach involves two distinct confusions.

First, concern with the parameters of identity is to misconceive the character of unionism by applying to it concepts relevant to the theory of nationalism. This theory holds as self-evident that the natural social unit is the nation, and that the individual nations of the world ought to find full expression in political self-determination. States ought to be conterminous with nations. For nationalists, therefore, it is important to detect difference and distinction, to examine the language, customs and origins of a people to determine not only its identity in terms of the sport of classification but its political destiny. However, this is no exact science, and the idea of the nation is elusive. Certainly, nationalist pre-occupations in no way constitute self-evident political truths. Nationa-lists invented nationalism and constructed "imagined communities" on the principle of natural exclusiveness. The fertility of the imagina-tion of Irish nationalists fabricated the myths of republicanism. Today it has become fixated, predictable and without solidity.

For instance, Jennifer Todd can perceptively illustrate the ideologi-cal identities of unionism, but tortuously cramps these into the wishful thinking and unexamined postulates of Irish nationalism. The salva-tion of intelligent unionists, she holds, lies in moving away from "a primary imagined community of Greater Britain to placing as much importance on an Irish imagined community as on a British imagined community – from Ulster British to British Irish".[37] This ignores a whole dimension of unionist sentiment and is narrowly deterministic. According to Arendt Lijphart, "Group identification and loyalty are not a zero-sum game."[38] Only if one is an Irish nationalist is there something intrinsically incompatible (an identity crisis) if one drinks Guinness, loves to holiday in Donegal or Killarney, supports an all-Ireland rugby team in Dublin, recognises that one is "Irish", and yet at the same time is a committed unionist. Nationalist presumptions cannot accept the distinction between "culture" (whatever that word may imply) and political value and allegiance. The young bandsman, whose ideas Todd would condemn as "approximating to a self-contained, closed system", is less dogmatic in his appreciation of the diversity of life than she is. The confidence he needs is not the security of a complacent national identity but the confidence that it is both proper and respectable to embrace a political allegiance that allows expression of whatever cultural values one likes. The idea of the Union is not reductionist in the way that the idea of the Irish nation profoundly is.

The second muddle may be called categorical irrelevance. This means the use of concepts and notions inappropriate to the understanding of the modern state (and therefore of the constitution). These may be in the form of analogies with the family or the various institutions of civil society. Such analogies are often taken to characterise the relations and identity of unionist politics to British politics as a whole. Anthony Kenny argues that the reasons for maintaining the Union fall into three classes: self-interest, sentiment and morality. His conclusion is that the first two are now redundant, so "it is clear that the argument for retaining the Union is now almost entirely a moral one".[39] Rather piously, he adds that this is the clinching reason. This argument would have interesting consequences if applied to other problems of British political life. As T.E. Utley remarked, if unionists "had a different coloured skin and lived in inner cities", such views would provoke a sense of outrage among the *bien-pensants*.[40]

Talk of sentiment and morality only blurs the issue and intrudes values relevant to personal relationships into the proper conduct of statecraft. If anything, it is precisely self-interest, a calculation of *raison d'état*, which has informed the policy of Westminster. But more than morality is involved: constitutional right is also. Here Kenny reveals a curious understanding of the political "self" and the interests that pertain to it. If it is the self-interest of the United Kingdom, then that explicitly involves the interest of Northern Ireland which has consistently expressed its determination to remain within the Union. If not, then what interest of which state does Kenny refer to? His thinking represents Great English "chauvinism, which is antithetical to the very idea of the Union and not merely to Northern Ireland's place within it. The aggravation that such remarks provoke is conveyed clearly by A.T.Q. Stewart. Unionists, he argues, have never considered the Union to be in the sole gift of Westminster, "to be granted or withheld at the pleasure of Britain". He goes on: "Nothing irritates an Ulsterman more than the assumption that the United Kingdom exists simply for the comfort and security of England and the English."[41] This is a point to which we return in the next section.

In sum, while the issue of culture and identity is a tricky one likely to ensnare the unwary, the character of unionism has little to do with the assumptions of nationalism. Like any idea that still has life and is not sterile, problems of "imagining" an identity commensurate with experience will continue. But these are not the same problems that exercise the imaginations of those who espouse the identity crisis thesis. The identity of unionism has little to do with the idea of the nation and everything to do with the idea of the state. It will not do to try to characterise this identity thus: "[the] existing relationship between Great Britain and Ulster has been well described as a loveless marriage."[42] The relationship has nothing to do with weddings, divorce or alimony but with the principle of the modern state itself. The relationship is not a civil one, nor is it based on arbitrary or private considerations.

The reference above to blacks living in Britain's inner cities was not made flippantly. For the theory of the state with its intrinsic principle of right is one employed by non-whites in the United Kingdom to attack the vicious racism of Little Englanders and the National Front, who formulate their arguments in terms of the integrity of the nation. Bhikhu Parekh systematically demolishes the nationalist thesis in his inimitable and fluid philosophical style and although his target is the "New Right", his conclusions are congenial to the intelligent unionist. Starkly, he argues that the modern state "does not depend on, and in fact has nothing to do with, a sense of nationality". To suggest that the modern state "should be based on the unity of nationhood in the hope of returning to a state of primitive simplicity is to understand neither its nature nor its wider context." The state does not depend upon any form of substantive identity at all. "The modern state is unique in that, unlike its predecessors, it has developed an autonomous principle of unity, that is one located in the very structure of the state rather than something lying outside or beyond it."[43] In other words, the modern state has transcended its dependence on extrinsic legitimations such as race, nation or religion, and is grounded in the political universals of right and the rule of law. In so far as those within the state accept the authority of the rule of law (justice being the impartiality of law designed for the general welfare), then there can be the fullest expression of ethnic, religious and social diversity.

The old Stormont regime was incapable of complying fully with this principle, since its substantive political identity of protestant élitism was exclusive. Irish unity, on the model available in the Republic (and there is no other), would clearly be regressive. This implies no disrespect for the proper administration of law in the Republic of Ireland; it is simply to emphasise that, despite the rhetoric of its politicians, in reality there is no popular desire for the state to "transcend" its constituted particularism. Given the choices before it, this would seem to be quite wise. This wisdom is acknowledged by those, like Conor Cruise O'Brien, who are not wedded to fossilised nostrums. Similarly any "settlement" within Northern Ireland that tried to accommodate the demands of protestant and catholic élitism – and dignified it with the appellation of government – would compound and not alleviate the problem. If the autonomous principle of the modern state is taken to be right (in the Hegelian sense), then the relevant political concept is neither religion nor nation but citizenship. The United Kingdom is a state which, being multi-national and multi-ethnic, can be understood in terms of citizenship and not substantive identity (which helps to account for the bandsman's muddle). And it is significant that the character of the British state has always been associated with the idea of law, common and statute. (In passing, it may be said that the apparently archaic unionist celebration of the Crown is as near as one can get to a theory of the British state.) The imperial notion of *"civus Britannicus sum"* has transformed itself into the democratic ideal of different nations, different religions and different colours, all equal citizens under the one government. It is to this notion that intelligent unionism, which embraces both protestants and catholics, owes allegiance. It was from this notion that the Republic of Ireland seceded to construct a state on the principle of national unity.[44]

The character of unionism must be understood in terms of this idea of citizenship; and the longer that protestant unionists and catholic nationalists are denied local state power, the more important it becomes as a universal organising political value. Thus "Equal Citizenship" is no mere cant slogan (although it may mean different things to different people); it is an idea that is struggling to make itself intelligible and coherent. At its heart is a claim to just treatment within the state of which all protestants and all catholics are part. The Solemn Covenant of 1912 talks of the "cherished position of equal citizenship in the United Kingdom". The crises which have dogged the history of Northern Ireland have been due to successive British governments systematically acknowledging this principle and systematically failing to act upon it. That ambiguity has fuelled nationalist intransigence and protestant bloody-mindedness.

If there has been a crisis of identity, it has been one experienced by all citizens alike in Northern Ireland. It is this: the establishment of the devolved state in Ulster was not a victory for unionism; it was a victory for unionists. This may seem a needlessly fine distinction, but its implications have been important. Unionists had both won and lost. They had been able to reject the exclusive world-view of nationalism but not to assert convincingly the right of equal citizenship within the United Kingdom. What ensued was the dialectic of political narrow-mindedness, sponsored by British governments equivocal about the principles and integrity of their own state and the hypocritical and irresponsible irredentism of Irish governments. What has been astonishing in the history of the Ulster crisis is the self-righteous tone adopted by ministers in London and Dublin – as if they had had no part in driving protestants and catholics apart.

A question of loyalty

A logical consequence of an interpretation that takes identity to be the criterion of unionist crisis is to conclude that unionism's notion of loyalty will be equally contradictory. In other words, if unionists are confused about who they are, they will also be confused about what it is they are loyal to. And since "being loyal" is part of unionist self-regard, and "loyalism" is often used interchangeably with "unionism", there has been wide scope for critical explorations of the vagaries and difficulties that this notion of loyalty has presented. Few such interpretations have been as influential as David Miller's *Queen's Rebels*, and the measure of its influence may be taken to be the wide dissemination of its central thesis in the press.

That the loyalty thesis shares much with the preceding view can be seen in Miller's assumption that the Ulster question is really a specific case of incoherent nationalism. He argues that "the central peculiarity in Ulster's political culture is that no community – not Britain, not the United Kingdom, not 'Ulster' and certainly not Ireland – has attained for Ulster protestants all the characteristics which a nation commonly possesses in the modern world."[45] As we have argued above, such an interpretation chooses the wrong foundation upon which to build, and is therefore substantially misconceived. It constructs an argument on ground congenial to nationalism, and so it is not surprising that unionism appears woefully inadequate as a political doctrine. Nevertheless, it may be that Miller's thesis is a valuable insight that holds true regardless of its intellectual origins. As such it deserves critical attention.

Miller's well-researched historical analysis begins with a conundrum and proceeds to develop a persuasive answer to the puzzle. The conundrum is that "few aspects of the contemporary Ulster problem are more perplexing to British and other outside observers than the 'conditional' character of the loyalty professed by those known as loyalists."[46] The resolution of this perplexity lies in the understanding of unionism in the past and in the present by reference to "a venerable theory of political obligation – that of the social contract thinkers" of the seventeenth century and especially "the peculiar Scottish variant of contractarian thought and practice, covenanting".[47]

What are the political implications of this distinctive brand of theorising? According to this point of view, unionist "loyalty" is a compound of the neat coincidence of religious belief and political self-interest. Loyalty is given not to particular governments but in effect to those constitutional prerequisites necessary to maintain and secure the protestant way of life in Ulster. Unionist loyalty, despite all its symbolism, remains theoretical and not concrete. It can never feel at home in the real world of political activity, and seeks refuge in meta-physical ideals – like the absolute values of the Williamite Settlement, the coronation oath and the Covenant of 1912. Far from being the hard-headed, unemotional figures of repute, unionists are full of fond imaginings, are essentially romantic and therefore incorrigibly "Irish". At the heart of unionism is an impossible political longing. T.E. Utley defined it, appropriately enough, as the search for some sort of indestructible safeguard against the danger that Irish unity would ever be achieved against its will.[48] Since there can be no permanent and absolute truths in political life (not even God's provi-dence), unionism is also at heart fundamentally unstable. It is at one and the same time completely loyal and completely rebellious. It prostrates itself before the Union Jack and every sympathetic utterance of royal and politician alike and takes to the street with an almost anarchic fervour at the slightest hint of its absolute values being "com-promised". No better example of self-contradiction could be found. Ultimately, unionism conveys little meaning beyond its own narrow confines, for its contradictions reveal it to be essentially self-serving and particular.

The sustained exposition of the contractarian theme in Miller is an important contribution to the theoretical literature on unionism. Like Bruce, Miller takes unionism seriously. While Bruce locates the central characteristics of the doctrine in evangelical religion, Miller places them firmly within a definite tradition of Western political thought. There is certainly an overlap, since covenanting may be understood as the political expression of evangelicalism. However, it is constitutional insecurity that speaks universally to unionists. This has predisposed them towards a political vision that has meaning for them, a vision that helps to resolve their dilemma. Unionists may never read John Locke, the American Founding Fathers or Thomas Hobbes – nevertheless, their assumptions are the same. For Miller the problem for unionism is that those assumptions are "anomalous in our own day".[49] The reason why the behaviour and arguments of unionists strike the outsider as being odd is that the central concerns of contrac-tarian political thought – the origins of government and the nature of political obligation – are ones which have been answered satisfactorily by the development of the modern state since the seventeenth century. If this were true, and if this were all there is to unionism, then it would be condemned as irrelevant. As we tried to show in the previous section, this is not all there is to unionism. Miller's interpretation fails to do justice to the subject.

The view that unionism suffers from an incompatible set of loyalties has two logical premises. The first is that contractarian thought is relevant only to those interested in the history of political ideas and is no longer appropriate to understand the practical problems of modern government; and the second is that a more persuasive political doctrine – i.e. nationalism or some sub-variant of it – has not only absorbed the wisdom of contractarian thinkers but also provided answers to their questions. We have already considered the notion that, far from being natural and progressive, nationalism itself is a doctrine that no longer corresponds to the modern idea of the state. At least one would have to question the universal claims made on its behalf by Miller. Even Woodrow Wilson recognised that the inveterate advocacy of national self-determination as the principle of political obligation was a form of lunacy.

A closer examination of the specific situation of Northern Ireland makes Miller's assumptions even more questionable. First, in so far as the basic constitutional position of Northern Ireland is in doubt, questions of political obligation and the duties of government are of immediate concern and not of merely antiquarian interest. Hence, speculation on the nature of the social contract between citizen and government would appear to be highly relevant. It is not the only intellectual framework within which the current problems of Ulster may be understood, nor may its conclusions even be viable for unionists, but it does suggest concepts that are readily intelligible in the circumstances. Indeed, it is not just unionists who find this so. Miller has scoured the writings and statements of unionist politicians assiduously for examples of contractarian thinking. However, it was an English Secretary of State for Northern Ireland, William Whitelaw, who, from his utterances, appeared to make contractarian ideas central to his whole political strategy. He seemed to define constitutional practice as a set of reciprocal rights and duties, and was not loath in his time at the Northern Ireland Office (NIO) to tell the people of Ulster this basic fact of life. If Miller is to be believed, Whitelaw was preaching to the converted. The difficulty with his formulation of con-stitutional propriety, given what he was trying to do, was that a ''right'' (in this case Ulster's Britishness) is a right as such and is not in the gift of a particular government. A ''duty'' has to be agreed and recognised by those who must fulfil it. The duties which Whitelaw and successive British governments have tried to impose on unionists as a condition of that ''right'' have been, for the vast majority of unionists, an intolerable qualification of that right. This is especially so when unionists are expected to recognise the duty of accepting a role for the

Republic of Ireland in the good government of Northern Ireland. In terms of reciprocal rights and duties, it may be claimed that such an acceptance would infringe a higher duty – the maintenance of the fundamental integrity of the United Kingdom. In this case unionists could claim the right to defy a government if it were failing in its duty.

Secondly, if conditional loyalty is at the centre of unionist political behaviour, Miller has left unanswered one major question in his exposition: namely, what is unconditional loyalty? Of course, he cannot really answer this question for it falls into that category of absolutes which is outside the scope of politics. The implication seems to be that one gets at least some inkling of it in the idea of the "nation"-state. In fact this comes close to a preference masquerading as a political truism. Surely one prime condition of the loyalty of the nation is that the state acts genuinely in the interests of the nation. This leads us to the interesting conclusion that Irish nationalism itself manifests a very similar notion of conditional loyalty. Militant republicans are loyal not to the Republic which exists but to the ideal of the Republic which has yet to be achieved; and constitutional nationalists in Ulster and are loyal only to the idea of a political nation which includes them. It may seem silly to make this point, but it is necessary to emphasise the partiality of an interpretation which places such weight on the singularity of the unionist attitude. It is no more conditional in its loyalty than any other rational political doctrine. Of course, a rational unionism can only be loyal to a United Kingdom which embraces it on the basis of equality. Rational nationalism in Ulster can only be founded on the understanding that eventually the six counties will be brought within the fold of a united Ireland. Neither unionism nor nationalism can assume some fairy tale of unconditional loyalty: this would presuppose a people so devoid of self-consciousness and self-interest as to be no longer citizens but mere serfs. Even serfs had recourse to tyrannicide.

Overall Miller's basic weakness (which applies to all those subsequent interpretations which have followed in his wake) is that two very different concepts are struggling for mastery. The one which is of limited utility for the understanding of unionism is that which is given prominence. The other, which illuminates much more of the character of unionism, is given only passing attention. The first is the idea of the nation; and the second is the idea of the state. Miller's commitment to structure his loyalty thesis around the former blinds him to the significance of the latter. Thus while he claims not to accept "the myth of nationalism which permeates modern political attitudes",[50] his critique of unionism seems to presuppose it. Of necessity, then, his approach is essentially negative, for he is truly concerned rather with what unionism lacks than what it may positively convey. Despite his best intent, he portrays unionist politics as somehow deviant, because originally protestants "avoided the more 'normal' course of investing the 'nation' - any nation - with the attributes of a divine right monarch".[51]

Only towards the end of *Queen's Rebels* does Miller begin to come to terms with the central issue in unionist politics - indeed the central issue in Northern Ireland's politics generally. By the 1970s, he writes, with the onset of the campaign by the Provisional IRA and unionist disaffection with British government policy, the "absence of a state became the essence of the Northern Ireland problem, subsuming all other candidates for the distinction of being *the* problem".[52] This acute insight is followed with this observation of the political situation in the mid-1970s: "Westminster in 1972-74 was unwilling to give meaningful assurances of a determination to make the United Kingdom the state in Northern Ireland."[53] Unfortunately he does not draw out the significance of this point and it becomes lost in his concern with the fog of "nationality assumptions".

Yet nationality assumptions and notions of loyalty based upon them rather confuse the motivation of unionist politics. To refer again to the distinction made above, unionism is concerned primarily with the quality of citizenship within the Union; it is nationalists who are agitated by ideas of nationhood and its extent. The political cohesion of the United Kingdom - its "identity" if you like - cannot lie in loyalty to the nation. There is no British nation; there are only British citizens. Loyalty, if it means anything, must mean loyalty to the idea of the Union: the willing community of peoples united not by creed, colour or ethnicity but by recognition of the authority of that Union. Certainly this formula allows for a wide scope of interpretation on the part both of the government and of loyal citizens. But no idea, however dogmatic, is without its ambiguities, nor is it unchanging.

To accept the authority of the idea of the Union (being loyal to the British state) means in effect that unionists must admit the prevailing political values of the state. However, this does not imply acceptance of the right of any particular government to weaken or to dissolve the Union. Internal reform, as unionists can well recognise, is not necessarily a strategy designed to destroy the Union; indeed the history of Northern Ireland since 1972, despite the inheritance of the Stormont-style of political thought, shows that internal reforms on the basis of general British norms have been implemented with little popular hindrance. As far as most unionists are concerned, the British government is acting within its right (whether they like it or not is a different matter). The principle of authority is not at issue. It only becomes so when the integrity of the Union seems to be under threat – that is, when governments attempt to involve the Republic of Ireland directly in the affairs of the province. Even in the traumatic early 1970s, as Sarah Nelson observed, when memories of Stormont were still strong, "there is little evidence that even those extremists [on the unionist side] who clashed with British troops rejected British authority". Nor did she find that most people were "prepared to contemplate changes in the relationship between Northern Ireland and Britain". She rejects such "simplistic" formulae as "conditional loyalty" to express the complexity of values involved in the unionist response.[54]

There is another way of understanding the politics of unionism without recourse to the supposed arcana of Hobbes, Locke and the Scottish Covenanters. As Miller himself admits, "social contract ideas were never intended to define the allegiance of an entire population participating in the politics of a modern society."[55] Nor need they. Unionists have access to a recognisably modern concept which has wide popular currency, namely the concept of the democratic will. One does not have to look far in unionist discourse to find this concept being used to challenge the policy of the British government and the claims of Irish nationalists. It has been acknowledged, after a fashion, by both British and Irish governments. This concept may be understood as corresponding with such terms as "wish", "desire" or "want". This is the way in which the British government chooses to recognise it, and which forms the basis for what is generously regarded as the "guarantee" to unionists. It is also the term used intermittently in its public utterances by the government of the Republic of Ireland. For instance Tom King, the Secretary of State for Northern Ireland at the time of going to press, agreed in the House of Commons debate on the Anglo-Irish Agreement that the "present wish of the majority in Northern Ireland is for no change in its British status".[56] The same expression is employed in the Preamble to the Agreement. Now this understanding – and not the principles of unionism – conveys conditionality; it treats political allegiance as somehow inherently fickle. Tomorrow, next month, in a few years, the majority may "wish" to be something else. The British government will be only too happy to facilitate that wish only so long as it means Ulster leaving the United Kingdom and becoming part of a united Ireland. No other wish of the majority would be accepted. Such use of constitutional language by the British government suggests an effeteness which cheapens the idea of the Union and certainly cheapens the value of its guarantees. Miller's thesis needs to be stood the right way up. It has been the consistent policy of London to be conditional in its loyalty to the United Kingdom. It has equivocated and vacillated and shown an infirmity of will. As that perceptive student of Ulster politics, Richard Rose, has noted: "In violation of the integrity of the United Kingdom as a state, Northern Ireland has been treated as a place apart."[57]

Rose is one of the few commentators who has recognised the crucial significance of the state in the politics of unionism. He does not confuse the state with the nation, and he understands the idea of the Union in a way that policy-makers do not. After 1972, instead of "removing practices anomalous by Westminster standards, the government sought to introduce new anomalies."[58] This further stressed the conditionality of constitutional commitment. Therefore Rose intelligently interprets unionist resistance to so-called constitutional initiatives as "evidence of a demand, enforced by extreme ultra-loyal actions, to defend the present boundaries of the United Kingdom".[59]

The other way in which the expression "democratic will" may be understood incorporates the insights into unionism which Rose explored, and is a deeper, richer and more full-blooded one. It has to do with the recognition of a common political life and of sharing a general good of civil, religious and political freedom (see McCartney, above); not just a general good from which Ulster people draw material benefits, but also one to which they have contributed and thereby helped to fashion. Unionists have willed the state not in the feeble sense of "wishing" to be British. They have willed it by their contributions in treasure, talent and sacrifice in both war and peace. Often this view is taken as hubris founded on the illusion that somehow the rest of the United Kingdom needs the unionists of Ulster. But in so far as one is concerned with the integrity of the state this is inadmissible. It assumes some sort of hierarchy of citizenship and of geographical priority. In principle, at least, no modern state could admit this (which is not the same thing as acting on principle). But given the degree to which the state does not act according to principle (cf. Rose), unionists are in their right to demand that it does. It is a legitimate demand, dating back to the Covenant and based on the notion of equal citizenship. Equal citizens who will the authority of the Union are entitled to equality of treatment and benefit in the state of which they are an integral part. In particular – and this is important if one is to comprehend the nature of unionist outrage – it is not in the gift of a government to alter the conditions of the Union, for it is not fully theirs to do so. It must be willed by those whom a change of the conditions will directly affect.

The usual argument against this is that such an interpretation denies the legitimate rights of catholics. It does nothing of the kind. The attempt to keep Northern Ireland at one remove from British political life did exactly that (at the same time pleasing nationalist politicians). There is no incompatibility at all between accommodating the diversity of Ulster life and accepting the principle of democratic will. To believe otherwise is to believe that all political arrangements, pending the event of Irish unity, are provisional and ultimately worthless; and this is simply to encourage the instability and mutual suspicion which has been at the heart of the Ulster crisis. At least the IRA is consistent in that it operates on this very premise. It is also consistent in recognising that the existing Republican state will have to be forced to be free as well. The hypocrisy of the Republican government in claiming the territory of Northern Ireland while having no practical interest in the responsibility of governing it has only encouraged such a disposition. One other criticism would be that unionists do not really care about such notions as democracy and will at all; that come the day when there is a majority in Ulster for a united Ireland, unionists would be as wilful in their opposition to this outcome as ever. But condemnation of unionists in advance for behaving like nationalist politicians in the present merely reinforces the unionist argument rather than destroying it.

The purpose of this Chapter has been to criticise the underlying assumptions of some influential interpretations of unionism. This is not to argue that these interpretations have no explanatory value; Steve Bruce and David Miller, especially, have much to say that is pertinent to the understanding of unionist politics. Rather, it is to argue that to reduce unionism to evangelicalism, an identity crisis or conditional loyalty does not adequately capture its character. It is also to observe that these particular interpretations tend to reinforce each other and to convey unionism as entirely negative and politically anti-quated. For instance, if the nation is the normal unit of state organi-sation, and unionists do not constitute a nation but an ethnic group, then all they have is their religion. Therefore the core of unionism can only be the protestant faith. Religious faith is an unacceptable basis for any claim to government; it is too exclusive and too bigoted, as the late Stormont regime demonstrated. And when that system of government fell – as inevitably it had to – then unionism suffered a crisis of identity. It had lost the political coherence which institutional power alone had provided. It was also forced to recognise the uncomfortable fact that Westminster no longer needed unionism or unionists. With that realisation the whole ideological fabric of loyalty collapsed. Unionism is a relic of political history and must accommodate itself to playing a new role in a new Ireland. Generally such a view betrays a fascination with contemporary nationalism, no better exemplified than in the failure of Tom Nairn to understand the dynamics of unionism. For him it is simply ''as aberrant substitutes for nationalism that these idea-systems have to be understood''. Unionism is a crude surrogate ''for a separate or national consciousness''.[60] There can be no other identity.

After the signing of the Anglo-Irish Agreement, it was no coinci-dence that the leader of Ulster's constitutional nationalists, John

Hume, began to talk of unionism's historic task of representing the protestant ethos in a new Ireland. This is consistent enough, for nationalists genuinely believe that this is all there is to unionist politics. What is surprising is that some unionist politicians should accept that definition – the political equivalent of wandering naked in someone else's dream. But there are always those in any style of politics who do not think beyond the self-satisfied, inward-looking level of Sinclair Lewis's Gopher Prairie. The reason why it is easy for unionists to assimilate the definitions of others is that they rarely bother to explore the political principles of their own belief. When they do, it tends to be a sort of back-handed compliment to nationalism. Hence the recent fascination for exploring and at times manufacturing a distinctive Ulster culture from the "Cruthin"* of pre-history to the Shankill Road of today. While the specific motivation of this ingenious effort may be understandable, it tends to compound that besetting sin of Ulster politics – its parochial self-indulgence. This is what nationalism is all about, but it need not absorb the energies of unionism.

As an idea, unionism has a place for localism; but it puts it in its place as part of a wider vision. The strategy of David Lloyd George in his Irish policy was to foist a devolved system of government upon unionists and thereby to encourage localism to triumph over the idea of the Union. In this he was partly successful. The Unionist party of the Stormont days got into the habit of thinking of the Stormont parliament as sovereign and of Stormont ministers as statesmen of international rank. At least Caligula's horse had the sense not to believe itself to be anything other than a horse. But the wider vision was never completely dimmed, and unionism has always been at its most sensible when it has understood that it is not an entire philosophy of life, as nationalism exclusively claims to be, but a theory of the state. As such, as we have tried to explain, it is intelligible and defensible. Indeed it is more appropriate in modern conditions than the romantic nostalgia of contemporary Irish nationalism.

It may be claimed that such a theory is too abstract and too far removed from what Karl Mannheim would have called the "social carriers" of this theory, namely flesh-and-blood Ulster protestants. My purpose was to examine unionism in terms of principles that could contest effectively with Irish nationalism at that level of abstraction at which the latter is usually considered (an aspiration). And if nationalism claims to be an ideology that transcends its social carriers – flesh-and-blood Irish catholics – then unionism merits a similar considera-

---

*The original people of Ulster, adopted by some loyalists to prove the right of Planters against the Gaels.

tion. Again we have tried to show that the idea of the state embraces this potential more positively than the idea of the nation.

NOTES

1. R. Scruton, *The Meaning of Conservatism* (London: Penguin, 1980), p. 11.
2. See W.H. Greenleaf, *The British Political Tradition*, vol. 2 (London: Methuen, 1983), pp. 189–95.
3. See S. Bruce, *God Save Ulster!* (Oxford: Clarendon Press, 1986) and John Hickey, *Religion and the Northern Ireland Problem* (Dublin: Gill and Macmillan, 1984). For a view congenial to the interpretation of this chapter see P. Brooke, *Ulster Presbyterianism* (Dublin: Gill and Macmillan, 1987).
4. G. Bell, *The Protestants of Ulster* (London: Pluto Press, 1976), p. 14.
5. M. MacDonald, *Children of Wrath* (Oxford: Polity Press, 1986), p. x.
6. C.C. O'Brien quoted in ibid., p. 12.
7. S. Nelson, *Ulster's Uncertain Defenders* (Belfast: Appletree Press, 1984), p. 9.
8. "Ulster's Diehards Strike Back", *New Society*, 7 March 1986.
9. Ibid.
10. See J. Madeley, "Politics and the Pulpit: The Case of Protestant Europe", *West European Politics*, vol. 5, no. 2, 1982, p. 149.
11. *Fortnight*, July 1986.
12. R. Wallis and S. Bruce, "Ian Paisley: Defender of the Faith", *Social Studies Review*, vol. 1, no. 4, March 1986, p. 13.
13. S. Bruce, *God Save Ulster!*, op. cit., p. 258.
14. Ibid., p. 258.
15. Ibid., p. 264.
16. *Fortnight*, July 1986.
17. *Spectator*, 5 July, 1986.
18. M.A. McIver, "Militant Protestantism as a Political Ideal" (unpubl. Ph.D. thesis, University of Michigan, 1984), p. 272. McIver's study covers the same ground as Bruce, but she does not arrive at the conclusion that evangelicalism is the essence of unionism. Her traditional approach has a certain advantage over contemporary sociology.
19. C. Smyth, "The DUP as a Politico-Religious Organisation", *Irish Political Studies*, vol. 1, 1986, p. 42.
20. S. Bruce, *God Save Ulster!*, op. cit., p. 148.
21. M. Elliott, "Watchmen in Sion: The Protestant Idea of Liberty", *Field Day*, no. 8, 1985, p. 25.
22. Ibid., p. 27.
23. P. Gibbon, *The Origins of Ulster Unionism* (Manchester: Manchester University Press, 1975), p. 146.
24. R.L. McCartney, "Liberty and Authority in Ireland", *Field Day*, no. 9, 1985, p. 5.
25. Ibid., p. 15.
26. A. Bairner, "The Battlefield of Ideas: The Legitimation of Political Violence in Northern Ireland", *European Journal of Political Research*, **14**, 1986, p. 638.
27. See W.H. Cox, "Who Wants a United Ireland?", *Government and Opposition*, vol. 20, no. 1, 1985, p. 38.
28. McCartney, op. cit., p. 27.
29. Bairner, op. cit., p. 638.
30. Lord Windlesham, quoted in J. Biggs-Davison, *The Hand is Red* (London: Johnson, 1973), p. 178.

31. T. Brown, "The Whole Protestant Community: The Making of a Historical Myth", *Field Day*, no. 7, 1985, p. 8.
32. Smyth, op. cit., p. 42.
33. Elliott, op. cit., p. 26.
34. Nelson, op. cit., p. 12.
35. Ibid., p. 108.
36. D. Bell, "Loyal Sons of Ulster March Anew", *New Society*, 19 July, 1985.
37. J. Todd, "Two Traditions in Unionist Political Culture", *Irish Political Studies*, vol. 2, 1987.
38. A. Lijphart, "The Northern Ireland Problem: Cases, Theories and Solutions", *British Journal of Political Science*, vol. 5, 1975, p. 94.
39. A. Kenny, *The Road to Hillsborough* (Oxford: Pergamon Press, 1986), pp. 135–6.
40. *Spectator*, 16 Aug. 1986.
41. *Spectator*, 11 Jan. 1986.
42. A.B. Cooke, quoted in J. Biggs-Davison, *Rock Firm for the Union* (Monkswood Press, 1979), p. 6.
43. B. Parekh, "The New Right and the Politics of Nationhood" in G. Cohen *et al.*, *The New Right* (Runnymede Trust, 1986), pp. 39–40.
44. For the currency of the academic interest in this notion, see E. Moxon-Browne, *Nation, Class and Creed in Northern Ireland* (Aldershot: Gower, 1983), ch. 1.
45. D. Miller, *Queen's Rebels* (Dublin: Gill and Macmillan, 1978), p. 4.
46. Ibid., p. 1.
47. Ibid., p. 5.
48. T.E. Utley, *The Lessons of Ulster* (London: J.M. Dent, 1975), p. 25.
49. Miller, op. cit., p. 5.
50. Ibid., p. 4.
51. Ibid., p. 6.
52. Ibid., p. 150.
53. Ibid., p. 164.
54. Nelson, op. cit., p. 96.
55. Miller, op. cit., p. 40.
56. *Hansard*, 27 Nov. 1985, col. 887.
57. R. Rose, "Is the United Kingdom a State? Northern Ireland as a Test Case" in P. Madgewick and R. Rose (eds), *The Territorial Dimension in UK Politics* (London: Macmillan, 1982), p. 125. See also the work of P. Bew and H. Patterson, esp. *The British State and the Ulster Crisis* (London: Verso, 1985).
58. Ibid., p. 115.
59. Ibid., p. 129.
60. T. Nairn, *The Break-Up of Britain* (1977), p. 236.

2

THE EVOLUTION OF THE AGREEMENT

There is about the Anglo-Irish Agreement that simplicity of conception which would encourage the impartial observer to ask – as one
always does of other modes of innovation – "Why did no one think of
that before?" The logic of the Agreement is such that it is likely to
appeal, on the grounds of rationality, to the uncommitted (and there is
little doubt that part of its rationale was to do exactly that). It appears in
all its articles as a triumph of statesmanship, of the art of compromise,
over the unruly passions of irresponsible prejudice. Nevertheless, logic
and wisdom are not necessarily inseparable; and if the notion of politics
as the art of the possible has any consequences for policy, a cautious
pessimism should at least inform the counsels of logic. Logic is a pro-
blematical term in political discourse since one person's logic is
another's insanity. In politics it may lead to the most calamitous of
unintended effects, however rigorous the intellectual preparation. The
historian is aware of the swiftness with which praise for the reason of a
judgement can turn into criticism of its fallacy. In this vein Conor
Cruise O'Brien reflected that the Agreement embodied "a remarkable
theoretical theory". As a prominent scholar of that realist and prag-
matist Edmund Burke, O'Brien is certain that Burke would have
despised it "for its excessive confidence in the power of documents and
institutional innovations to change human attitudes and passions".[1]

Since Burke's whiggish conservatism is truly the paradigm of British
constitutional practice, this may raise doubts as to the appropriateness
of such a departure from tradition. Where Ireland is concerned, British
governments have always been prepared to make exceptions.
Generally it has happened that when it comes to abstract thought and
schemes based on it, British politicians in charge of Northern Ireland
have shown themselves to be incompetent. They are ill-equipped for
the task. T.E. Utley has argued persuasively that the failures of British
policy since 1969 may be attributed to the fact that "those responsible
for that policy have fallen far short of the standards of sensible medio-
crity for which the British are traditionally supposed to look in their
statesmen".[2] Both O'Brien's and Utley's comments make specific
reference to relations within Northern Ireland. The Anglo-Irish
Agreement (as its very name suggests) is also concerned with relations
between two sovereign states. This provides a different perspective
altogether on the "logicality" of the enterprise. Rather than theoretical precision applied to the situation in Northern Ireland in the

31

expectation that experience will conform to principle, logic in this other sense is figurative. It suggests the necessary consequence of assumption and conclusion. Whereas political logic in the first mode implies self-evident truths in advance of activity, the latter implies a political condition arising out of the practical engagements and partial understandings built up in due course between participants. Such understandings are always subject to revision or even repudiation, for they rely all too clearly on the willingness of the parties involved to recognise the imperative obligations of such "logic". This is only to repeat the caveat that everything in politics is by its nature provisional – logic being no exception.

The Agreement is an achievement of the latter sort of political development. It represents a slow and painful recognition by British and Irish governments of what – very broadly, and for a time – constitutes their mutual advantage. However, the statement must be qualified, because the evolution of the Agreement involves temporal considerations, a crystallisation of viewpoints which events might dissolve; and, of course, it cannot be divorced entirely from Northern Ireland's internal circumstances. Yet it has a solidity that does not lie in theory at all but in something very conservative and pragmatic. Brendan O'Leary captures this understanding when he writes that an institutional approach best reveals the logic of the Agreement. He goes on to argue that from this point of view – the point of view of the manner in which officials and agencies define problems and solutions – the Agreement, "far from being a radical departure on the part of the British and Irish governments, was, in fact, the outcome of the policies and actions of state institutions."[3] There is a historical perspective here which appreciates the development of "compatible strategies" on the part of both states, despite the clear zig-zags in tactics.

Anglo-Irish relations in general disclose, in the words of Paul Arthur, an "asymmetrical relationship and a long history of mutual hostility". The asymmetry lies in Britain's power and historical significance and in the Republic of Ireland's weakness and historical insignificance. The source of much of that hostility is Northern Ireland. According to Arthur, any progress on this latter issue would have to transcend "the myths and prejudices" ingrained in the minds of officials in London and Dublin. As it stands, this interpretation is somewhat loaded since it apportions blame equally for the "myths and prejudices". It accords the Republic's posture more justice than it deserves. Our argument in this Chapter is that the confusions are almost entirely peculiar to the Republic, since it is trapped by an ideological obsession of which the British show hardly a trace. Arthur's account of the history of this relationship illustrates that up till 1969, neither government had given much constructive thought to the Ulster question. This may be politic neglect on the part of London, but it seems like irresponsibility and incompetence on the part of Dublin; it was Dublin, after all, which claimed to speak for all Irish people. Whatever the judgement, the civil disturbances which broke out in that year came as something of a bolt from the blue to both governments. In such circumstances political leaders tend to fall back upon received wisdom rather than setting about amending or re-defining their ideas. Indeed, where Paul Arthur is concerned, even received wisdom was at a premium; neither government, he argues, had "a sufficient repository of knowledge about the problem to engage in radical solutions".[4]

"Radical solutions", like the notion of political logic, is an ambiguous term. To this bald statement we need to add that neither London nor Dublin had enough understanding of its own priorities to establish an effective medium of inter-state cooperation. Nor were the terms of compromise sufficiently clear to either party to allow such an understanding to emerge. It was to take more than a decade for the "compatible strategies" of London and Dublin to be woven into a putative solution to the Ulster question. The purpose of this Chapter is to explore the confluence of these compatible strategies in terms of their underlying assumptions. It considers the intellectual trend in both countries moving towards a "sovereign authority" approach to the problem, and reflects on the significance of the Agreement in terms of the priorities of the two governments.

The parties to the Agreement
THE BRITISH GOVERNMENT

The policy of the British government in response to the political crisis in Northern Ireland exhibits a number of configurations since 1969, of which the strategic intent of the Agreement is the most significant. During the debate on the Agreement in the House of Commons on 26–27 November 1985, some Conservatives described their government's initiative as a "quantum leap" in policy. They were reflecting upon the broad engagement that had been entered into whereby provision for the good government of Northern Ireland was no longer to be the exclusive concern of the sovereign authority in Westminster. Yet despite the clear historical import of this phase of British policy, there are four major assumptions informing it which are far from new. Having been relatively constant in the political disposition of successive governments, they find explicit expression in the articles of the Agreement.

The first assumption, simply stated, is that Northern Ireland is "different". This was an article of faith for Merlyn Rees, Northern

Ireland Secretary in 1974–6.[5] In a note to his Prime Minister, James Callaghan, he wrote that "history and geography distinguish it from other parts of the UK, as does the presence of two separate communities. Its problems are not those of Scotland and Wales and therefore do not necessarily require the same treatment."[6] It would seem natural in a diverse state like the United Kingdom for there to be a variety of local political cultures; in this it is no different from European states such as Italy, where the politics of South Tyrol bear little resemblance to the abiding concerns of Calabria; or France, where what agitates the Corsican seems quite alien to the Norman. So whatever concurrence the characteristics of political life in Ulster may be seen to have which would distinguish them from those of the Home Counties, no single or obvious conclusion need logically flow from such a perception. Clearly Rees (and here he expresses a popular intuition) believes that the specific style of Ulster politics requires an unusual form of government. The assumption usually is that Northern Ireland ought to have its own distinctive form of devolved government with wide powers over local affairs, supposedly to make the administration of the province more responsive to local needs (to use the cant phrase). On the other hand, it could suggest any number of other administrative procedures which would not involve hiving off legislative competence from Westminster. Nevertheless, it is argued forcefully that there is difference and there is *difference*. The socio-political differences of Scotland, Wales and North-West England are qualitatively unlike those of Northern Ireland, and, as Rees argues, require separate treatment. A consistent unionist (either from Ulster or from the "mainland") could accept that up to a point; but there is that point beyond which any unionist becomes suspicious of the litany of "difference". Haunting the mind is the well-grounded fear that London means something else entirely: namely, that it would be more convenient for the political establishment if Northern Ireland were out of the Union altogether, taking its "differences" with it.

The second assumption of British policy is an extension of the first in that it has tended to exclude the possibility of absorbing Ulster's problems within the prevailing procedures of the state. It is that the politics of Northern Ireland ought, as far as possible, to be isolated and abstracted from mainstream debate at Westminster. Generally the tendency of British MPs is to find the whole Ulster question a tiresome distraction and something of an anachronism. (For the moment we will not address the question of whether this is because of the particular way in which these two assumptions have informed British policy hitherto.) It is a tiresome distraction because the ideological lines of political division in Great Britain are social and economic, and rarely constitutional and nationalist. To the political ear attuned to discourse on the intricacies of financial management, to the debate between collective provision and self-reliance, to the arguments over energy and the environment, the fervent constitutional passions of Ulster's representatives are quite an alien phenomenon. Indeed the half-century of devolved government in Northern Ireland before 1972 seems to have entrenched this assumption like a dogma in the public mind. And since the major British political parties do not organise and compete electorally in the province, there has never been a pressing need or incentive to assimilate the parochial tensions into a wider framework, a point taken up with some animation by thoughtful unionists after the signing of the Agreement.

It is an anachronism because unionist professions of loyalty to the Crown and to the British way of life, its vivid language of wartime sacrifice and imperial heritage, echo as the redundant ideology of a former ruling class in the harsh and unfamiliar tones of the Ulster accent. The language of those elected representatives of unionism at Westminster confirms every leftist suspicion of unionism's "reactionary" and sectarian nature; and it embarrasses Conservatives, for whom such notions usually serve as electoral rhetoric rather than constituting a living ideal. On the other hand, the whole thrust of Irish nationalist argument is to take the affairs of Northern Ireland out of the chamber at Westminster entirely and to vest them in the care of some form of all-Ireland institution. In this sense, at least, constitutional nationalists like John Hume* present a case which runs along the grain of certain British political sensibilities.

This was not always so. In the years before the First World War, the politics of Ulster had encapsulated the preoccupations of an empire and inspired the verse of its most celebrated poet, Kipling. After that war things were different, and the British establishment was animated by other concerns. It was weary of the Ulster question, which appeared peripheral to its strategic interests. This sense of exasperation is well captured in Winston Churchill's famous passage about the "dreary steeples of Fermanagh and Tyrone emerging once again" from the deluge of war which had changed the whole map of Europe. "The integrity of their quarrel is one of the few institutions that have been left unaltered in the cataclysm which has swept the world."[7] Churchill may have had a personal axe to grind, but his sentiment was a commonly held one. Therefore the contending Liberal Unionist, Conservative and Liberal factions were relieved to have Lloyd George "conjure" the Ulster question – which, as far as possible, they wanted to forget – out of existence in 1920. As Hugh Roberts succinctly puts it: "From 1920 to 1972, Northern Ireland was obliged to operate a form of devolved

---

*Leader of the Social Democratic and Labour Party (SDLP).

government which kept it at arm's length from the political life of the rest of the United Kingdom, a system which was imposed against the wishes of the Ulster Unionist leaders, who predicted with complete accuracy what the result would be: the institutionalisation and perpetuation of sectarianism."[8]

Even when the Stormont system of devolved government collapsed and ushered in the current prolonged spell of Direct Rule, no provision had been made to assimilate procedures relevant to the consideration of Northern Ireland legislation into the pattern appropriate for either Scotland or Wales. This procedural pattern would in no way contradict the notion of Ulster's political difference, but it would at least recognise those differences as consonant with being a full part of the British state. Instead, legislation is approved on the basis of Orders in Council. Parliamentary scrutiny of such Orders is perfunctory, and attendance at the debates minimal. Conveniently for the managers of the parliamentary timetable, it allows Northern Ireland business to be despatched with little or no disruption to normal business. As Roberts notes, underlying this procedure is the "assumption that Northern Ireland is not an integral part of the United Kingdom, but a place apart, for which special arrangements need to be made, whether these enjoy the consent of its population or not".[9]

The third assumption is that some form of Irish unity is natural, inevitable and, for convenience's sake, desirable. Of course to assume the inevitability of a political outcome does not mean that one will do anything to facilitate that end. It proved expedient for London not to do anything about the Stormont political system until it became too much of a problem; it was content to quarantine the province and label it "unfinished business". What it does mean is that no one is prepared to do anything which would avoid the "inevitable". As far as British policy in Northern Ireland is concerned the sin has not been one of commission but of omission. Since 1972 its assumptions have perpetuated instability, the constant trembling on the edge of chaos, which has afflicted the citizens of the province.

British policy-makers would legitimately complain if they were being accused of trying to force unionists into a united Ireland or of disregarding entirely their fears and wishes. Yet they have been consistently opposed to initiatives which would pull against the tide of "historical inevitability", so deeply entrenched has that particular prejudice become. Alternatives which the British government has been prepared to countenance have been measured against this unspoken, deterministic index of the naturalness of Irish unity. It has exhibited a profound reluctance to subscribe to a definitive expression of Ulster's "Britishness". To do so, it is held, would be to commit a great political error – in short, to be wrong-footed by history. There is nothing which the magniloquent mandarinate at the centre of British public affairs despises more than a conviction or a commitment that is no longer fashionable (when the mandarins speak, a gaggle of academics and journalists is ready to spread the word). The message that goes out is that the British establishment lacks the will or the purpose to fulfil its obligations to Northern Ireland as a part of the United Kingdom – a message not lost on those prepared to use force to achieve a united Ireland. Westminster thus exercises a reluctant sovereignty, one based on necessity and expediency rather than expressing a sense of common will.

This condition is remarked upon by W. Harvey Cox, who describes the position of the British government since 1920 as "quite extra-ordinary". It is "that 1 ½ million citizens of the state, with the territory they inhabit, are free to stay in the state if they so wish or to secede if they so wish. Britain is officially impartial in the matter." Cox has captured the spirit of the government's position, but such an inter-pretation is misleading. It suggests – falsely – that Ulster people, protestant and catholic, have an absolute right of self-determination. In fact, they have the right to self-determination so long as they determine to become part of an Irish Republic. For unionists this is no right at all. However, Cox grasps the consequence of this for Ulster political life; he acknowledges that it is "highly destabilising, leaving the Ulster unionists in a perpetual position of distrustfulness, crying out for reassurance to British policy-makers perpetually stymied by their inability to supply it in sufficient measure".[10] Nothing could give the lie better to ideas of unionist "conditional" loyalty, and put the blame more squarely where it belongs – not in the "inability" of policy-makers to provide constitutional reassurance, but in their unwillingness to rid themselves of a pernicious dogmatism.

An excellent consideration of this "official mind" in London is provided by Jim Bulpitt, who adopts a machiavellian perspective, untainted by constitutional sentimentalism. For him British politics is to be understood in terms of a dual polity which exhibits "a centre seeking relative autonomy from, and 'quiet subordination' in its periphery". As he argues, all the traditions and precepts of the English "official mind" are against the construction of a "highly integrated union".[11] Further, the centre (the political class in London) "never developed any positive Unionist culture. The idea that the United Kingdom was 'one and indivisible' was absent."[12] Bulpitt must apply this understanding not only to Northern Ireland but to the United Kingdom as a whole: when this is done, the Ulster question becomes one extreme example of the equivocation of modern British govern-ments when faced with the claims of the democratic revolution in popular sensibilities over the last century. The idea of the Union as a "partnership of peoples" (to use Tom Nairn's phrase), and subscribed to by Ulster unionists, is one aspect of this revolution. Hence the unionist advocacy of a positive and full-blooded idea of the Union is part and parcel of a popular struggle which takes a number of forms throughout the United Kingdom. While in Ulster the particular idiom is primarily constitutional, it shares the same idea of justice as the social and economic claims of Scotland, Wales and the North of England for equal treatment within the United Kingdom. The unionist disposition may be conservative, but it is a radical conservatism. Just as the citizens of the British regions fear a sell-out of their social and economic rights, so the unionists of Northern Ireland fear a sell-out of their constitutional right to equal citizenship. As Bulpitt concludes, "whatever the morality of the issue", unionist "fears of a 'sell-out' seem justified".[13]

That the British centre has remained in thrall to this notion of the inevitability of Irish unity has led to consequences which would be curious and quaint if they were not so tragic. After the demise of Stormont – that institution which, *par excellence*, revealed the unionist paranoia produced by British stubborness – there was every opportunity to secure the positive integration of the province in the name of security and justice. On the contrary, it continued to operate on the basis of that "strange doctrine", as Alistair Cooke calls it, which submits to the tender consciences of the Social Democratic and Labour Party and the government of the Republic. It has obliged the government of the United Kingdom "to prolong the maladministration of one part of the state because a faint possibility – no more than that – existed that in a future generation the boundaries of the state might be changed."[14] The Agreement was just an extension of that peculiar state of mind.

The fourth assumption, which embodies the other three, has been the operative basis of British policy in Northern Ireland since 1969. It is that stability will be achieved by the establishment of political balance. The Stormont system – despite having been forced on unionists by the British government – is regarded now as having had the seeds of disequilibrium implanted from its birth. It was a majoritarian democracy which pitched a consolidated protestant political power against a dissident minority of catholics. From this premise, enlightened policy must seek to redress the sectarian and religious imbalance and thereby achieve some legitimate framework within which a tolerant respect for opposing views may be fostered. This might appear a fair and liberal concern rooted in the best traditions of British political life; yet such tolerance, laudable and worthy in itself, must be understood in the light of the preceding assumptions. This assumption has consistently conflated two quite separate notions: on the one hand, it has led policy-makers to believe that unionist and nationalist, or British and Irish, or protestant and catholic "identities" (the terms are often used loosely and interchangeably) are of equal validity in terms of ideals, cultural expression and so on; and, on the other, it has convinced them that conditions – these different conditions in Northern Ireland – demand that these identities should somehow have a balanced *constitutional* expression. The conclusion is that it is necessary to institutionalise these identities in a fixed and permanent fashion within Northern Ireland (i.e. some form of con-sociational democracy). More than that, there is a conviction that a balance must be struck between Northern Ireland as a part of the United Kingdom (its Britishness) and the claim made upon it by the *ersatz* home of northern nationalists, the Republic of Ireland (its Irishness).

This is an assumption which severely qualifies the idea of the Union in two very contradictory ways. First, it casts the British government in the role of a neutral arbiter of sectarian political demands. In abstract terms, this is reasonable – so long as it is recognised that such neutral arbitration implies an assertion of sovereignty. In practice, what it has meant is that the government has equated political right with political aspiration, and fatally blurred the distinction between them. To make this point is not to condemn ways of seeking reconciliation *within* Northern Ireland; nor does it suggest any derogation of the rights of catholics. It stresses the point already made: that the sovereign authority is essentially indifferent as to whether Northern Ireland remains a part of the Union or not, and that this indifference has been inimical to the value of rights in general in Northern Ireland. Secondly, the idea of a political balance between Britishness and Irishness being somehow sponsored by the respective authorities in London and Dublin is a political monstrosity. It is a betrayal of the whole idea of the modern state, for it implies a partiality at the heart of public administration. The British government could not claim to be both pro-unionist and sovereign and retain any credibility, for that is a mutually incompatible position. Clearly the British government cannot be taken at its word – if only because it cannot simultaneously be neutral and partisan.

Reasoning such as this, on the other hand, has always been congenial to constitutional nationalists even though hitherto they have remained suspicious of British motives. "Power-sharing" within Northern Ireland has been coupled with some sort of demand for a wider frame of political reference which would institutionalise their "aspiration" for a united Ireland. What is more, the basic thrust of British policy has tended to pay obeisance to this nationalist defini-tion of the Ulster question. In particular, it has officially sanctioned a

constitutional uncertainty which can only have one credible denoue-
ment – a united Ireland. It has done so in a delphic manner which has
demented unionists, frustrated constitutional nationalists, encouraged
the IRA and confused the Republic of Ireland.

Frank Wright analyses this disposition with some perspicacity only
to fall victim to its logic, which leads him to an insupportable
conclusion. He argues that the distance of Britain from unionism (he
really means unionists) ''certainly has some positive effects''. These
are held to be that the British government ''makes more of an effort to
behave neutrally between opposed blocs than it would if it treated the
North of Ireland as a touchstone of British nationality.'' (The nationality fetish again!). He goes on: ''But the desire to keep a distance from
unionism has also prevented Britain from taking full responsibility for
reforming Northern Ireland for fear of being unable to shed that responsibility if the effort failed.'' One could have no clearer statement of
London's pusillanimous dereliction of duty. This insight notwith-
standing, Wright goes on to make the judgement that both ''national
groups'' ought to be put in a ''symmetrical relation to state power'' in
Northern Ireland. ''As this means institutionalising the guarantor role
of the Irish Republic on behalf of Northern Catholics, it also means
that Britain must fulfil the same role in relation to Unionists.''[15]
According to this, the idea of the state as objective right is completely
transgressed while two sectarian political camps lose all need to reform
themselves. In principle, they have big brothers to call on to get them
out of their own mischief; but in practice, and in the light of the
preceding assumptions of British policy, there could be no honour or
interest in this for the intelligent unionist.

These four assumptions have meshed together to form a policy disposition which has given a definite character to the enterprise of the
British government in Northern Ireland. The pattern of this enterprise
is at times unclear, and does not unfold smoothly; it has been presented
in this Chapter in a way that certainly represents an abridgment of a
convoluted process. None the less, one detects the lineage of the Anglo-
Irish Agreement in previous policy engagements. Since London has
operated from the outset on the basis that direct rule is a temporary
arrangement pending some sort of local settlement, there has never
been an adequate focus for political coherence in Northern Ireland.
There is a direct relationship between the fixity of government assumptions and the instability of Ulster politics. The frustrations of British
policy have been largely self-imposed, but could easily be blamed on
the natives. Out of this self-imposed frustration emerged the realisation of the advantages to be gained by a direct political relationship
with the government of the Republic of Ireland.

THE GOVERNMENT OF THE REPUBLIC OF IRELAND

The Irish government asserts a direct interest in, and a sovereign claim to, the territory of Northern Ireland, as stated in the Irish Constitution of 1937:

Article 2: The national territory consists of the whole island of Ireland, its islands and the territorial seas.

Article 3: Pending the re-integration of the national territory, and without prejudice to the right of the Parliament and Government established by this Constitution to exercise jurisdiction over the whole of that territory, the laws enacted by that Parliament shall have the like area and extent of application as the laws of Saorstat Eireann [i.e. the current territory of the Republic] and the like extra-territorial effect.

The spirit animating the Republic's discourse on the problems of Northern Ireland has been the spirit of those two articles, yet despite their superficial clarity and the formal solemnity of the territorial claim, one has to be cautious about taking them at their political face-value. The apparently unequivocal commitment to the ideal and principle of Irish unity must be qualified by the practical experiences of partition: hence the revealing admission in the Report of the New Ireland Forum in 1984 that both the government and the citizens of the Republic tended to treat Northern Ireland as a "place apart". Thus while the historical development of both parts of Ireland may not have affected the emotional symbolism for good nationalists of the words of Articles 2 and 3, it may have modified their exact meaning. Distilling from the broad flow of the Republic's policy since the late 1960s, four major assumptions may be said to inform its disposition towards the Northern Ireland crisis.

First, governments have proclaimed the idea of the geographical integrity of the island of Ireland. National determination is taken to be determination for the whole island and not for two separate parts. The "fourth green field" may have been fenced off by the machinations of British policy, but there is absolutely no question as to where it naturally belongs. The further one is away from Ireland (for instance, the United States of America) the more logical does this claim become, for it appears to go against all common sense that such a small island should be divided into two. This perception is because geographical contours are more easily recognised and understood than political ones; to understand the latter demands some thought as well as interest. But far from being concrete common sense, the territorial claim is incorrigibly abstract and contentious: it confuses the land and the name applied to it with the political will of the people who inhabit it. Of course the logic of this simplistic and untrammelled geographical understanding is a sovereign and independent united Ireland.

As D. George Boyce reveals, this view was crucial to the internal political stability of the newly-independent Ireland, a sort of comforting ideological balm involving an idea of destiny. In his opinion, "one of the most important unifying themes of southern politics after the 1920s was *Hibernia Irredenta*."[16] This theme helped to broaden the historical discontents of the new state by linking them to a general European malaise of territorial frustration – the experience of Italy, Germany and Austria among others. However, as the Constitution suggested, territorial integration could wait, and anyway there was nothing that southern nationalists themselves could do about it. Yet despite this realisation, "uniting territory" remained more important for the authorities in Dublin than "uniting people" (to use Conor Cruise O'Brien's felicitous phrase). How much simpler it was to deprecate a line on the map than to have to address the real resistance of Ulster unionism. This assumption still remains an important component of nationalist thinking. However, there has recently been a slow and partial movement towards reversing the emphasis; this, according to Peter Mair, represents a definite decline of "territorial nationalism". He supplements: "To be sure, the commitment to unity remained part of the everyday political rhetoric, and a minority of voters and political activists would continue to accord it primacy, but in general the demand for unity was pushed to the margins of the new consensus, and the vision of a green, gaelic and/or united Ireland became a thing of the past."[17] Mair might be going rather far in this conclusion, but the general thrust is clear. It is also a politically intelligent course for governments in the Republic to follow. But to move from territory to people as a focus of nationalist claims does not necessarily destroy the impetus to political unity. Indeed the distinction between territory and people can be one without meaning. If the "Irish people" is defined as those who live on the island of Ireland, then the geographical consideration remains paramount.

The second policy assumption is that, regardless of the "artificial" division of the national territory, the government of the Republic has an abiding responsibility for its people who happen to be under the rule of a foreign power. This takes two different and, in reality, antagonistic forms. The first is an inclusive one, assuming that all Irish people in Ulster, protestant and catholic, are the concern of Dublin. It further assumes a rather pious and patronising view of unionist values with Unionism being understood as the false political consciousness of Irish protestants who mistakenly identify with the foreign power. Nor is defiance or intransigence held to be the very nature of the protestant attitude to Irish unity. Rather, it is due to the sad constitutional status of the North which allows animosities and bitterness to fester between fellow Irish people which would be resolved amicably within an all-

Ireland political system. The second is an exclusive concern for the interests of the catholic minority in Northern Ireland – what Paul Arthur has dubbed the Republic's "guarantor" role. Throughout most of the history of partition, Arthur explains, Dublin could do little more than act as an "ombudsman" for northern nationalist grievances.[18] And it did so without any great enthusiasm, although the moral obligation could not be shirked. Dublin's concern for catholics in Ulster was legitimate enough, given London's lack of interest in taking responsibility. The major problem was that its own national strategy was specifically designed to threaten, antagonise and alienate unionists, thereby helping to provoke those very features of Ulster life which it condemned; indeed, the encouragement of catholic alienation within Northern Ireland was instrumental to the cohesion of the idea of *Hibernia Irredenta*. The inclusive and exclusive interpretations of Dublin's role are really the two sides of the unstable and contradictory nature of Southern Irish nationalism in its decadent phase. The significance of the Anglo-Irish Agreement lies in its confirmation that Irish nationalism is nothing other than the political expression of catholicism with the prime minister of the Republic cast in the role of political pontiff to the Ulster flock and the foreign minister as his nuncio.

These two aspects of nationalist populism reveal an opposition at the very heart of its ideology, one which exposes "the contradictory nature of Irish nationalism. Its political theory advocated the incorporation of all Irishmen, whatever their origin, within the Irish nation; but its popular appeal, and its organisational strength, lay not in nationalist philosophy but in a process of political socialisation, begun under O'Connell and continued into the twentieth century, and founded on historical myth."[19] That myth is the myth of a Gaelic, catholic island unsullied by unionism or protestantism. Or as Girvin's cold, clear and unsentimental analysis of nationalism, democracy and Irish political culture substantiates (*pace* Bruce), the close association between "Irish nationalism and religion prevented the development of political forces within the island which could appeal across religious boundaries".[20] Despite efforts (such as the New Ireland Forum) to modify the definition of Irish nationalism, the reality of the Republic's catholic conservatism has not changed to accommodate the new definition. This means either that the citizens of the Republic do not want to attract unionists, but merely want to coerce them; or that the citizens of the Republic are content with the character and integrity of their own state and want to keep things the way they are. Both notions probably coexist, but it is the latter which seems the only credible interpretation. For politicians the idea of Irish unity is still more powerful than the realisation that it is probably not worth the candle. The idea of Ireland for the Irish (however exclusive that phrase may be) still has magical potency in the politics of the Republic.

The third assumption is one which severely qualifies the immediacy and necessity of the first and second. A product of experience and pragmatism rather than pure ideology, it has never been as articulate as the other two, but it may be said to have more substance. Basically it holds that the Irish unity so fondly conjured up by the geographical and populist imperatives will not, indeed should not, happen tomorrow. This is the truth of the Forum Report's remark about Ulster being a "place apart". The unquestioned justice of a united Ireland meant that the problems of unification went unexamined and the exact nature of the new Ireland was not unconsidered. In the mean time, politicians and administrators could devote themselves to the pressing task of developing the distinct and independent entity of the Republic of Ireland. Let the issue of the assimilation of the North be left till the day after the British depart – when everything would be different anyway. With this comforting circular reasoning, practice did not need to conform to rhetoric.

The Republic, in common with all states, has evolved its own distinctive political style and mode of socio-economic management, with the result that a network of interests and groups have become locked into the system of government radiating from the Dáil in Dublin. Officials, public representatives, ministers and pressure-group activists have invested time, energy and reputation, and expect to reap appropriate rewards. These expectations and the political fortunes which depend on them would be severely disturbed if 1½ million Northerners were brought within the national fold. This very pragmatic assumption implies that Northern Ireland should remain a place apart until such time as the Republic can absorb the consequences of unity without undue disruption to the fabric of state. Since the calculation is that no *Anschluss* could take place without difficulty (to put it mildly), the political establishment in the Republic is saddled with a dilemma of its own making, and one to which it cannot admit. In this instance, Sinn Fein's critique of Dublin's policy seems highly accurate; the IRA is right to be suspicious of the motives which inspire its nationalism.

A number of commentators have remarked on the hypocrisy or (if that is too strong) the ambiguity of the stance of the Republic's governments. For instance, Clare O'Halloran has subjected nationalist assumptions to sustained and withering criticism, especially in her exploration of the self-righteous political pomposity of republican introversion.[21] She attaches great significance to the fact that while the language of nationalism has retained its long-standing rhetorical character, the substance of popular nationalism in the Republic has changed. This has been highlighted by Mair, who perceives "the emergence of a new nationalism which derives its legitimacy from the 26-county state itself."[22] In his opinion, the overall conclusion is inescapable: "The vast bulk of Irish voters are not interested in Northern Ireland, and are not interested in pursuing Irish unity – regardless of the means being advocated."[23] What this seems to represent is a willingness – unfocussed but detectable – on the part of the citizens of the Republic to throw off their state's perniciously dependent political culture. It is dependent because it has for too long been sustained by the myth of British influence in Ireland (while at the same time defying it); and has relied upon the Ulster protestants as an excuse to set about reforming its own social structure – belatedly, and with little success. Popular attitudes reflect a growing political maturity of the average southerner, and intimate a clear preference for the direction in which the Republic should develop. An idea, adopted from the German experience, is struggling to give itself concrete form: namely, to retain a loyalty to the idea of nation, while acknowledging the reality of two separate states. This is something with which unionists could happily come to terms. Unfortunately, the backward political culture of the Republic has consistently frustrated the emergence of this possibility; it has made amicable relations with Ulster unionists almost impossible, and encouraged the political intransigence of the SDLP and the violence of the IRA. The nationalism of the Republic's political leadership encourages a renewal of tunnel vision on the part of each new generation of party activists. This, rather than the so-called unionist veto, is the real tragedy for everyone who lives in the land of Ireland.

W. Harvey Cox has investigated the question of who really wants a united Ireland. His conclusion, from surveys of Southern opinion, is that only about one-third of the electorate would accord it priority.[24] This was confirmed by an MRBI poll carried out in the early summer of 1987 and published in the *Irish Times* on 1 September. Only 49 per cent of the Republic's voters believe that there will ever be a united Ireland, and less than 30 per cent believe it will happen within fifty years. More significantly, only 39 per cent were prepared to make any financial sacrifice to achieve this possibility. The percentage of Ulster catholics prepared to make the same sort of material sacrifice for a united Ireland is probably even less (although the IRA ensures that everyone pays a price for not having one). The political energy devoted to an eventuality which only a minority seek to realise is probably without parallel in modern European constitutional history.

The corollary of the growing political distinctiveness of the Republican state is the growing "alienness" of Northern Ireland, which the military campaign of the IRA, the emergence of protestant paramilitarism and the insecurities of everyday life in the North since the early 1970s have exacerbated. As Liam de Paor succinctly put it: ''The duration and character of the violence in the North pointed up both the difference in experience between the people of the Republic and the people of Northern Ireland and the difference in outlook that had developed over half a century.''[25] The fourth green field – the province of Ulster – has unfortunately become infected with a most unwelcome form of ideological pollution, and while Belfast may be attractive as a city in which to buy consumer goods at a reasonable price, the average citizen of the Republic has little desire to import its politics. So in practice this third assumption of policy ironically brings the thinking of the Republic into line with that of the British government. Both happen to believe in the distinctive and unusual nature of Ulster politics. Both want to avoid the disruption of normality which a full integration of Northern Ireland, with all its pressures and demands, would immediately entail. And both, for these reasons, have a vested interest in containment.

The fourth assumption has come to embody the previous three, and is the operative disposition of successive administrations. Very simply, the Republic would welcome a concession or commitment from the British that would satisfy to some extent the ideological and sentimental aspiration to unity without going so far as to thrust the problem – immediately – into its lap: Irish unity sometime but, please God, not in our lifetime. The mission of historic and ideological destiny could remain, while the difficulties of Ulster could be kept at a very politic arm's length. What that concession might be has been a controversial issue within southern politics. Fianna Fail has tended to articulate a more traditional nationalist line, while Fine Gael and Labour have been more inclined to revisionism, but a revisionism which does not abandon the ultimate goal of Irish unity. The two approaches have been personified in the figures of Fianna Fail's Charles Haughey and Fine Gael's Garret Fitzgerald.

The divisions in Irish politics north and south have tended to encourage what the French would call *''la politique du pire''* and others a ''worst case scenario''. For instance, unionist politicians have always preferred the hardliner Haughey. They know where they stand with him and believe that he is so anti-British that London will consequently realise what a friend they have in loyal Ulster. Those like Fitzgerald, with their sentimentalism and goodwill and efforts to ''understand'' unionists, are likely to encourage the British government to do something silly. In the actual evolution of the Anglo-Irish Agreement, both leaders as Prime Minister tried to further the public role of the Republic as a ''guarantor'' for the good government of Northern Ireland. Haughey was Taoiseach when the process of Anglo-Irish summitry got under way in 1980, and it was he who encouraged the

British commitment to give consideration to "the totality of relationships within these islands" including "possible new institutional structures" to involve Dublin and London.[26] Fitzgerald then carried forward the process which had been set in motion, and which culminated in the Anglo-Irish Agreement. What both leaders and their officials seemed concerned to achieve was some sort of direct involvement by Dublin in the administration of Northern Ireland but without immediate or even medium-term responsibility for the costs of such a role. This does not mean that there is agreement on the form which that relationship should take. As Mair writes, while the new summitry was progressing and a mutual accommodation with London appeared in the offing, the same period also witnessed "the emergence of significant inter-party divisions on the Northern Ireland issue". Briefly, Fine Gael and Labour laid stress upon the uniting of peoples by "consent" (though that "consent" might be encouraged, if necessary, by the British coercing Ulster unionists into seeing "reason"), while Fianna Fail emphasised territorial unity prepared by a declaration of intent to withdraw by the British government.[27] This split was not necessarily because of any great ideological divide; it was because of the demands of politics within the Republic.

The Haughey line is firmly grounded in the tradition of the dependent political culture which has been suspicious of any British diplomacy short of a farewell note. The feeling has always been that the Republic cannot enter into agreements with the British without being cheated; it expresses the sort of mentality shown by the representatives of the Irish Sovereignty Movement who can discern the hand of England in every Irish misfortune.[28] It is not without its own perspicacity. To be hardline on the Northern Ireland issue, for instance concerning unionist sensibilities or a unitary state, is sensible for there is obviously nothing to attract unionists to the idea of Irish nationalism. Why, therefore, risk alienating a section of one's own support in a fruitless endeavour? More important, there is the severe risk of being accused of collaboration in the British occupation of Ulster and betrayal of republicanism in trying to have direct influence on the Northern Ireland polity, a danger of which Haughey is well aware. It has little to do with helping England maintain her hold on Ireland, an absurd notion though one that is often expressed. It has to do with the integrity of Southern politics. Not only does an arrangement like the Agreement allow Dublin a role in Ulster's internal affairs, but it also brings those affairs into the day-to-day politics of the Republic. Every time the SDLP gets upset, Dublin cannot simply make the usual noises about failed political entities or about the "nationalist nightmare" in the North; it is obliged to try to do something about it. Mixed education in Ahoghill may exercise the attention of the Republic's government and divert its energies from its own pressing needs. Nor (rightly) is Haughey keen to see the Social Democratic and Labour Party (SDLP) MPs John Hume or Seamus Mallon materially affecting the course of the Republic's foreign policy. This is not the sort of bargain for which republicans like Haughey have wanted to settle. In the stakes of all or nothing, it has always been more satisfying for the dependent culture to have nothing rather than to have something; or to appear to have everything without having to give anything in return. Hence the salience of maintaining a "principled" stance on the status of Northern Ireland.

The Fitzgerald line has been to try to deal with the problem in terms of a limited engagement that would contain the virus of Ulster politics and control its symptoms. Explaining his perception and his political strategy, Fitzgerald admitted that the political calculation involved in the process of negotiating the Agreement was part of "the completion of a process through which the Irish state has had to go in order to face a reality it did not want to face: that Partition was not going to end in the foreseeable future; could only end in consent; that this consent could only be secured over a long timescale and with radical changes in our state; and that, in the meantime, something had to be done to end the violence in Northern Ireland."[29] Most significant is his phrase "completion of a process', implying that it could only be achieved by attaining a victory over unionism. The catch was that by attaining a victory over unionism the Agreement would set in motion another process sponsored by IRA violence and SDLP triumphalism, and over which the Republic would have little control. And despite all his fine phrases about reforming the state in the South, Fitzgerald's experience has shown that that is precisely what no Irish politician has been able to achieve. The failure fully to comprehend unionist objections to unity and to recognise the profoundly negative opinion of the Southern state held by both protestants and catholics in Northern Ireland is part of the complacency of a nationalism made even more self-satisfied because of its attempt to put a conciliatory gloss on the same old ideas.

That brief sketch is a simplistic abridgement of two differing approaches, but may serve to indicate the contentious characteristics of nationalist argument. It may also indicate the ambivalent elements of any direct co-operation with the British government in the administration of Northern Ireland. The Fitzgerald approach acknowledged and stressed the opportunities, while that of Haughey emphasised the difficulties. Significantly these opportunities and difficulties had to do with the affairs of the Republic and not with the fate of Ulster catholics – there was much to play for in terms of nationalist kudos and, more important, in terms of political success in the Dáil.

As the fallout of violence and instability from the North imposes some cost on the Republic, it is to its advantage to engage in close security co-operation with Britain to protect its own interests, if not the lives of Ulster people. Yet without a British accommodation of the Republic's claim on Northern Ireland there are real political limits to such functional co-operation; for example, it would be seen to facilitate the "occupation" of the North against the spirit of its own constitution. Therefore, without an open gesture from London to legitimise the Republic's interest in Northern Ireland, the growing fear in both capitals was that the ideological assumptions of Irish policy could work against and frustrate its more pragmatic considerations – to no one's advantage. The acknowledgement of mutual benefit and compromise led both governments to the position where they decided to formalise their relationship with regard to Northern Ireland. A first example of this was the Anglo-Irish Intergovernmental Council in November 1981, which had grown out of the earlier summits. This was an institutional framework within which ministers could maintain cordial relations and officials could share experiences and co-operate on joint studies of a functional nature. It helped to establish the idea of "sovereign primacy"; that is, it encouraged the view that a "balanced" undertaking by Dublin and London could establish those conditions in which protestants and catholics within Northern Ireland could be galvanised into some form of political compromise. The Irish wanted to help John Hume to humiliate the unionists and thereby reduce support for Sinn Fein. The British too were keen to undermine the Union while piously professing the opposite intention.

The immediate background to the Agreement

In the three years before the signing of the Agreement at Hillsborough on 15 November 1985 there was renewed debate on the nature of alternative constitutional strategies for Northern Ireland. Nevertheless, up to almost the very day of signing, it was unclear exactly along what lines the British and Irish governments were proceeding. The discussions had been held over an eighteen-month period in the strictest secrecy, and only when the details were released did it become plain that an Anglo-Irish establishment consensus had emerged, based on the common assessment of the threat of militant republicanism and the rise of Sinn Fein. Besieged by pleas from the SDLP both to restate the case for constitutional nationalism and to encourage the Northern Ireland Office to make concessions to head off Sinn Fein, Fitzgerald's government had not only to act but to be seen to be acting positively. Similarly, the British government was aware of the potential domestic and international repercussions of a majority democratic mandate among catholics for the IRA (however unlikely this prospect was).

In the light of what the Agreement contained, two reports indicate aspects of the intellectual consensus developing in the Republic and Great Britain. The New Ireland Forum Report, published on 2 May 1984, was the Republic's response to SDLP pressure and involved the three major parties of government in the South, along with the SDLP, in a presentation of "modern" nationalism. In fact there was little that was new in the Forum Report, but it helped to put the Irish dimension back into focus. Its language was moderate and conciliatory enough to allow the British government to use it as an opening to the South. This was followed by the report of the Kilbrandon inquiry – an independent investigation of the Forum Report by the British-Irish Association – published in November 1984. Kilbrandon had no official status, nor did it have the political weight of the Forum. Its significance lies in its intellectual tone and the indication of a style of thinking in the British establishment sympathetic to those ideas which were to find expression in the Agreement.

The stated purpose of the New Ireland Forum, which held its first session on 30 May 1983, was to consult on the manner in which "lasting peace and stability could be achieved in a new Ireland through the democratic process and to report on possible new structures and processes through which this objective might be achieved."[30] The Report had things to say about constitutional forms for the new Ireland which were rather predictable and stale and have been exhaustively commented upon. What was interesting was the critique of British policy in Northern Ireland, which the Report condemned for its lack of purpose and consistency. Strangely and significantly it was not the principles of British policy which were condemned but the fact that its intentions had never been matched in practice. An inkling that the assumptions of British policy are conducive to nationalism's advantage is clear in that perception: the British ought to recognise the logic of their position and recognise the nationalist heritage by some direct and effective linkage of Northern Ireland with the Republic.

But how was this to be achieved? The Forum Report was rather coy on this point – but establishing agreement first *within* Northern Ireland was not seen as a priority. The first step had to be some binding agreement between the sovereign governments to effect a change of political context "within which urgent efforts can be undertaken to resolve the underlying causes of the problem".[31] This leads to the most ambiguous of all the articles of the Report and illustrates the source of conflict to come with unionism over the Anglo-Irish Agreement. Article 5.8 reads:

Constitutional nationalists fully accept that they alone could not determine the structures of Irish unity and that it is essential to have unionist agreement and participation in devising such structures and in formulating the guarantees they required. In line with this view, the Forum believes that the best people to identify the interests of the unionist tradition are the unionist people themselves. It would be thus essential that they should negotiate their role in any arrangements which would embody Irish unity. It would·be for the British and Irish governments to create the framework and atmosphere within which such negotiations could take place.[32]

At first reading, this appears a benevolent demonstration of nationalist good faith and an indication of the bold thinking for a new Ireland. Read in the light of the Hillsborough Agreement, its implication is much more sinister. It can be taken to mean, first, that the two sovereign governments should establish a constitutional *fait accompli*, setting up institutions compatible with the idea of Irish unity; and secondly, that the British government should use the resources at its disposal to "encourage" unionists to come to terms with it. Then, and only then, could unionists negotiate the guarantees required to safeguard their "identity". Constitutional nationalism is revealed once again as discounting all that unionism means and as understanding democracy in a way which takes account only in passing of the majority in Northern Ireland. To unionists, excluded from the Agreement deliberations and presented with what they see as a *diktat*, this is precisely what has happened. The argument of the deed of 15 November 1985 is already intimated in the argument of Article 5.8.

The Kilbrandon inquiry team were not unanimous in their final recommendations as to what the response to the Forum Report should be. None the less, they were agreed on the analysis of the situation in Northern Ireland. Where they differed was on the "*appropriate degree* of the association of the Republic with the administration of the province"[33] (my emphasis); but there was no disagreement on whether or not the Republic should have any association with the administration of the province. This distinction is supremely important. To their credit, the minority felt that sovereign co-operation between Dublin and London was important, but that it should not go to the lengths of confusing responsibility. Certainly Dublin should not have a say in the internal affairs of Northern Ireland, for that was against the direction in which the majority – who wanted to please the powers that be – felt things ought to move.

The starting-point of Kilbrandon's analysis is the assumption that the Irish dimension must not be obscured, for it will not go away. "It must in fact be given some substance, not least because a thing of substance is more easily accepted than a lurking ghost."[34] This defence of the involvement of the Republic is very similar to that provided by the Secretary of State for Northern Ireland, Tom King, in his speech on the Agreement to the House of Commons[35] (clearly it had become received wisdom). Old apparent certainties were now being reinterpreted in a convenient way for British policy-makers. For instance, the British "guarantee" (a term which, on its own, suggests that Northern Ireland is some form of political merchandise) was not so unambiguous as we had all thought: according to Kilbrandon, it did not rule out the possibility that "while continuing to be a part of the United Kingdom, the province should also become part of the Republic of Ireland".[36] The majority report favoured a "suitably modified form of joint authority" which would involve the co-operation of both governments at the highest level of effective decision-making in Northern Ireland. If Ulster politicians – i.e. unionists – failed to co-operate, then London and Dublin should persevere with their own priorities even to the point of "joint direct rule".[37]

In summary, then, one may argue that a persuasive intellectual consensus was developing among politicians and officials in London and Dublin and their academic minions in favour of joint action by both governments as a first step towards the resolution of the Ulster crisis. Clear-sighted as usual, Bulpitt recognised what the British were up to. The process of intergovernmental discussion was important for London because it forced the Republic to state its position clearly. Moreover, the British were keen to explore "its potential impact on Dublin's official mind regarding unification". He continued: "In a sense summits can be regarded as a subtle device to offload some responsibility for Northern Ireland on to Irish governments." It was forcing Dublin to face up to the key question of the whole problem: "the terms of the future contract which Dublin would offer the majority community in Northern Ireland to bring about unification".[38] As it turned out, the Dublin government was not prepared to make any offer at all. It continued to talk of the nationalist Sugar Candy Mountain while Fitzgerald bumbled incoherently about his Protestant mother; it remained beautifully stretched out between wishful thinking and cold realism; it hoped for the best of both worlds – to face up to the "realities" of modern Ireland without letting go of the dream. Even if, following the "Out! Out! Out!" Anglo-Irish summit of November 1984, the Forum's alternative structures for a new Ireland were rejected, this did not mean that many of its recommendations, suitably reinterpreted, would not be congenial to the longer-term calculations of British and Irish officials. After all, as we have tried to show, there was a potentially similar frame of reference within which each government could orient their remaining differences. It took a year and a half for these differences to be smoothed out.

The Anglo-Irish Agreement

A week may, as Harold Wilson once said, be a long time in politics, but eighteen months is a short time in Anglo-Irish relations. What is perhaps remarkable about the Agreement is not the delay between conception and signing but how rapidly official attitudes on both sides coalesced into a firm commitment, and how far that commitment went. Of course there were the usual alarums and excursions which attend such an enterprise, and these have been well covered in a number of commentaries.[39] On the Irish side, there was much concern about the concessions the Republic might have to make on security; in return it wanted clear promises from the British on the reform of the judicial system in Northern Ireland. The "ambiguities" of the engagement are nowhere better illustrated than in the subsequent political controversies over these very points. The problem for the British Foreign Office and the Cabinet Office was, as it has been throughout her premiership, that the Prime Minister, Margaret Thatcher, actually happens to believe in ideas such as the Union. When the established wisdom of officialdom is to attenuate the Union of Great Britain and Northern Ireland, this is unfortunate. As Enoch Powell has laconically reported, the civil servants were worried momentarily lest the Prime Minister would spoil their preparations: "Three times she lay down between the shafts," as one put it, "but we got her whipped up again."[40] Apparently the Prime Minister was sold the package on the basis of both improving security in Ulster and strengthening the Union. Clearly the persuasive powers of the Whitehall mandarins are formidable.

The interests of the British government have been served by playing down the constitutional significance of the Agreement while the reverse has been true for the Irish government. Neither side is being entirely truthful or accurate in the presentation of their case. In general, however, the following considerations have been established to the immediate satisfaction of both. For the British, Northern Ireland's political distinctiveness compared to the rest of the United Kingdom is further underlined: the discussion of its affairs is set further apart from the Westminster norm and constrained by the obligations of an international treaty. The Agreement embodies all the familiar notions of political balance designed to capture the imagination of world opinion. To balance unionist and nationalist "aspirations" the Anglo-Irish Conference has been established. This primary balance is designed to create the framework of discussion within which local parties can come to some form of mutual accommodation. The second balance is the aim of fostering a devolved power-sharing administration between protestants and catholics which would be responsible for a wide range of legislative functions. The Irish dimension, then, has been partly absorbed into the whole texture of government in Northern Ireland, and London's willingness to facilitate an eventual united Ireland is set out in black and white in the Agreement itself. That third assumption of British policy had become explicit.

For the Republic, the aspiration to eventual Irish unity is in no way circumscribed. It was not even obliged, given the generous British negotiating position, to revise or withdraw Articles 2 and 3 of its Constitution. That the government of the Republic has a special role to play in representation of nationalists (or is it catholics?) in Northern Ireland is also acknowledged. This only recognises the sectarian nature of Irish nationalism and not its universal claims. However, since we are in the new age of political realism, the Republic was prepared to go along with it while doing its best not to admit it. What longer-term consequences this admission has for Irish nationalism remains to be seen. Ironically, this significant admission has been ignored by unionist politicians. They have failed to recognise, as have most of the advocates of "guarantor" politics, that this acceptance by the Republic of the exclusive nature of its interest makes any united Ireland – in principle – insupportable. How, unionists may well ask, can Dublin ever guarantee them political equality when the Agreement has defined its role as a sectarian guarantor? If the Agreement has given unionists few practical opportunities, it has handed them this valuable ideological ace – there, in black and white, in an international treaty. In the mean time, the Republic's government has managed to acquire a direct influence in the decision-making process in Northern Ireland without responsibility for the execution of policy. Britain retains nominal sovereignty. Thus Northern Ireland can remain (to a degree) a place apart. So in the terms of our assessment of the policy assumptions of both governments, the text signed at Hillsborough incorporates most of the elements of an optimal solution. It is little wonder that they have indicated their determination to see the Agreement firmly established whatever the immediate resistance it engenders, for, in principle, it coincides neatly with British and Irish *realpolitik* and offends neither party.

The Anglo-Irish Agreement consists of thirteen Articles and a preamble setting out the broad principles accepted by both parties. Its brevity does not belie its critical import for unionism. As academic commentators have observed, the preamble concedes the definition of the Ulster crisis advocated by Irish nationalism.[41] For example, the text proclaims the "need for continuing efforts to reconcile and to acknowledge the rights of the two major traditions that exist in *Ireland*" (my emphasis). Reconciliation in such terms is not between the contending parties within Northern Ireland but within the framework of Ireland as a whole. The language here is the language of the Forum Report, and it implicitly abandons any idea of encouraging catholics to support the Union.

Article 1, concerning the status of Northern Ireland, makes this even clearer. Both governments affirm "that any change in the status of Northern Ireland would only come about with the consent of a majority of the people of Northern Ireland", and both recognise that for the moment such a majority does not exist. When it does, both governments "will introduce and support in the respective Parliaments" legislation to give effect to the wish for a united Ireland. This Article is ambiguous in vocabulary but unambiguous in the direction in which it points. First of all, the Agreement makes a manifest change in the status of the province; it reflects the Kilbrandon style of sophistry and takes liberties with the interpretation of the 1973 Constitution Act. Secondly, the historical inevitability of Irish unity is promoted because the text acknowledges no other possibility or eventuality. The idea of self-determination is not recognised. The Agreement suspends Northern Ireland in an ante-chamber of the Union (the term coined later was the "window-ledge of the Union") and gives notice that it will stay there until proper deeds of transfer have been drawn up. The democratic façade of the Agreement hides its true spirit – it resembles more than anything else a land deal between two fedual dynasties.

Article 2(*a*) sets up an Intergovernmental Conference to deal, on a regular basis, with political and legal matters, security and cross-border co-operation. Article 2(*b*) states that the Conference will be mainly concerned with Northern Ireland. The British government acknowledges the right of the Republic to "put forward views and proposals on matters relating to Northern Ireland". In the meetings of the Conference, "determined efforts" will be made to resolve differences, although it is added that there is no derogation of sovereignty on either side. Article 3 establishes the structure of the Conference: it is jointly chaired by the Secretary of State for Northern Ireland and the permanent Irish ministerial representative (usually the Foreign Minister), other officials and ministers attending as required. The Conference is serviced by a permanent secretariat in Belfast, composed of civil servants from both states.

The setting up of the Conference suggests a form of sovereign power-sharing which at first sight seems curiously loaded; it appears to concede to the Republic a degree of influence without commensurate responsibility. Thus, while the frame of reference for Conference deliberations is Ireland as a whole, the effective sphere of operation is Northern Ireland in particular. British commitments at the level of administration are specific; Irish ones are hypothetical. Whatever "determined efforts" the Republic's government must make to fulfil its part of the political bargain remain self-motivated. Nor is there any duty binding on Dublin to associate itself with the priorities of London in the government of the province, although clearly the British expect to involve Dublin in a process which will encourage it to underwrite and legitimise security measures to deal with republican terrorism. Since, as we have argued, Britain already exercises a reluctant sovereignty, it is not averse to the Republic getting the balance of advantage. It is quite pragmatic about such principles. On the other hand, the Republic, flattered by the old enemy and revealing its spiritual dependence on it, may have got more than it bargained for. Fitzgerald may have put his signature to the Agreement, but it is Haughey's scenario which may in the end prove accurate.

The scope of the Conference is to consider the whole range of affairs in Northern Ireland from the day-to-day to the constitutional. Article 4(c) gives to the Conference the power to assess and to determine the "modalities of bringing about devolution in Northern Ireland", which is the declared aim of both governments within the province. Power-sharing devolution would reduce the extent of the operation of the Conference, but would not mean its demise. Indeed, the prospect for devolution seems even less inviting for unionists than ever. Along with the usual stipulations about cross-community support, which impose external considerations upon the internal search for compromise, there is now a significant change in the balance of political forces. For the first time, the definition of what the appropriate form of devolution ought to be is partly vested in the government of the Republic. Devolution has become a function of the Irish dimension rather than, as previously, vice versa.

Articles 5, 6, 7 and 8 outline the representative function which the Dublin authorities should play. Generally its task is to ensure fair play and equal recognition of the nationalist ethos in Northern Ireland. This gives substance to the point stressed earlier, namely that the Republic's role is an exclusive one, that it has accepted formally that Irish nationalism no longer includes protestants. On proposals "for major legislation and on major policy issues" (which issues are not major in Northern Ireland?), the Irish government will expect to be consulted and to present the minority viewpoint. This is important for two reasons. First, it allows the Republic to fix nationalist priorities within the legal order in Northern Ireland and thus to control the "organic" fusion of the two parts of Ireland. In other words, and in principle, it can set the pace of unity, provided events within Northern Ireland become stable and predictable. Secondly, the involvement of the Irish government at such a high level and in such sensitive issues as the mouthpiece of the minority in the North (whether catholic or nationalist is not stated) is a virtual admission by

London that it has no interest in properly governing its own citizens. The text of the Agreement makes bland and innocuous what is a quite amazing confession by a modern state – that it cannot determine adequately and alone the welfare of a proportion of its people.

Article 9 is designed to make more effective cross-border security. Successes against republican terrorism would help the British government to contain violence in Ulster and perhaps enable it to sell the Agreement to unionists. For the Republic it would help to confine the violence to Ulster and prevent it spilling over into its own territory. It is a position at once sensible and cynical, but it is one which shows little concern for the real tragedy of loss of life and destruction of property in Northern Ireland. The suspicion remains that the Republic has never been assiduous in its pursuit of terrorists so long as they have confined their activities to north of the border. And if the government does subscribe to a universal concern over terrorism, why has it taken the Agreement to make it do anything special about it?

Assessment of the Agreement

The Anglo-Irish Agreement has asserted that common ground exists between London and Dublin, and embodies their priorities concerning the long-term political development of Northern Ireland. Those most likely to engage in compromise are those who do not believe passionately and absolutely in their respective causes. This applies to the Agreement, for neither London nor Dublin fully subscribes to either the unionism or the nationalism of the citizens of Ulster. In a rationally calculated fashion, each has tried to affirm a general purpose over and above the exclusive loyalties of Ulster unionism or catholic nationalism. The governments invested the Agreement with all possible solemnity to impose the vision embodied in it. Yet the sovereign compromise cannot be divorced from the passions of Ulster politics, and this external settlement has made any proper internal resolution even less likely.

It has legislated for the absurdity we noted in the analysis of Wright: of the British government being the sponsor and protector of unionists while the Republic steps in to play the same role for nationalists. That is a constitutional monstrosity. Mrs Thatcher herself proposed such a scenario at the press conference following the signing ceremony, yet a moment's reflection reveals its folly. Are legal judgements to be meted out on the basis of unionism or nationalism or on the basis of justice? Given the very existence of the Agreement and the way it was negotiated without their consultation or their consent, unionists could not trust the goodwill of their "own" government. Apart from those specific considerations, the very notion itself is a corruption of the idea of the modern state. Nor is there any likelihood that it will achieve its avowed objective of peace, stability and reconciliation. W. Harvey Cox, in his survey of the Agreement, came to the conclusion that its "main characteristic was the attempted introduction into Northern Ireland's governance of a novel, though modest, measure of necessary ambiguity". It is clear that Cox does not have to live with these "necessary ambiguities" and the violence they encourage, nor does he explain what they are necessary for. Far from stabilising constitutional argument in Northern Ireland, Hillsborough has created an open-ended uncertainty and insecurity, the result of which has been a partial outbreak of unionist atavism and an inspiration to republican terror.

Cox is confused by the verbal fog of the Agreement, and indeed he has reversed the truth: "The pity of it is that the United Kingdom and Ireland, while together embarking on a fine and imaginative political enterprise, were themselves too much in thrall to their own inheritances of simplistic concepts of sovereignty and territoriality, which ill-fitted the peculiarity of Northern Ireland; and out of which the two regimes had done far too little in the past to educate their respective Northern Irish clients."[42] Cox is in thrall to stale clichés on the Ulster crisis. Protestants are not, and never were, "clients" of the British government but, along with catholics, are citizens of the state. To imply otherwise is a misuse of the terms of political science. Nationalists and the British government may not like this, but it is a fact they should recognise. It has been the Republic which has helped to perpetuate divisions within Northern Ireland with a territorial claim it has had little stomach to fulfil – except in the very unlikely circumstances that unionists themselves embraced unity. It is the Republic which has formally adopted a clientelistic role as part of its nationalist strategy which it sees as a means of enabling it to muddle along, trying to reconcile its bombastic nationalist irredentism with its integrity and interest as a modern European state.

The British government continues to argue that its ultimate sovereignty has not been infringed. This is what Mrs Thatcher believes. Yet her officials in the NIO and in the Foreign Office are working to ensure that the way is open to ever greater constitutional "ambiguity". There are any number of euphemisms for lack of integrity, and this one may serve the purpose. The aim is fatally to weaken the Union. Fitzgerald's government trotted out the expected phrases about historic achievements for nationalism and new beginnings. For the Republic the professed purpose of the Agreement was to allow it to help settle the long-running sore in Anglo-Irish relations. This is a noble aim, but the Agreement was also designed to allow it to keep all the old shibboleths intact. The potential this gave to any future government to play the Green Card was to be fully exploited by Haughey over extradition. Thus to argue that an intelligent understanding of the limits of nationalism helped to inform the Fitzgerald approach is not to argue that the "aspiration" to unity has evaporated from the political culture of the Republic. The old contradiction between maturity and honesty and dependence and illusion remains. On 15 November 1985, the Irish government and most of the citizens of the Republic felt that they had got the best of both worlds. Their confidence is probably misplaced for the fundamental dishonesty of the Agreement, and the indifferent quality of the Republic's political establishment, are a recipe for difficulty.

For the Republic the Agreement is an attempt to regulate an ideological passion of which its own fundamental principles are a part. Within the framework of the Agreement it has lost absolute control over the modulation of that passion. The nature of Anglo-Irish relations can now be determined not merely by the interests of the Republican state – as Fitzgerald expected – but also by the sectarian demands of the SDLP and the sectarian acts of the IRA. Ironically the old criticism of the unionist tail wagging the British dog may today be applied to the SDLP tail wagging the Irish dog. Unless the Republic shows greater acumen in confronting the contradictions of its nationalism, then it will have bargained away its integrity for a prize which reason would suggest it ought not to want. That is if the Agreement can survive the contradictions not only of its basic dishonesty but also of the reality of a fundamentally anti-British state collaborating directly with London on that very issue central to its own – contradictory – meaning. The long-term prospect of Dublin, in terms of the Agreement, accepting British "insensitivity" (read: the British government actually behaving like a sovereign authority) and London retaining patience with Dublin's nationalist atavism (read: Dublin politicians finding it irresistible to make capital out of the North) was hard to imagine without some great crises attending the process. And attend it they did, for at the time of the review of the Agreement in the winter of 1988 the whole structure of Anglo-Irish relations had degenerated into bitterness.

But in the long term, as Keynes once sagely remarked, we are all dead. The immediate purpose of the Agreement has been more mundane. It is an exercise in containment and an attempt to cow unionists. At that level there have been differences of emphasis between Dublin and London, yet enough community of purpose to ensure that the whole hypocritical enterprise has not come crashing down. Unionist anger and opposition had to be faced down. The unionist "boil" had to be lanced (to use the felicitous phrase of the new nationalism). This meant humiliating the majority in Northern Ireland to the extent that their political will would be eroded from within. Unionism would become so discredited by the actions of the reactionary few that the many would be happy to accept the new dispensation provided for them by the Agreement – forced "consent" to help facilitate Irish unity. The ability of unionism to confront this challenge was not just a case of organising an effective British-style campaign of civil disobedience. It was also a case of intelligently assessing the situation and formulating the appropriate aspects of its character into a formidable political argument. For the power of the Agreement's philosophy is the ingrained prejudices held about catholics, protestants and the state. And if these cannot be addressed and shaken, then the game is well and truly up for the Union and those who support it.

Therefore, the Agreement was not just an immediate threat. It was also a vital intellectual challenge – in some ways, a necessary one. Slogans might encapsulate the defiant spirit of people who feel betrayed, but slogans are nothing without the deeper political reflection to sustain them. For too long unionism had remained speculatively passive and inarticulate. The crisis provoked by Hillsborough was to stimulate an exciting and acrimonious reconsideration of what, after 15 November 1985, unionism actually meant.

NOTES

1. C.C. O'Brien, *Time and Tide*, Winter 1986, p. 28.
2. T.E. Utley, *The Lessons of Ulster* (London: J.M. Dent, 1975), p. 148.
3. B. O'Leary, "The Anglo-Irish Agreement: Meanings, Explanations, Results and a Defence" in P. Teague (ed.), *Beyond the Rhetoric* (London: Lawrence and Wishart, 1987), p. 24.
4. P. Arthur, "Anglo-Irish Relations since 1968: A Fever Chart Interpretation", *Government and Opposition*, vol. 16, no. 2 (1983), pp. 157–8.
5. M. Rees, *Northern Ireland – a Personal Memoir* (London: Methuen, 1985), p. 99.
6. Ibid., p. 329.
7. W. Churchill, quoted in A.T.Q. Stewart, *The Narrow Ground* (Belfast: Pretani Press, 1986), p. 179.
8. H. Roberts, *Northern Ireland and the Algerian Analogy* (Belfast: Athol Books, 1986), p. 11.
9. Ibid., p. 10.
10. W. Harvey Cox, "Managing Northern Ireland Intergovernmentally: An Appraisal of the Anglo-Irish Agreement", *Parliamentary Affairs*, vol. 40, no. 1 (Jan. 1987), p. 94.
11. J. Bulpitt, *Territory and Power in the United Kingdom* (Manchester: Manchester University Press, 1983), p. 97.
12. Ibid., p. 157.
13. Ibid., p. 230.
14. A. Cooke quoted in J. Biggs-Davison, *Rock Firm for the Union*, op. cit., p. 60.
15. F. Wright, "The Reconciliation of Memories" in *Northern Ireland: A challenge to Theology*, Occasional Paper no. 12 (Edinburgh: Centre for Theology and Public Issues, 1987), pp. 48–9.

16. D. George Boyce, *Nationalism in Ireland* (Dublin: Gill and Macmillan, 1982), p. 23.
17. P. Mair, "The Irish Republic and the Anglo-Irish Agreement" in P. Teague, op. cit., p. 88.
18. P. Arthur, "Northern Ireland: The Unfinished Business of Anglo-Irish Relations" in P.J. Drudy (ed.), *Irish Studies (5): Britain and Ireland since 1922* (Cambridge: Cambridge University Press, 1986), p. 167.
19. Boyce, op. cit., p. 387.
20. B. Girvin, "Nationalism, Democracy and Irish Political Culture" in B. Girvin and R. Sturm, *Politics and Society in Contemporary Ireland* (Aldershot: Gower Press, 1986), p. 5.
21. C. O'Halloran, *Politics and the Limits of Irish Nationalism* (Dublin: Gill and Macmillan, 1986).
22. Mair, op. cit., p. 86.
23. Ibid., p. 105.
24. W. Harvey Cox, "Who Wants a United Ireland?", *Government and Opposition*, vol. 20, no. 1 (Winter 1985), pp. 29–47.
25. L. de Paor, *The Peoples of Ireland* (London: Hutchinson, 1986), p. 319.
26. *Irish Times*, 9 Dec. 1980.
27. Mair, op. cit., p. 99.
28. See, for instance, A. Coughlan, *Fooled Again* (Cork: Mercier Press, 1986), esp. pp. 34–5.
29. Fitzgerald quoted in *Northern Ireland: A Challenge to Theology*, p. 59.
30. New Ireland Forum, *Report*, 2 May 1984, p. 1.
31. Ibid., p. 24.
32. Ibid., p. 30.
33. Lord Kilbrandon (chairman) *Northern Ireland: Report of an Independent Inquiry* (London: The Independent Inquiry, 1984), p. 5.
34. Ibid., p. 22.
35. *Hansard*, 27 Nov. 1985, col. 888.
36. Kilbrandon, op. cit., p. 29.
37. Ibid., p. 55.
38. J. Bulpitt, op cit., pp. 227–8. For Bulpitt Mrs Thatcher was doing her duty by the dual polity and abandoning the integrationist thrust of the Conservative Party's 1979 manifesto.
39. See, for instance, B. Girvin, "The Anglo-Irish Agreement" in Girvin and Sturm, op. cit.
40. *Spectator*, 11 Oct. 1986.
41. See, for example, M. Connolly and S. Loughlin, "Reflections on the Anglo-Irish Agreement", *Government and Opposition*, vol. 21, no. 2, 1986, p. 148.
42. W. Harvey Cox, "Managing Northern Ireland Intergovernmentally", op. cit., p. 97.

3

THE UNIONIST RESPONSE

Surveying the Northern Ireland scene in the immediate aftermath of the Hillsborough Agreement, Paul Arthur argued that the response of unionists to the new dispensation would be crucial. "The future of the Anglo-Irish process centres largely on this community as to whether it accepts willingly, with others, its subordinate status or whether we shall be forced towards the 'dreary steeples of Fermanagh and Tyrone' again." In one of those neat phrases with which authors try to encapsulate a situation and do justice to their own perspicacity, Arthur goes on to describe the new asymmetry in Anglo-Irish relations as one which involves "self-confident Catholics and demoralised and divided Unionists".[1] This interpretation of the post-Hillsborough situation contains a number of assumptions which need to be addressed for they characterise a certain disposition common to a number of popular criticisms of unionist opposition to the Agreement.

To begin with, the use of the term "subordinate status" implies that before 15 November 1985 unionists occupied a superior political status. Nowhere is any evidence for this cited; indeed the very use of the term "status" in the context of Arthur's argument is meaningless for it stands without relation. Nonetheless it is a common assumption assiduously propagated by those unsympathetic to the Union that in Northern Ireland unionists dominate catholics. Fionnuala O'Connor, while hardly sympathetic to unionism, is generally careful and reflective in her journalism; yet she wrote that unionist mobilisation against the Agreement would find it difficult to hide the real motive – pain and anger "at the loss of supremacy".[2] Anthony Coughlan put forward a similar view, arguing that the "main constituent in unionist hostility to Hillsborough was the venom of a politically privileged caste at learning it was losing its privileges".[3] These assertions are left judiciously vague. The intention is clear enough: to suggest that whatever the nature of unionist complaints and disaffection, they really had good reason to expect what had happened, and not before time.

Politically, such facile jibes are about two decades out of date. They might have been applied with some justice to the old Stormont order when unionists did feel that, where possible, they were entitled to preference as true and willing citizens of the state. But since the universal provisions of post-war welfarism treated willing and unwilling citizens alike, the extent of such discrimination has always been exaggerated. It manifested itself most evidently in local government; and what was true of unionist-controlled districts was equally true of nationalist-controlled ones. After 1972 the idea of unionists any longer being a privileged caste or in a position of supremacy does not bear close examination. Their determination to maintain the Union with Great Britain did not change, but that is something quite different. That determination is not intrinsically supremacist, nor does it entail a superior status; to suggest that it does only distorts our political language. The critical weakness of the ''status'' argument is that it inevitably confuses the issue of national identity and the issue of justice within the state; or what Bew and Patterson call the national question and the democratic question. The latter has to do with ''those historic and current practices which discriminate against'' catholics; the former with the very different issue of whether Northern Ireland should be part of the United Kingdom or not. Since 1972 there is every indication that although certain sections of unionism are far from pleased with the progressive elimination of sectarian discrimination undertaken by Westminster, there is no pressure at all within unionism to return to the old order. So long as Northern Ireland is unequivocally recognised as part of the United Kingdom, unionism will have proved itself a remarkably complaisant political force. Yet it at once becomes intransigent and defiant when the government tries to qualify or circumvent the popular will to maintain the Union. In the words of Bew and Patterson, ''the liberals and the neanderthals make common cause.''[4] A common subordinate status is certainly implied by the Anglo-Irish Agreement insofar as it means that unionists will be represented in the Conference by a government minister over whom they have no control and nationalists by a government minister whom they have never had a chance to mandate. But these democratic assumptions are far from the minds of those who advance the supremacy thesis.

The second point concerns the new relationship between the communities in Northern Ireland. In the nature of things, such an impression is hard to confirm or deny, although, in the analysis of the recent intimacy between the governments in London and Dublin, Arthur has been more accurate than most. This much can be said. The intent of the Anglo-Irish Agreement is precisely to foster the division and demoralisation of unionism; and no doubt for the SDLP leader John Hume and the catholic establishment in Dublin it would be a good thing if their co-religionists could notch up a victory over the other side. Conor Cruise O'Brien captures the essence of this. The Hillsborough accord is understood as the Micks having put one over on the Prods. Of course this is not the sort of language Hume himself would use. ''The idea is to sound conciliatory, to the Brits, in order the better to screw the Prods. Mr Hume is a virtuoso of this kind of conciliatoriness, and the Anglo-Irish Agreement is Mr Hume's *chef d'oeuvre.*[5] So much for self-confident catholicism and constructive statesmanship. In reality it transpires that it is the small change of sectarian politics writ large in the affairs of international negotiation. Nor is the policy of creating divisions within unionism anything new in British policy. It has been a consistent strategy in London since it was forced to involve itself in Ulster politics in 1969, to foster a "moderate" unionism, defined not in terms of its willingness to accept reform within Northern Ireland but in terms of its willingness to compromise the Union. A measure of the rigidity of policy-makers is that they have ignored all the evidence which shows that such "moderate" unionism is impossible to sustain for the purpose intended. In the pursuit of this impossibility, they have missed opportunities to reform thoroughly certain unacceptable features of Northern Ireland society. What is novel about the Anglo-Irish Agreement is the extent to which the British government has been prepared to engage in the morally dubious exercise of power to humiliate and demoralise unionism. This is popularly known as calling the unionist bluff. Those whom the government wish to divide and rule they first try to make mad. Part of this strategy of calculated demoralisation was to release the furies of unionism and thereby to destroy respectable opposition to the Agreement from within. And it was confidently expected that this would be in the shorter rather than the longer term. So one has to be careful about taking Arthur's epigrammatic excursion at face value. Catholics may not be so confident about their future in the sort of world the workings of the Anglo-Irish Agreement might produce – especially if it meant accepting the civil liberties and living standards of the Republic; and the idea that unionists had become divided and demoralised is hard to reconcile with the almost universal rejection of what the Agreement implies. In the opinion of Brendan Clifford, instead of "intensifying unionist demoralisation, Thatcher's betrayal dispelled a nagging demoralisation which has persisted around the fringes of unionism since the late sixties."[6] A.T.Q. Stewart illustrates this new mood vividly (albeit histrionically) when he writes that "all was changed utterly on 15 November 1985. A terrible, unwished-for duty was born." And for the moment a novel solidarity emerged: "One thing is particularly striking; the attitudes of Protestant anti-Unionists. Marxists, socialists, radicals of every description, are saying things which would make followers of Dr Paisley put their hands over their ears. . . . Even the we-mustn't-bite-the-hand-which-feeds-us Unionists are as deeply hurt as the we-will-eat-grass variety."[7]

Stewart captures the immediate atmosphere of the post-

Hillsborough period, although his terminology is somewhat confused and misleading. It was not just anti-Unionist protestants, i.e. those who had never before expressed any party political allegiance, who rallied to the defence of the Union; significantly, non-protestant unionists – those who supported the Union but were atheists, catholics, muslims or whatever – were equally outraged by the Agreement. Indeed, it was this latter group who were to play an important role in providing intellectual substance and coherence to the unionist protest. Thus it may be argued that the trauma of the Agreement had injected a critical determination into unionism for the first time in fifty years. But such unity – and also such diversity – brings with it its own problems: a critical and politicised following could not be satisfied with the parrot-phrases of calmer times. Massive unity itself is subject to the virus of discouragement if success is delayed; and unionist leaders were presented with the difficult task of formulating a strategy that satisfied everyone and maintained the spontaneous momentum of opposition, a task that proved all the harder to achieve given that time was definitely on the side of the supporters of the Agreement. It is also important to realise that if the Agreement had provoked a profound anger in the heart of the average unionist, it had also severely wrong-footed the leadership of the two Unionist parties. At this political level, Arthur's estimation of demoralisation (in the immediate term at least) may apply with some force, and it is to this factor that we now turn.

The calm before the storm

In the history of the Anglo-Irish Agreement, what is surprising is not the intensity and duration of the unionist opposition but the rather belated realisation of what was actually afoot. In Patrick Keatinge's opinion, what gave added edge to the response after 15 November was the humiliation of the unionist leadership who had expected "well into the autumn, that the negotiations would not succeed".[8] With the wisdom of hindsight, it seems remarkable that government dissembling so effectively blinded the Official Unionists and, more surprising perhaps, the Democratic Unionists, to the true extent of its dealings with Dublin. They miscalculated the persistence and the purpose of British interest defined by the Foreign and Cabinet Offices. To be fair, events did not seem to portend any dramatic change in Anglo-Irish relations. First, the Republic's (popular) decision to break the EC's imposition of sanctions against Argentina during the Falklands War demonstrated its dependence for self-respect on traditional anti-Britishness. Afterwards the Foreign Office were happy to put this down to Haughey's personality as the British government and media set about cultivating his successor as Taoiseach, Dr Garret Fitzgerald. The Falklands episode was put down to a hiccup in the behaviour of the new Ireland. Unionists believed that Mrs Thatcher was not amused and that her fury could only work in their favour. Secondly, the Chequers summit of November 1984, when the British Prime Minister summarily dismissed the three Forum Report options for solving the Northern Ireland problem, pleased and encouraged unionists. It was too easily assumed by them and many others that the Anglo-Irish "process" was proceeding no further. Finally, the replacement of Douglas Hurd by Tom King as Secretary of State for Northern Ireland in September 1985 suggested that the British government did not place great emphasis on being sensitive to Dublin's belief in its own importance. The unionist leadership was simply behaving in accordance with the implication of these signals.

For instance the leader of the Official Unionist Party (OUP), James Molyneaux, was well aware of the rumours and intimations of a deal, but believed that these were manoeuvres designed to "unnerve" unionists, a sort of Anglo-Irish flanking attack to entice them into a power-sharing arrangement with the SDLP. More important, Molyneaux had placed his faith in the goodwill and good sense of the Conservative Prime Minister. He was sure that "she will not yield to pressure. She is far too realistic to be fooled by any of that stuff."[9] Molyneaux has always been a Westminster man and is well respected for his honesty and integrity and his competence at the parliamentary game. His way of defending the Union was the undemonstrative, the quiet and patient, cultivation of sympathy behind the scenes. And he believed that Mrs Thatcher would block any attempt to attenuate the Union. This was the word coming from those close to her like her Parliamentary Private Secretary Ian Gow. Addressing the Annual General Meeting of the Ulster Unionist Council on 30 March 1985, Molyneaux could sincerely tell his audience to be of good cheer for, despite the rumours, "the rats have been chewing at the bog-oak timbers for decades but all to no effect". Summing up the constitutional wisdom of unionism, he argued that the problem for the "diplomats is that Northern Ireland is a part of the United Kingdom itself and cannot be in and out at one and the same time." Unfortunately for unionism and the syntactical proprieties of politics, the diplomats of the Agreement were engaged precisely in the resolution of that conundrum: Repudiating the idea that unionism has a small and shrinking support in the House of Commons, Molyneaux concluded: "So members of the Ulster Unionist Council, when you return to your constituencies later this day, and you are asked by those who sent you here – 'What is the state of the Union?' Tell them the Union is secure – because the Union is in safe hands."[10] Nine months later the trusting naivety of those words were an acute embarrassment to the Official Unionist leader.

This false sense of security (as it subsequently proved) was not confined to the respectable parliamentary style of the OUP. The Democratic Unionist Party (DUP) was also caught off guard, despite Ian Paisley's mobilisation of opposition to the original summits in the "Carson Trail" of 1981. In the local current affairs magazine *Fortnight* of 4 February 1985, Peter Robinson, the deputy leader of the DUP, wrote that achieving an equitable settlement in Northern Ireland meant that there had to be an "acceptance of some realities". The first of these realities was the "Thatcher reality". This means that "Northern Ireland shall remain a part of the United Kingdom as long as that is the wish of its people." That, according to Robinson, was established beyond doubt at Chequers. "We all know what that means," he continued, "but let me spell it out." For the DUP in early 1985, spelling out reality meant that "any structures set up in Northern Ireland will recognise Ulster as an entity within the United Kingdom. This must be accepted without any blurring of the edges, without circuitous and circumventive small print or surreptitious language. In constitutional law this principle is a legitimate and honourable ordinance, a self-evident trust, and incontrovertible reality. They call it self-determination."[11] Robinson underestimated the scope of official sophistry and how quickly that incontrovertible reality was to change; but included in his brief statement are all the elements of the unionist sense of justice which Hillsborough was to offend.

In early 1985, Molyneaux and Paisley were, in fact, making overtures to the SDLP, encouraging Hume and his followers to take their seats in the Northern Ireland Assembly which had been set up by James Prior in 1982 and which the SDLP, like Provisional Sinn Fein, had boycotted. There was even conciliatory talk about recognising the interest the Republic has in events in Northern Ireland and making efforts to help the British government improve consultation with Dublin. This may be attributed to "a clever ploy" on the part of the unionist leadership;[12] it also shows a certain optimism regarding the trend of the times and an appreciation (misplaced, as it turned out) of the difficult position of the SDLP. The unionist strategy was to bring the SDLP back into the Northern Ireland political fold from the Anglo-Irish wilderness, and to sound conciliatory enough to prevent Hume losing too much face and too much support to Provisional Sinn Fein.

But it was not only unionist politicians who misjudged the times. Journalists and academics were also misled by the course of events. As late as June, the main unionist newspaper, the *News Letter*, was able still to interpret the words of Douglas Hurd to mean that "Dublin's influence is likely to be almost totally excluded from the affairs of

Northern Ireland''.[13] For most of the summer, its editorials repeated more or less the same message. Even *Workers' Weekly*, which was normally the most illuminating political journal in Northern Ireland, got it completely wrong. In May it believed there was nothing for unionists to worry about: "No initiatives, just common sense, pragmatism and stylish patting of little catholic nationalist heads. Things are certainly looking up."[14] By mid-August, that optimism was still there. Continued negotiations between London and Dublin were interpreted as a "Machiavellian scheme by Thatcher and Hurd to appear to be extremely reasonable to Dublin, in the knowledge that Fitzgerald will eventually pull out of the talks when he realises that he would end up with responsibility for government policy."[15] Such was the general consensus – underpinned, as it appeared, not by wishful thinking, but by thorough analysis. Even Bew and Patterson, in their standard text on *The British State and the Ulster Crisis* believed that the Chequers summit had marked the end of an era "when discussion had been dominated by highly speculative proposals of the joint authority type". In their opinion, the "Irish political establishment and its sympathisers deserved little better than the rebuff it received" by Hurd and Thatcher.[16] For most observers sensitive to the prevailing attitudes in Ulster political life, it was genuinely hard to believe that the British government, or indeed the Irish government, would commit itself to the profound absurdity of the Anglo-Irish Agreement as a recipe for good government in Northern Ireland.

It was not till the beginning of August that the leaders of the two unionist parties showed signs of anxiety. They had already begun to formulate a common front, although this had not to do with the Anglo-Irish talks but with the presence of Provisional Sinn Fein in the council chambers. They now turned their attention to what was being negotiated in secret over their heads. On 2 August, Molyneaux and Paisley issued a joint statement making clear that any consultative role for the Republic in the affairs of Northern Ireland would be in breach of the British government's assurances of self-determination. It was agreed to set up a new "think-tank" – the Joint Unionist Working Party – to monitor the progress of the talks and to prepare the unionist response.[17] On 29 August the two leaders met Mrs Thatcher at Downing Street. They demanded that, in the negotiations with Dublin, the Republic should be pressed to repeal Articles 2 and 3 of its constitution and to recognise the right of the people of Northern Ireland to self-determination. By the middle of September, it was clear what the detail of the Agreement would be, even down to the siting of the Conference secretariat in Belfast. Nevertheless there was still a sense of disbelief among unionists at what appeared to be on the cards.

At a press conference held at the beginning of October, Molyneaux and Paisley accepted the need for close co-operation between the governments of the United Kingdom and the Republic of Ireland. This was not a last moment attempt to head off the inevitable; we have already seen that the acknowledgement of the Republic's interest in Northern Ireland was no longer being disputed by either party. However both were adamant that the idea of any permanent secretariat having a day-to-day involvement in the province was a clear infringement of sovereignty and completely unacceptable to unionists. It was also made plain that there could be no deal on devolved government for Northern Ireland if it coincided with any specific arrangement with Dublin.[18] But since unionists were not being consulted, they were effectively out of the game until such time as the Agreement was presented to them. They were reduced to echoing Paisley's words and his hope that "the unity of unionism would be the rock on which a deal would be shattered".[19]

Meanwhile, the SDLP leadership, who had been taken into the confidence of the Dublin government all along, was preparing for its moment of triumph. At the party conference on the weekend before the signing of the Agreement, Hume berated unionists for "hiding behind unrealistic and uncompromising demands"; while Seamus Mallon, not hiding at all, proclaimed that "Irish unity cannot be put on the back burner."[20] The juxtaposition of these phrases illustrate what was to be a feature of political argument in the post-Hillsborough era. The two SDLP leaders at least distinguish the cynical abuse of conciliatory cliché from the real purpose it is intended to serve. Mallon's honest spleen is the perfect antidote to Hume's bilious benevolence. On the other hand, the British and Irish governments were to torture political language with a sinister "newspeak". In his usual direct style, Coughlan expresses this well:

Henceforth in Ulster reality was to be imaginary and the imaginary was to be real. Words were to mean the opposite of what they said. Loyalty was to mean rebellion, sovereignty was to mean sharing responsibility with foreign governments, consent was to mean what the politicians decided it would mean and talk about peace was to hasten preparation for civil war. Truly a statesmanlike achievement, concocted by the most creative political minds of Britain and Ireland.[21]

This is the frustrating, Kafkaesque, political situation with which unionism had to engage after 15 November 1985.

The immediate response

The Anglo-Irish Agreement was designed to be proof against unionist opposition. Those responsible for it may not have understood the idea of the Union, but they had learnt a thing or two about crisis management. (Ironically, the parties to the Forum Report who had been so critical of British policy for being nothing but "crisis management" were now praising and encouraging exactly that policy.) Therefore, no provincial institution was erected as the keystone of the Agreement which could be destroyed by unionist pressure. There was to be no repeat of 1974 when the Ulster Workers' Council "constitutional stoppage" brought down the painstakingly constructed power-sharing Executive and frustrated the whole Sunningdale accord. The intergovernmental Conference was to be beyond the reach of unionist protest; the "Irish dimension" had outflanked it. Not only were the structural arrangements of the Agreement different from Sunningdale: the British government had also calculated that the political atmosphere of the 1980s was not that of the 1970s. In the straitened circumstances of the Northern Ireland economy in the mid-1980s, it believed there would be few workers willing to sustain a long general strike. More than that, it now had experience of unionist protest. The practice of political boycott (which is what the UWC strike had amounted to) had shown diminishing returns after 1974. When Paisley tried to repeat that success in the strike of 1977, it was an embarrassing failure. Moreover, the government had been gratified by the lack of widespread response to the "Carson Trail" campaign of 1981. The potency of the 1974 stoppage had lain in its novelty: no one then knew how far the strikers were prepared to go. 1977 dispelled all that. Once government and opposition know the limits, threats become mere posturing. And the government calculated that fundamental unionist opposition to the Agreement would burn itself out in posturing rather than action.

The government's greatest strength has lain in self-knowledge, and this self-knowledge is a powerful mixture of indifference and commitment. It was embodied in the very character of Nicholas Scott, the NIO junior minister, who proved that the liberal Toryism he espoused on the London cocktail circuit was compatible with the arrogant intolerance he showed in Belfast. Indifference has shown itself in attitudes to the notion of majority consent, and to the reality of increased divisions, intimidation and sectarian suspicion which the Agreement has brought in its wake. There has been commitment, in that the government has invested too much capital in Hillsborough – political and personal – to be able to pull back without severe loss of face. Like most other actions of the Thatcher government, this commitment exhibits a stubborn purpose, and Mrs Thatcher has been nothing if not stubborn. With the Agreement signed, the logic was then to confront any unionist resistance and exploit to the full the hesitations and contradictions of that opposition. The government, in other words, assumed there were definite constraints to the pursuit of any anti-Agreement campaign. With the institutions of the Agreement firmly secured, the expectation was that those constraints would be revealed with startling clarity, and unionism would be forced to accept the new dispensation (its "subordinate status"). This was something which Peter Robinson had not considered, but which opinion polls after 15 November revealed to be a factor very much to the fore in popular estimation of the potential success of any unionist campaign.[22]

How, then, were unionists to respond to the challenge thrown down by Hillsborough? This was a question that concerned not only tactics and organisation but also the ideas that were to inform the campaign. Of course, there was a long tradition to draw on. As the editor of the *News Letter* put it: "The Anglo-Eire dialogue has revived an Irish Protestant tradition of resistance to an authority perceived to have betrayed a sacred trust."[23] And as we argued in Chapter 1, the contractarian philosophy is peculiarly relevant to the conditions of the Agreement and its unilateral terms – whether that contract is understood in the radical terminology of popular will and consent, or in the conservative terminology of the eternal contract between the living, the dead and the yet to be born. Also stimulated were the folk-memories of the anti-Home Rule struggles of previous generations.[24] However, history never repeats itself – it only stutters. What may appear a familiar set of events and conditions is invariably something very different. Not to recognise the implications of this would be like generals preparing to fight a new war using the tactics of the last one, with every likelihood of disaster. Or first time as tragedy and second time as farce (*Einmal ist keinmal aber zweimal ist einmal zuviel**). Unionists too had learnt the lessons of 1977. The wisdom of tradition was no real substitute for the intelligent judgments and choices which unionist leaders were now called upon to make and to bear responsibility for.

In an alternative summit held in the Assembly buildings after the signing of the Agreement at Hillsborough, Molyneaux and Paisley unveiled their initial plan of campaign. In a statement bitterly attacking the diminution of sovereignty contained in the Agreement, the two leaders claimed that, in essence, "this accord represents the end of the Union as we have known it and the beginning of joint London/Dublin authority". The immediate call was for a referendum to be held in Northern Ireland on the same principled basis upon which referenda on devolved government had been allowed to the people of Scotland and Wales in 1978. If the government refused this, then all unionist MPs would resign their seats and put themselves forward for re-election as a test of popular support for the Agreement. There was a

---

*"To do something once means nothing. To do it twice is once too often."

promise of firm leadership and a "course of action designed to derail this monstrous conspiracy". This would involve the withdrawal of consent to be governed under the terms of Hillsborough (since unionist consent had not originally been sought) and a redefinition of the role both parties would play in the Assembly and in the local district councils. Unionist councillors would withdraw from public service boards, and all politicians were called on to boycott Northern Ireland Office ministers.[25] The statement was a reasonable expression of unionist anger, but it was hardly a declaration of war or a declaration of independence. It reveals clearly the narrow lines within which unionist protest would be conducted. It was a declaration of politically restrained defiance, and reflects a clear dilemma. As Christopher McGimpsey succinctly put it, the dilemma "which faces the unionist community is how to maintain opposition to the agreement which does not, as a by-product, also weaken the union."[26] Any sign that opposition was weakening the Union would seriously split unionist solidarity itself. Correctly, Molyneaux, Paisley and their colleagues recognised that the campaign would have to be constitutional and be seen to be constitutional. Two options, one a mode of opposition and the other an ultimate sanction, were therefore immediately ruled out.

The first of these options was violence. Clearly there will be violent elements who are beyond the control of any disciplined campaign, and violence did attend the early stages of the unionist campaign. However a significant feature of the conduct of unionist protest has not been the disorder and assault which has accompanied it but the absence of serious violence. To those unfamiliar with the character of unionism, this might be rather surprising. One of the lessons of the Agreement, or so many people felt, was that violence pays. In a *Spectator* article, Enoch Powell claimed that Mrs Thatcher had been "bombed into submission" by the IRA.[27] There was a prevalent attitude that if the Anglo-Irish Agreement was a political victory for John Hume and the SDLP, it had been gained thanks to the military skill and determination of the Provisional IRA. And while the Provisional IRA did not like the Agreement, they certainly believed that it had come about because of them. They are probably right. Thus, simple logic might suggest that if unionists wanted to redress the balance, then they should copy their opponents. This is indeed what a number of English observers did think was happening. For instance, Andrew Gimson thought that "Mrs Thatcher, by signing the Agreement, has ensured that it is the most horrible and vicious loyalists who are strengthened, and the decent, honourable, law-abiding loyalists who are left without hope, all constitutional expedients exhausted." In his view "thuggish loyalists take as their tutors in exerting pressure on the British Government the IRA."[28] Gimson was commenting here on the attacks that took place in March and April 1986 on policemen's homes and on the increased intimidation of catholics living in protestant estates. The rapidity with which such violence ceased is a measure of unionist distaste for measures which cast them in the role of "rebels".

Commenting on the one-day strike against the Agreement in March 1986, Martyn Harris argued that the unionist leadership had lost control of its supporters. For him, the disorder which accompanied the strike presaged the take-over by the shadowy groups of paramilitaries and pan-unionist groupings intent on violence. The wish was evidently father to the thought. Harris reported apocalyptic scenes in which the fascist power behind the "three-piece-suitniks of unionist authority" had taken its true shape. The evidence for this seemed to be one burned-out car and a street disturbance on the Newtownards Road in East Belfast.[29] In the history of the Troubles in Northern Ireland, the one-day strike on 3 March was not a day of violence but one of intimidation. Certainly, the police did not feel that some sort of loyalist rising was in the offing. Sensible journalism recognised the limited impact and intent of the strike, but even then could not resist the temptation to suggest that a sinister conspiracy was lurking in the wings. There was the suggestion that the paramilitaries were more independent and less politically naive than they had been in either 1974 or 1977. This time, they would allow the politicians to exhaust all constitutional methods and then, when these were seen to have failed, take over.[30] James Molyneaux himself half-heartedly implied that if the British government did not accede to the demands of the unionist leadership, then it was pushing the "red button" for extra-parliamentary activity.[31] After the strike, in a statement to the Prime Minister, both Molyneaux and Paisley made what capital they could by noting the "first worrying signs that our control might be slipping and our authority eroding."[32] However, Molyneaux did not mean indefinite and violent action, and the British government knew he did not. Indeed, he formally announced that he would not associate himself with any further plans for strike action. *Fortnight* remarked, perceptively for once, that "the repeated '*Après nous le déluge*' pleas from the OUP camp would be just so much hot air."[33] The key question was: from which part of the unionist "family" would such a consistent campaign of political violence conceivably come?

Loyalist paramilitaries would seem the obvious source. From the late 1970s, groups like the Ulster Defence Association had only been engaged intermittently in offensive military action. Instead, the UDA claimed to be preparing for a "doomsday situation" when unionism would be faced with the ultimate crisis and would need disciplined and militant leadership to confront it. Preparation for doomsday became an alternative to political violence in the present. The trouble with doomsday scenarios is that doomsday is always perceived as being the day after tomorrow. The Anglo-Irish Agreement would appear to have provided the UDA with conditions for entering into its own in a way not experiencèd since the early 1970s. Yet this did not happen. Some individuals within the organisation, like John McMichael, who had thought long and hard about Ulster politics, expended much energy in encouraging and "permeating" resistance to the Agreement (though not with the aim of creating fronts for some paramilitary *putsch*), and took on the task of acting as a ginger group to demand action as well as words from unionist politicians. This did not unfold as a coherent strategy, though an idea of the sort of Northern Ireland the political wing of the UDA wanted was to be presented later. In reality, the UDA was prepared to support any political policy that was popular and authoritative. This was a great disappointment to the media, who were looking for unionist bogeymen. The chairman of the UDA, Andy Tyrie, stated that his organisation would "support anything the unionist leaders and politicians suggest. We want to do what is right." This was hardly the stuff to inspire insurrection. The media were forced to look elsewhere for the villains of the unionist campaign. They discovered the Ulster Clubs.

The origin of the Ulster Clubs lay in the 66-member Action Committee set up in Portadown at the beginning of July 1985 to protest against the re-routing of traditional Orange Order marches. This was directly related to the Anglo-Irish talks, since it was believed that the re-routing policy of the Royal Ulster Constabulary was a direct result of intervention by Dublin. From this Committee developed the United Ulster Loyalist Front, the chairman of which was Alan Wright, a young Orangeman and member of the Salvation Army. The purpose of the UULF, as its name suggests, was to bring together all strands of protestantism in defence of the loyalist heritage. As rumours of an Agreement increased in the late summer of 1985, it was decided to form a network of local groups to mobilise resistance to any Anglo-Irish "sell-out". The motto was "Hope for the best and prepare for the worst". But the essential confusion of the Ulster Club philosophy was revealed at the rally held at Belfast City Hall on 1 November, when the organisation was publicly launched. Alan Wright made two demands: first, that the government should recognise the right of Ulster people to be full citizens of the United Kingdom; and secondly, that there should be an end to the erosion of the protestant heritage. In principle there is nothing contradictory in these two demands, but in practice, the Ulster Club philosophy was founded on those assumptions of protestant supremacy found in the Orange Order, and the second demand was therefore fundamentally at odds with the first. In short, the first represents a defensible, just and universal claim to equality of citizenship in the state; the second represents an indefensible, insupportable and particular claim to set the conditions of that citizenship. Protestants, like catholics, have a right to expect equal treatment and equal respect in the United Kingdom, but they do not have the right to stage provocative marches wherever they like, whatever traditional expectations and common prejudice might demand. And of course the same rule applies for nationalists.

Members of the Ulster Clubs were prominent in street protest, helping to enforce the one-day strike, confronting the police at the site of the Anglo-Irish secretariat at Maryfield in Belfast, providing flying pickets to harass officials and ministers of the Northern Ireland Office, and resisting attempts to re-route Orange parades. As such, they were the familiar face of massed-ranks loyalism under a new name. Their chairman admitted that the Clubs were not in being to act for the sake of violence, but were prepared to use violence if the Agreement were forced on the people of Northern Ireland. What they meant by the term "violence" was left undefined. Alan Wright may have said in the abstract that the Clubs would use violence, but it was unclear exactly which individuals were prepared to do so and how. Throwing bricks at the police and pulling at the gates of Maryfield was hardly the same thing as the insurgent war of the IRA which had produced the Agreement in the first place. Indeed there was a protestant exclusiveness about the Clubs, and a particular religious spirit, which was hardly compatible with a campaign of premeditated violence. Although it was reported that Ulster Club "talk of warlike preparations spoke nothing but the truth", that is all it remained – talk.[34] Giving the impression of militancy while shrinking from violent acts created an ambiguity that neutered the success of the Clubs. The Clubs were at once too respectable and not respectable enough to give positive leadership to the anti-Agreement campaign. In fact the organisation, as a loyalist umbrella group with a nominal membership of around 8,000, was too diverse to be politically effective. Its leadership adopted the same sort of doomsday mentality as the UDA. Politely, they awaited "the decision and the call from the leaders" of the unionist parties.[35] Such a call would not come in the way which the Ulster Club leader expected. Instead, the Clubs became part of the DUP's exhibitionist politics.

It might also have been expected that Ian Paisley would have come into his element with the signing of the Anglo-Irish Agreement, because his rhetoric was that of a radical protestant tradition which thrived on persecution and challenge. Authors have defined him as a malign influence, a man of wrath lusting for power in Northern Ireland, and manipulating the Troubles to achieve that goal. The Bruce thesis devotes much effort to promoting Paisleyism as the bottom line of Ulster unionism. Hence the argument that it "should occasion little surprise . . . that in the current disagreement between the Government and Unionists in Ulster, Paisley has once again shown that he can command the support of an extremely substantial body of Ulster Unionist voters. Paisley has emerged as the leading Unionist politician alongside, and often dominating, James Molyneaux."[36] This is only superficially true. No one doubts Paisley's ability to command a substantial body of unionist support; and it is also true that on the public platform, like the mass demonstration at Belfast City Hall on 23 November 1985, he has greater presence than his OUP colleague. But appearance should not be confused with substance. Paisley has not been the dominant figure in post-Hillsborough unionism; because of his efforts to make a success of James Prior's Northern Ireland Assembly, the Agreement came as a severe blow to Paisley's prestige and credibility, and left him exposed and betrayed. His performances after 1985 have been a bit tired and flat. Certainly he was not going to orchestrate violent opposition to government policy. He is not that sort of politician, despite the caricature common in nationalist writing and in the British media. His flirtation with Ulster Resistance does not disprove this thesis but confirms it.

The formation of Ulster Resistance on 10 November 1986 appeared to be Paisley's attempt to take a more militant line and prepare for armed conflict with the forces of the state. The mass rally at the Ulster Hall, which launched the movement, was conducted with that mixture of religious piety, showmanship and aggressive political voice which is Paisley's unique style. The immediate impact of this event, however, was ambiguous. It was possible to read into it and the subsequent sub-rallies a new and ominous development in opposition to the Agreement – yet on the other hand one could dismiss it as a publicity stunt. The message was direct enough and is familiar to Paisley-watchers: namely, that Ulster Resistance "will therefore embark upon a province-wide recruitment of men willing and prepared to take direct action as and when required. Such action will be strictly disciplined, calculated and controlled."[37] An estimated 1,500 people, many of them Ulster Club members, were present at the first rally when Paisley donned the red beret, the emblem of Ulster Resistance. For a time it seemed as if words were going to become action, and confrontation with the government would move to a new level of violence.

Paisley did not see it that way. Ulster Resistance was designed to keep up some sort of anti-Agreement momentum, with the DUP at its head. It specific aim was to lever political concessions from the Conservative government, and its activity would be entirely subordinated to that constitutional purpose. It was a reluctant Paisley who had to put on the red beret. His heart was still in the Assembly which the government had so unceremoniously dissolved in June that year. He was trying to retain control of that very radical protestant tradition to which his whole career had been dedicated, and to ensure that hot-headed elements in his party, without an Assembly within which to focus their energies, did not go over the top. He has been a moderating influence in this case, and successfully so. The Paisley manner was well grasped by Ian Sutherland, who observed a loyalist rally in Glasgow, held to encourage support in Scotland for the unionist cause. Discounting the tone and listening to the words, Sutherland pointed out that "Paisley makes what is, in effect, an appeal for peace, stability and the maintenance of the status quo." He went on: "This man will lead a protest, but will have no truck with a revolt."[38] This is the heart of the matter, known to British intelligence – despite the stance adopted by Ulster Resistance and the Ulster Clubs. No one was preparing for armed confrontation with the forces of the state. Since Paisley did not play the part expected of him, the media looked around for someone else and came up with Peter Robinson, his deputy. Yet despite his fiery speeches and his leading the "invasion" of the village of Clontibret in Co. Monaghan within the Republic, Robinson, like his leader, is a constitutional politician above all else. He is intelligent enough to know the limits of militancy and what unionist opinion will stand for. The (almost) unvarnished truth was that expressed by Frank Millar, general secretary of the OUP: "that violence has no part to play in our campaign against the Agreement."[39] It was to play no part, because no one was prepared to organise it or to legitimise it.

The second option effectively ruled out was to take political opposition to the Agreement to the length of a negotiated, or even unilateral, declaration of independence. This is not to say that such notions were completely without appeal to some of those who felt betrayed by the Hillsborough accord. A number of commentators mistook rumination on the idea of independence for a considered option in reaction to the Agreement, but this was to deal in fantasy rather than reality. The idea of independence appealed to two very different frames of mind. One was a form of political emotionalism and the other was logic taken to extremes.

To take the first, nearly every unionist politician worth his or her salt would argue that the alternative to the Union is not some form of united Ireland – at least, not while there is a unionist majority in Northern Ireland. Whenever unionism is challenged and the "naturalness' of a united Ireland suggested, this is usually countered by the proposition that the alternative to the Union (which cannot be a united Ireland) is an independent Ulster. Underlying this response is a theory of the right to political self-determination. If unionists are going to be cast out of the Union, then they must have the right to decide for

themselves the form of governance under which they should live. The
emotionalism lies not in the argument itself but in the images conjured
up of the sturdy character of Ulster folk, their industriousness, the
common enterprise in adversity which will make the desert of the local
economy bloom, and so on. Ulster becomes the centre of its own
empire. Reality has little bearing on this nostalgic vision.

The second argument was to be found in the pages of *Workers' Weekly*
and *The Equal Citizen*. Here the advocacy of independence was the
logical development of an idea, one considered element of a consistent
political doctrine. And the influence of these journals, precisely
because they did think logically and coherently, was widespread within
unionism after Hillsborough. If the Ulster Club motto was "Hope for
the best, prepare for the worst", then the motto of logical independence was the rather Gramscian "Optimism of the will, pessimism
of the intellect". It can be no better expressed than in the following
extract from *Workers' Weekly*: "At present we are being threatened with
the idea that if we go too far in opposing the Anglo-Irish Agreement we
are headed for Independence. We must make clear that while that is
not what we are working for, we are not afraid of it."[40] That is clear
enough; it is not an argument against the Union but the advocacy of
thorough opposition to the Agreement. What both notions of independence advocate is a valid concern with the quality of the Union.
The Union is an idea, and not simply a temporary constitutional
arrangement which the government of the day has seen fit to impose
upon a number of its citizens. The idea of the Union embodies rights
and values that cannot be traded in any agreement without the willing
consent of those to whom that agreement applies. Independence,
whether emotional or logical, is a claim to be treated as equal British
citizens. It may be a convoluted way of saying it, but it is so
nevertheless.

That "forms of independence" were mooted, as Paul Arthur
observes, by Harold McCusker of the OUP and Peter Robinson of the
DUP at the beginning, and again at the end, of 1986 is beyond doubt.[41]
Yet it is misleading to leave that observation without further qualification, for it implies an intent which was not there. Take McCusker, for
instance: if anyone within the unionist leadership could qualify for
Arthur's description of "demoralised", it would be McCusker. In
what must be one of the most eloquently passionate and frank speeches
the House of Commons had heard for some years, McCusker had
poured out his sense of betrayal at the hands of the Conservative
government over the Agreement. As he said to the House, "I have
suffered the systematic humiliation of being excluded from the government of part of the country to which I belong because I thought that the
price was worth paying to be a British citizen." The Anglo-Irish

Agreement, he went on, "is too high a price to pay." Succinctly conveying the idea of the Union to MPs too complacent to understand it, he addressed the question of Ulster being a charge on the British exchequer (a claim consistently put about by nationalists and academics): "I can accept money from the richer parts of the United Kingdom being given to Northern Ireland if it is the decision of the Parliament of the United Kingdom to redistribute the United Kingdom's wealth to the poorer parts. However, I cannot accept, and I do not want United Kingdom charity. I do not want money to be offered to me to buy my acquiescence."[42] It is in this notion of the integrity of citizenship and the nature of the modern British state that, ironically, McCusker's transient dalliance with independence lies. In fact it is intrinsically unionist and has little to do with knee-jerk supremacism.

McCusker's remarks regarding a negotiated independence for Northern Ireland must be read in the light of the reasoning behind them. This reasoning was a mixture of logic and emotion. Thus the Agreement had so distorted the relationship between Great Britain and Northern Ireland that the present form of the Union "is not a Union worth fighting for and certainly not worth dying for". The reason is that "Ulster is treated like an early 19th century English possession, governed long-distance with condescension and ill-concealed contempt."[43] This is a point upon which, till very recently, both nationalist and unionist were in full agreement. McCusker's moot point about independence is a plea to be treated equally, not differently. Independence is the mental shadow which casts into relief the value of the Union, and McCusker revealed it.

Yet one vital element is missing in all this talk of independence, and that is a sense of proportion. This takes two forms, one conceptual and the other practical. The first was illustrated in inimitable style by Enoch Powell. It is this: Unionists, even if they wanted to, could not choose independence, which depends upon recognition. An independent Northern Ireland, despite the mumblings of a James Callaghan, would be recognised by nobody, least of all by the United Kingdom and the Republic of Ireland. Powell, in his rejection of the conceptual absurdity of independence, advocated the true idea of the Union which is the positive case of the majority in Ulster. Faced with the Hillsborough accord, unionists have only one course, which is "to reject it, to repudiate it, to affirm their right to continue as British citizens represented like all others in the Parliament of the United Kingdom and entitled to the same rights and status as all the rest".[44] Talk of independence, while emotionally and even logically understandable, was actually a distraction from that main issue.

The second factor is the corollary of the first. If you cannot negotiate independence, then you are going to have to declare it and maintain it. That would demand a degree of popular and military organisation not seen in Northern Ireland since the days of Carson and Craig at the beginning of this century. The conspiracy theorist might point to both the Ulster Clubs and to Ulster Resistance as a pan-unionist network ready and prepared for such an eventuality. For instance, the Clubs had as one of their original tasks to prepare for the take-over and control of local areas in the event of a prolonged strike, a breakdown of law and order, or an offensive by the IRA. In other words they could be understood – however stretched the metaphor – as loyalist people's soviets which might provide the organisational nucleus of an independent Ulster. Ulster Resistance and the UDA could provide the military muscle in the initial days of disorder, perhaps in the expectation that the local security forces might feel a tug of loyalty and side with those mobilising for independence. In the early days of the Agreement, these notions did undoubtedly circulate. They had all the self-deceiving attraction of plans formulated on a grandiose scale and in the abstract while skipping over those unfortunate but resistant facts of political life. In short it was, and is, an absurdity.

For instance, Padraig O'Malley argued that the final stage of unionist escalation in opposition to the Agreement "would be the threat of UDI – going to the brink and hovering – a rational action". Further, and privy to objectives not found in any speech or proposal, O'Malley believed that unionists "calculate that the threat of UDI to Britain's national and strategic interests would outweigh whatever advantages Britain might achieve from strict adherence to the agreement".[45] But it is only "rational", indeed it is only possible, to go to the brink of a unilateral declaration of independence if you are willing and capable of doing so. Similarly the British government will only be worried about unionist threats if it believes that they can be carried out. There is no evidence of this in either case. British intelligence knows all too well what unionists are capable of, and the Cabinet Office knows within days what unionists are thinking.

So the Peter Robinson who mooted schemes of independence and coined the phrase that Northern Ireland was now on the "window-ledge" of the Union was the same Peter Robinson who argued that unionists should not jump off that window-ledge. He was in favour of taking every "practical step to get back to good order and government".[46] For him the aim of unionism should continue to be "the Union, the whole Union and nothing but the Union."[47] No clearer indication could be given of the essential conservatism of the radical mode of Ulster unionism. Paisley also made it plain that independence was not an option, and the idea had little impact at all in the OUP. Frank Millar might argue that "we don't want membership of the

United Kingdom at any price'', but this was not an argument for independence but for justice.[48] To rub home the point, even those most maverick and aggressive loyalists, the outlawed Ulster Volunteer Force, came out against independence and declared unequivocally in a leaflet handed out at the City Hall rally in November 1985 that ''Ulster is part of the United Kingdom''.

Without a strategy of violence and without the design of independence, the unionist leadership was compelled to tread a cautious and circumscribed path in the full knowledge that there were few, if any, sanctions they could bring against the government. Even the moral argument – that unionists had suffered a great wrong because an agreement had been imposed upon them without consultation – depended upon it being recognised as such by public opinion. However, there is little evidence that political opinion in Great Britain was prepared to concede that Ulster unionists qualified for the same consideration as the black people of Zimbabwe. So the unionist leadership was limited to the following tactical mode. First, it was imperative to establish a rational and principled set of arguments against the Agreement. Secondly, it was important to maintain a consistent, popularly acceptable opposition to it and to avoid precisely that division and demoralisation intended by both governments. Thirdly, it was vital not to get ensnared in some temporary and cobbled-together compromise which might confuse and dissipate unionist solidarity. And finally, unionists would have to hope that the subtle ambiguities of the Agreement would translate themselves in practice into irreconcilable differences, and that the process set in motion by Hillsborough would destroy itself. Within that constrained prospectus there was still obvious potential for disagreement and disaffection. It is necessary to consider each of these points in turn.

The case against the Agreement

In his speech to the House of Commons during the two-day debate on the Anglo-Irish Agreement, James Molyneaux advanced a central proposition of the unionist case – ''equal British rights for all British citizens''. No fancy franchises and no intricate constitutional arrangements ought to modify the full enjoyment of those rights – rights which apply irrespective of religion or political interest. Endorsing the view of the OUP policy document of April 1984, *The Way Forward*, Molyneaux repeated one of its crucial arguments: ''Only rights can be guaranteed, not aspirations.''[49] The aspiration to a united Ireland is not denied to any individual or political organisation in Northern Ireland. There is no legal disability preventing anyone from advocating or campaigning to attain that end. But this political aspiration cannot be equated with the constitutional reality of the United Kingdom, which is not the same thing as saying that unionists are "correct" and nationalists are "wrong". To conflate these very separate points is to muddle one's thinking. The substance of the unionist critique of the Agreement is that these points have been muddled by the British and Irish governments, and conveniently so, in order to circumvent the democratic will of the majority in Northern Ireland. The just notion of equality of respect and treatment for all citizens has been transformed into the inadmissible proposition that nationalist aspiration should have equal constitutional weight with the fact of the Union. For unionists that is a distortion of political thought that makes nonsense of the idea of equal citizenship. For unionists the injustice lies in this: nationalists want to continue to enjoy the rights that are theirs by virtue of living within the United Kingdom, but shirk the responsibility of acknowledging the authority of the source of those rights. The whole philosophy of right has been stood on its head, and justice is mocked. What was said in reply to that point during the debate in the House of Commons indicated the atrophy of precise constitutional reflection in British politics. The thrust of this critique is the denial of majority right and the privileged status the Agreement accords to nationalist politicians. As Millar put it: "As a unionist I seek nothing for myself which I will not gladly share with all my fellow-citizens. But I am equally adamant I shall have none with privilege over me."[50] The delicious historical irony is that the phrase adopted by unionists – "British Rights for British Citizens" – was the very one used to discomfit the Stormont regime by civil rights activists (like John Hume) in the late 1960s.

A second theme of the case against the Agreement was the principle of consent, which logically complements the preceding point. The argument was twofold. First, there was the fact that unionists were not consulted as to the terms of the Agreement, which was presented to them as a *fait accompli*. This was the more unacceptable in that it was clear the SDLP had materially influenced the negotiating position of the Dublin government. Secondly, the Agreement having been signed, it should have been ratified by the people of Northern Ireland themselves in a referendum. As Robinson put it: "Our citizenship of the United Kingdom must be on the same basis as applies in any other part of the United Kingdom. If, for whatever reason – be it good or ill – the Government decide that Northern Ireland must be treated differently from the remainder of the United Kingdom, that can only be done if there is consent, and the consent not only of the Government and Parliament, but of the people of Northern Ireland."[51] To do otherwise is a fundamental breach of constitutional propriety and an act of misrule. On these grounds, unionists may legitimately withdraw their consent to be subjected to misrule, and try to bring the institutions of state back to their true principles. Once again this is a clear example of that characteristic conservative radicalism of unionist thought. As Enoch Powell succinctly expressed it: "The demand is not that the Government should break its word or be untrue to its professions. The demand is that it should keep its word and be true to its professions."[52] That the Agreement was all too consistent with the government's intent was something which Powell also recognised.

A third proposition was that the Anglo-Irish Agreement was not the law of the land and that there was no obligation on the part of the citizens of Northern Ireland to accept an alien imposition. This is an involved argument which produced a number of interpretations. David Trimble, a member of the OUP and a lecturer in law at Queen's University, Belfast, propounded the thesis that the "Treaty of Union and the Acts of Union specifically provide that in all treaties the people of Northern Ireland are to be on the same footing as the people of Great Britain. It would be wrong therefore for the government to enter into a treaty which treated Northern Ireland differently, for if it did it would be breaking the Treaty of Union." Developing the topic of the one and indivisible nature of the modern state, he asked: "If one part of the Union goes, how does the rest stand?"[53] The former argument had no support in the British legal establishment, and the latter found little positive resonance within the political class. It did represent a widespread feeling among unionists that the Agreement was a repudiation of the spirit of the Union; or, perhaps a unilateral alteration in the contract between government and citizens (both phrases are taken at random from the many speeches by unionist politicians of all ranks) and was an unwarranted and intolerable exercise of state power. There was more to the Union than merely being subject to the sovereignty of parliament, as if all that sovereignty meant was a set of injunctions addressed to a meekly grateful people. This notion of sovereignty is another muddle attractive to those who want to ignore questions of right but are keen to exercise power. Sovereignty has nothing to do with terms like unconditional authority; it has to do with the quality of authority and the nature of the political association in which that authority is recognised. Sovereignty is the whole body of the association at one in the acknowledgement of the legitimate conditions of rule. To change the status of one part of that association without the agreement of that part may be a policy of government with the support of parliament, but it is far from being an act of sovereign authority.

Enoch Powell presented an argument intimately related to this latter point: "To send Members to sit in Parliament is to accept the right, and the exclusive right, of Parliament to make the law under which oneself lives." To make law, and for that law to have the proper character, definite and recognisable constitutional procedure must be followed. Powell expands the logic of this point, and should be quoted in full:

This House, by resolution, has no power to make law, nor has the other place by resolution any power to make law. Law is made in this country only in a particular way, by both Houses through a certain legislative procedure that eventually receives the assent of the Crown. It is not true to say that if the motion that is before the House is carried tonight the law of the United Kingdom will have been altered. All that will have happened will be that approval has been given, perhaps by a majority, to the action of the Government in entering into an external contract – a contract between this Government and another Government – although admittedly, a contract in respect of what we would say are the internal affairs of the United Kingdom. But no one will be able to say after the Division tonight that the people of Northern Ireland are under an obligation to accept – whatever might be the meaning of the term 'accept' in that context – the Anglo-Irish agreement that has been made between two Prime Ministers. We are again straining beyond its moral limit the authority of this House when we demand that by a resolution of the House we shall have the power to impose the will of the Government upon a portion of this country differentially from the rest.[54]

However the subtlety of the Agreement lay in the fact that unionists did not need to consent to it. When the House of Commons voted by 473 to 47 in favour, it was accepting the formal word of the government that there was no detraction from British sovereignty in Northern Ireland. As Mrs Thatcher put it, the "fundamental point" on which there "can be no misunderstanding" was that the "United Kingdom Government, accountable to Parliament", remained responsible for the government of Northern Ireland.[55] Unionists might reject the Agreement as not being the law of the land – but the laws of the land still had to be obeyed. A campaign of civil disobedience would have to be one of thorough extent if unionists were fully to withdraw consent to their governance under the new "framework" established by Hillsborough. Such a campaign would fall outside the parameters of opposition which the two leaders expected to lead. What they confronted in the conduct of parliament and government was what Lord Hailsham, when in opposition, had once called "elective dictatorship".

After 1985 a fresh term was coined by Brendan Clifford – "parliamentary despotism". The rejection of this despotism was to be one of the mobilising principles of radical unionism. Clifford repeats the distinction, common in unionist discourse, that the Anglo-Irish Agreement is policy but not law. "Therefore what is required of the Ulster unionists is not that they should not break it. It is government policy, and they are required to co-operate in implementing it."[56] This perverse state of affairs requires a kind of compliance with the will of parliament that no constitutional politician in the rest of the United Kingdom would dream of tolerating. "In its initial character the Hillsborough Agreement is an insidious conspiracy of state against the people of a region which is supposedly an integral part of the state, and no words used in condemnation of it can be excessive. But it is possible that in the long run Hillsborough will be significant as an act of despotism against the people of Northern Ireland which dispelled their illusions" about the inequity and the iniquity of their position.[57] Unfortunately for those who expected this new realism to mark the beginning of a thorough-going separatist trend, the opposite was the case. Clifford's arguments were employed by groups of activists to propound a more thorough integration of Northern Ireland into the United Kingdom polity. Parliament, it was asserted, could only act in such a despotic manner towards Northern Ireland because the citizens of the province were excluded from participation in the vital element of parliamentary politics – the British party system. The injustice of exclusion from the major parties of state and the right to participate in the affairs of those parties which would be responsible for the government of Northern Ireland became a particular, though significant, aspect of the general, broader claim to equal citizenship.

What angered unionists above all was the constant invocation of parliamentary sovereignty by the SDLP in general and John Hume in particular, in effect to undermine the true meaning of that sovereignty. It was ironical to find the notion of sovereignty used against those who accept the state and in support of those who do not. It is the sort of situation which Pirandello would have appreciated. In one of his short stories, *Signora Frola and her Son-in-law, Signor Ponza*, the citizens of Valdana are presented with a serious problem of determining which of these two characters is mad. Both claim to be sane, and both claim that the other is mad. Both appear to engage in rational discourse. The Agreement has created the same sort of madness in which language has lost its integrity. As Pirandello observed: "To deprive people of all foundation for any kind of judgement, so that they can no longer distinguish between fantasy and reality. It's sheer agony. You live in a state of perpetual bewilderment." As the British government said one thing about Hillsborough and the Irish another, and while Hume professed the sovereignty of Westminster and the legitimacy of the Dáil, the citizens of the British Valdana were justified in asking: "Which is mad? Where is the reality? Where the fantasy?"

What was being asked of unionists was well grasped by the *The Equal Citizen*. It argued that the incantation of parliamentary sovereignty presented unionists with a Catch-22 (another association with madness). "This one goes as follows: you call yourselves unionists and say that you want to remain within the United Kingdom, therefore you

must accept the will of the United Kingdom Parliament, which wants
to manoeuvre you out of the United Kingdom. To be a thoroughgoing
Unionist you must acquiesce in the breaking of the
union – Catch-22.'' The journal went on to deny that this was a real
dilemma, for parliament "has no more right to tell us to surrender to
the dictatorial government of a secret intergovernmental conference
than it had the right to impose devolution on Scotland and Wales.''
The analogy might not be entirely sound, but the implication for
unionism was clear. "We will refuse to accept Parliament's attempt to
impose dictatorship upon us and we will be the better unionists and the
better democrats for it.''[58] Revealed once more is the conservative
nature of unionist dissent. The task of unionism is to bring the
parliament of the United Kingdom back to its true principles. The
argument of unionism is that a great wrong had been done, not just to
the citizens of Ulster, but to the whole British way of political life.

The plan of campaign

On Saturday, 23 November, over 200,000 people gathered at the City
Hall in Belfast to demonstrate their opposition to the Anglo-Irish
Agreement. They heard Paisley shout that unionists would "Never!
Never! Never!" accept what had been done at Hillsborough and
witnessed the leaders of all the unionist parties pledge their total
commitment to its undoing. The task facing the leaders was to keep
their support together and to sustain its morale. This was not going to
be easy, since there was little they could do and the government showed
no sign of being attentive to their criticisms. In fact the campaign has
not been one that has moved from one stage to another in a crescendo
of opposition. Rather, it has been one in which the original rejection of
the Agreement has been repeated in a number of different ways. The
substance of the unionist campaign has been to demonstrate and re-
demonstrate that fundamental resistance. In a sense it has been to
engage in a permanent referendum on the one issue. As Molyneaux
was at pains to make clear (although in the circumstances few
commentators cared to listen), the task of unionist leadership was not
to inflame further a situation already sufficiently fuelled by government insensitivity. It was to calm it. This was a wise course, but one
with an obvious disadvantage. It could not of itself provide unionism
with a lever to encourage the British government to reconsider the
Hillsborough accord. This was bound to create a sense of frustration
and ineffectiveness – that opposition to the Agreement was going
nowhere. Precisely. The unionist leadership, and Molyneaux in
particular, were determined not to let the campaign "go" anywhere,
because they believed that it could only go in a direction inimical to the

Union itself. Unity and unionist solidarity were the watchwords of the authoritative line of policy. At times this advocacy of unity became a substitute for critical and intelligent choice, especially in the General Election of June 1987. Otherwise, it has served unionism rather well. The campaign has followed its restrained but persistent course in an atmosphere of stalemate. There has been no indication that the government is about to change its mind, and there has been little relaxation in unionist hostility to the Agreement.

The first move was that, after the outcome of the House of Commons vote, all fifteen unionist MPs resigned their seats to force a mini-General Election in Northern Ireland. The object was to attain the equivalent of what the government had refused to concede – the holding of a referendum. According to Jim Allister of the DUP, this was the deployment of the "ultimate weapon of democracy".[59] Yet in the unionist manifesto it was implied that, if it were the ultimate weapon, it was not going to have much impact. It was hinted that the verdict of the ballot-box would be ignored, for the leaders had undertaken – in advance – to head "a continuing campaign of opposition embracing every form of legitimate political protest". The by-elections were held on 23 January 1986. In a rigorous analysis of the result, Sidney Elliott observed that if "the overtones of a referendum were present, then the vote passed the most stringent test yet set by Parliament." That test had been the 40 per cent of the electorate, as laid down in the Scottish and Welsh devolution referenda: 418,230 unionist votes were cast for candidates against the Agreement or 44 per cent of the electorate as a whole. If the anti-Agreement Sinn Fein votes were added to the total (though these are uneasy bedfellows), then the total anti votes came to 457,051, or 78 per cent of the poll and 48 per cent of the electorate. The votes in favour were 127,937 – 22 per cent of the poll and 13 per cent of the electorate.

Of course, there are difficulties in reading the poll result as a referendum. Only 15 of the 17 seats were contested, and many supporters of the Agreement might have stayed at home rather than vote for dummy "Peter Barrys" (the fictitious pro-Agreement candidate, named after the Republic's Foreign Minister, put up in a number of unionist–held seats to make sure a poll actually took place). Certainly, both the government and the media tended to concentrate on the loss by the unionists of one seat, Jim Nicholson (OUP) being beaten by Seamus Mallon (SDLP) in Newry-Armagh. They also had no compunction about pointing to the failure of the anti-Agreement vote to reach 50 per cent of the electorate, implying that this was politically significant. And whatever the outcome, it was evident that the British political class had already decided to shrug it off and talk of the sovereignty of parliament. Elliott's conclusion, however, is worthy of note. "The government strategy since the early 1970s has been based on a fragmented unionist community and building the political centre. But unionists are now united, the centre is becoming smaller and divided, and government policy is faced with a very negative environment."[60] Since the by-elections had made not the slightest impact on the Agreement, the remaining fourteen unionist MPs conducted a boycott of Westminster. Enoch Powell alone did not fulfil that boycott to the letter, and the only general exception to the rule was when Ulster unionists returned to the Commons to help defeat the Sunday Trading Bill in April 1986.

That same April, the unionist parties revealed what was called their anti-Agreement "battle plan". There was little in this which differed from the intimation of action outlined in the Assembly meeting on the day the Agreement was signed. All that was changed was the number of points in the strategy. There were now twelve. One of them was a day of prayer for deliverance from the Agreement to be held on May 3. (Unkind observers suggested that, of the twelve points, the day of prayer has been the most effective.) Another advocated that as an act of civil disobedience rates should be withheld or delayed. The economic effect of this was less important than the direct engagement of average people in political defiance.[61] More significantly, in the absence of any real influence at Westminster, it was clear that the front line of unionist political resistance would be the protest conducted by elected councillors. Where unionists were in control (in eighteen of the twenty-six local councils), public business was to be consistently disrupted.

The council protest campaign, however, was not one precipitated by the Anglo-Irish Agreement. It had begun in May 1985 after Sinn Fein had won 59 council seats in the local elections. But it was a protest originally designed as much against the attitudes of the Northern Ireland Office as against the political wing of the IRA itself. Thus NIO ministers refused to have any dealings with the representatives of Sinn Fein because the latter did not disassociate themselves from the "armed struggle" of the Provisional IRA. However, unionist councillors, whose constituents and colleagues were being gunned down or directly intimidated by the IRA, were expected to sit in the same council chambers and on the same committees as members of Sinn Fein. The hypocrisy of the NIO was as offensive as the presence of apologists for the IRA. So the impact of the Agreement was simply to accentuate and regularise a protest already in being.

From the beginning, the council campaign was a bitter struggle, and a number of councillors were unhappy at being thrust into a position of liability for the failure to discharge their legal responsibilities. Refusal to strike a rate and the adjournment of meetings *sine die* were the two main weapons employed. But such are the minimal powers of local government in Northern Ireland that this was no more than a minor irritant to the government. In November 1986, the unionist councillors balked at a suggestion that they should resign their seats and withdraw from Area Boards. In the words of one, it was like "shooting yourself in the foot".[62] There were those who felt that the whole council protest had been like that; that the victims had been neither the NIO, nor Sinn Fein, but the local community. Indeed, in January 1987 Frank Millar was describing the protest campaign as "a shambles". Divisions between DUP councillors and some OUP members were making the rigid adherence to boycott counter-productive. Yet, despite all these obvious drawbacks, the council campaign really provided the only "form of legitimate political protest" in which unionists could express their rejection of the Agreement. Protest in the council, as someone like Molyneaux saw it, was of more advantage to the unionist cause in the long run than protest on the streets. But there were others who believed that the government had to be shown something more than the unionist ability to deny car parking facilities to Sinn Fein at council meetings. They were to get their way in the one-day strike or "day of action" on 3 March 1987. We referred to the strike above when we considered the absence of any strategy of political violence in the unionist campaign. It is unnecessary to go over the same ground again, except to emphasise the reluctance of both Paisley and Molyneaux to press ahead with the strike, and to recognise how hard they worked to devise some sort of face-saving compromise with the government to avoid it. This was almost their undoing.

With a usual regard for respectability and deference, the strike was not to be the child of paramilitaries and rough-hewn proletarians. It was to be co-ordinated by what was known euphemistically as the "primary tier" of the unionist anti-Agreement network – MPs, Assemblymen, councillors and constituency party chairmen. The complaint by activists after the strike – as always on such occasions – was that the political notables did not pull their weight but preferred to skulk in their tents (in some cases this was true). What was more to the taste of the leadership was another example of the permanent referendum. This was the petition to the Queen announced at the first anniversary rally at the City Hall, Belfast, on 15 November, 1986. The petition, collected on 23 January 1987, received more than 400,000 signatures and was delivered to Buckingham Palace on 12 February. As Molyneaux quaintly put it: "Our respectful plea to Her Majesty is that arrangements be now made for a referendum to ascertain whether the Agreement is acceptable to the people of Northern Ireland."[63] As the Minister of the Crown constitutionally responsible for the affairs of Northern Ireland, Tom King received the petition and promptly ignored it. Parliamentary sovereignty was to remain untrammelled.

By the end of the first year of the Agreement, things had settled down somewhat. There was now a certain dull predictability about it all. After the initial dramas, the Molyneaux doctrine had governed the relationship between unionism and the state. That doctrine (the term is used loosely) was spelled out when he addressed the women of the Ulster Unionist Council on 26 June 1986: "It is a near miracle", he said, "that Ulster's unity has been maintained for seven long turbulent months, given the diversity of attitudes within the vast array of opinion ranged against the Anglo-Irish Agreement. That body of opinion must retain its essential sense of direction to ensure that the Agreement is nullified, but because of its diversity it can only be led from the centre. Skirmishing units have an exciting and colourful role in the battle but the confidence which wins wars can come only from steady, cool-headed guidance."[64] This theme of unity, moderation and leading from the centre is one to which he returned in his address to his party conference on 8 November the same year. And despite the political theatre of Ulster Resistance, the histrionics of some members of the DUP and the Ulster Clubs and dark mutterings about new relationships between Northern Ireland and Great Britain, Molyneaux's pervasive restraint was felt throughout the campaign. This was largely in accord with popular unionist sentiment.

Therefore, at the end of the first year of the protest campaign, when the local journal *Fortnight* ran an article entitled the "Fragmenting of Unionism", it was evident that it had not found any serious fragmentation at all. There were no indications to justify the claim that what remained of the "unionist monolith" had broken up under the pressure of the Anglo-Irish Agreement. *Fortnight*'s editorials on the Agreement have turned wishful thinking into a political doctrine. This is not to say that there were no differences of opinion within unionism; but these differences of opinion were not about the iniquity of Hillsborough. The greatest danger of fragmentation had come in the first few months of 1986. Unionist leaders were still disoriented by what had happened, and seemed prepared to advance their own conciliatory proposals, which could easily have locked unionism into the operation of the Agreement. If these proposals had been taken up by the British government, the result would have been that precipitation of the division and demoralisation of unionism upon which the pro-Agreement forces were counting. It was an opportunity they missed. It was a consequence unionism narrowly avoided.

The politics of accommodation

In the early part of 1986, in the words of Bew and Patterson, "the Unionists, both OUP and DUP, were apparently running scared. The Protestant political leadership had felt the chill wind of British dis-approval and for the first time was somewhat uncertain; it dropped its demand for the scrapping of the Anglo-Irish Agreement and called instead for its 'suspension'."[65] It appears that the Executive Committee of the OUP agreed on 28 February to make the suspension of the Agreement, rather than scrapping it, the party's negotiating position. About this time, too, the DUP was coming to the same decision. The proposal of both parties by early March was this: that suspension of the Agreement should be accepted by the British and Irish governments to create the right atmosphere for talks to begin "without prejudice". There could then be a round-table conference on proposals for the devolution of governmental responsibilities to Northern Ireland on a basis acceptable to the minority (which was taken to be code for power-sharing). When a new government of Northern Ireland was established, talks should then begin between Belfast, Dublin and London on a framework of British-Irish relations to replace the Hillsborough Agreement.

Indeed, an inkling of a possible engagement in talks about talks had emerged from the meeting of Molyneaux and Paisley with Mrs Thatcher on 25 February. (Musings on the possibilities of talks about talks had been common since early January, as had suggestions by McCusker and Robinson for a tripartite Agreement, which would bring unionists into some new Conference structure.) That meeting had been designed to get a concession from the Prime Minister so as to head off pressure for the day of action. The Prime Minister had made it clear that the Agreement was to remain. The government was prepared to consider ways of consulting unionists on the work of the Conference and improving the conduct of Northern Ireland business in the House of Commons, and it was willing to "consider" the idea of round table talks on devolution. But there could be no shifting on the principles of Hillsborough. After the encounter, both men talked of a "limited victory" and a moving away from deadlock in Northern Ireland. However, the outcome of the Downing Street discussion did not meet with the approval of the Joint Unionist Working Party, and it was decided that the strike should go ahead as planned. In retrospect, the purpose of the strike may have been to let off steam and thereby to establish a more congenial atmosphere in which talks about talks could take place. In this way the strike was not to be the beginning of a campaign but was to mark its end.

The pessimism, almost fatalism, of this period is captured in a

speech delivered in Armagh on 14 March by the General Secretary of
the OUP. Millar argued that the "Ulster Says No" campaign was not
enough; there was the need to put forward positive proposals which
would unify both unionist parties. The task facing the OUP and the
DUP in the post-Hillsborough era was to "establish what *other* terms
for citizenship of the United Kingdom are to be had" (my emphasis).
Millar was not talking merely about terms other than those under
Hillsborough. The implication was that terms other than equal British
citizenship would have to be sought. "The painful truth", he went on,
"is that Mrs Thatcher has not bought the Unionist diagnosis and will
not prescribe a purely Unionist panacea." Millar did not seem to be
willing to try to sell that diagnosis, and thus the unionist negotiating
line emerged logically from this defeatist frame of mind. "We do not
ask that the Agreement be abandoned but rather that it be suspended.
And we should go to the Conference table painfully aware that should
we fail the British and Irish Governments could and would reactivate
the Agreement."[66] This was an absurd strategy and at that time could
only have done serious damage to the credibility of the unionist leadership. It would have given the pro-Agreement parties all they could
have asked for, and more; and that without unionism even having
made an effort to confront intelligently the political prejudices which
had created the Hillsborough accord. They would have been negotiating from a position of despair. If unionists were to discuss the future of
Northern Ireland, it could only be done sensibly when they had
regained some dignity through opposition. It could only be done when
they had had an opportunity to reveal the impossibility of the
Agreement working in its present form.

   Workers' Weekly was sound in its criticism of this negotiating position.
As its editorial argued, even if the Agreement were suspended and the
Conference secretariat moved from its provocative position at
Maryfield in East Belfast, it would still be stupid for unionists to enter
into negotiations on devolution. "In those circumstances they would
be negotiating under duress in the full knowledge that if they failed to
'compromise', the Agreement would be reinstated in all its glory with
unionists once more portrayed to the world as intransigent bigots."
The only sensible policy open to unionists was to continue to insist on
the scrapping of the Agreement and "on securing our democratic
rights (the democratic rights of *all* the people of Northern Ireland,
Protestant and Catholic) within the United Kingdom". The same
editorial was perceptive in recognising what prevented the unionist
leadership from digging their own grave and falling into it: the only
thing saving them from disaster "is the intransigence of the adherents
of the Agreement who have as yet refused to find a formula" to allow
the unionist leadership to decently betray itself.[67] It was at this critical

point that the British and Irish governments and the SDLP, as Bew and Patterson also acknowledge, mightily overplayed their hand. The strategy of humiliating the unionists had gone a little too far.

Peter Barry, the Foreign Minister of the Republic who was responsible for policy in the Conference, dismissed out of hand the precondition of suspending the Agreement. He announced categorically on Ulster Television's current affairs programme "Counterpoint": "I don't think any concession is necessary to unionism. This agreement in no way threatens them." Despite Hume's intelligent and calculated tactic of offering "unconditional talks" – so long, that is, as the Agreement remained in place – the triumphalism of the SDLP could not be suppressed. Seamus Mallon dismissed bluntly any notion that there could be any softening of attitude towards the unionists. By the middle of March it was clear that there would be no face-saving formula to encourage unionists to score the deciding own-goal. Molyneaux and Paisley received a serious rebuff from the Prime Minister over the conditions for round-table talks. All Mrs Thatcher was prepared to concede was that the Agreement would be implemented with "extra sensitivity", but extra sensitivity could not assuage the outrage which unionists felt. The rather cringing reply of Molyneaux and Paisley was that "our request, which was of a most reasonable nature – no further implementation of the Anglo-Irish Agreement while the round-table conference takes place – she has rejected."[68] Obviously they did not realise their good fortune – and what a favour the Prime Minister's stubbornness had done them. Even a month later Paisley was still seeing chinks of light and expressing his concern not to alienate anyone lest talks should not get under way. It seemed that the Big Man was losing his touch, and it was probably just as well for him that he did not move towards his vision. By the summer of 1986 the pending crisis in unionism had been averted even though some, like Millar, continued to hanker after some elaborate set of talks in the name of political realism. Yet, as Bew and Patterson have observed, unionists had by this time got used to the shock of living on the window-ledge of the Union. There was little pressure to do a precipitate deal with the government and the SDLP. The widespread assumption was that a period of protracted struggle lay ahead.[69] Rather than a dull acquiescence falling over unionist politics, a dull defiance settled in instead.

Agreement difficulties

On 3 December 1985, the Secretary of State for Northern Ireland, addressing a business lunch in Brussels, said that the government of the Republic of Ireland had accepted "for all practical purpose and into perpetuity'' that there would never be a united Ireland. He linked this to the principle ''that the will of the majority in Northern Ireland must predominate and that Northern Ireland, which is our fervent wish, remains part of the United Kingdom.'' Tom King was new to the job. He had not yet been briefed by his officials that British ministers were not allowed to say such things. It was a rather contrite Secretary of State who had to apologise to the House of Commons and to the government of the Republic for his inaccuracy. The furore which this speech created in Dublin, so soon after Hillsborough had been signed, appeared to augur well for unionists. Their hope and expectation was that the fabric of deceit contained in the Agreement would quickly unravel. Yet, for commentators like Harvey Cox, this was just a ''gaffe'', a symptom ''of a crippling inability of outsiders to attempt to persuade one Irish audience without another one overhearing''.[70] But the Secretary of State ought not to be an ''outsider''; rather, he should be a minister responsible to Cabinet and to the people of Northern Ireland. But in what did the gaffe consist? Was what he had said not true – as Dublin, the SDLP and, later, King himself admitted? Or was it true, and that everyone had lied? Or did no one really know but, like the Ulster Clubs, was hoping for the best but preparing for the worst? And if it were the case that you cannot tell the truth to one side and a lie to the other at the same time (which, Cox implies, is the real problem in Northern Ireland), then the Anglo-Irish Conference seems the perfect recipe for confusion and mutual suspicion – which is exactly what unionists have said. Whatever the judgment, very quickly both the Fitzgerald and Thatcher governments smoothed over the King affair and set about stabilising the Agreement's foundations.

Unionists, on the other hand, prepared to wait for something else to turn up. In particular, they looked to the fortunes and vagaries of electoral politics to change the circumstances within which the Agreement would operate. For instance, the Fianna Fail leader, Charles Haughey, had opposed the terms of the Agreement and was committed to seek their renegotiation, especially the so-called recognition of Northern Ireland's status in Article One, and to ensure improvements for nationalists in Northern Ireland in the fields of security, justice and employment.[71] A Haughey election victory within a year or year and a half of the signing of the Agreement might be the required shock to Anglo-Irish relations that would save the day for the unionists. Yet, as opinion polls in the Republic showed, the Agreement was popular, and it was unlikely that such a consummate populist as Haughey would hasten to incur the displeasure of his electorate by undermining it. Alternatively, unionists might hold the balance of power in a hung parliament at Westminster. In 1986 it did not look as if either the Labour Party or the Conservative Party would be able to get a majority of seats in a General Election. Would either party – if it needed unionist votes in the House of Commons to form a government – put the Anglo-Irish Agreement before the attainment of political power? What such speculations really revealed was that there was little that unionist politics itself could do to affect the Agreement. And while hope springs eternal, no one was prepared to put much faith in either Charles Haughey or the British Labour leader, Neil Kinnock.

What did decrease the pressure on unionism and raise the hopes of unionist politicians was the Referendum on Divorce held in the Republic on 26 June, 1986. Bew and Patterson put this in context: "The decisive rejection of even an extremely restricted legislation of divorce by the Republic's electorate in the referendum in June 1986, was a major shock to the pro-Agreement forces in the British state."[72] The proposal to amend the constitutional ban on divorce was announced by the Fitzgerald government in April 1986, much to the surprise of his own people. He was, in honourable fashion, trying to deliver within the spirit of the Agreement some sort of indication that the Republic was no longer the catholic state of unionist fears, and could face up squarely to the challenge of modern pluralism. Perhaps it was also a means of testing the water for some revision of Articles 2 and 3. (Tom King admitted to a Bow Group fringe meeting at the Conservative Party conference later that year that he had pressed Fitzgerald for the removal of Articles 2 and 3.) But the catholic church in the Republic had different ideas about pluralism. Anglo-Irish relations were one thing for which the state may claim an independent competence; ensuring the moral conformity of the nation was another. During the Divorce Referendum the *Irish Press* was to accuse the church of using the pulpit to ensure that its flocks would vote "No". Indeed what was surprising to opinion, not only in liberal Britain but in conservative Ireland, was the scale of the rejection. On a turnout of 63 per cent the amendment was defeated by 63.5 to 36.5.[73] It was plain to the British government, if nothing else was, that there was no desire among the citizens of the Republic to change their social and religious climate for the convenience of Whitehall mandarins. Whatever view might be held about the issue of divorce and the power of the priesthood, this was the right and proper attitude to take; it is what sovereign independence means. In the Divorce Referendum the citizens of the Republic exercised their constitutional right, and did so in a way that served to stress the exclusiveness and distinctiveness of the social order. However, it also implied that the citizens of the Republic should accept a self-denying ordinance and confine their political vision to the limits of the twenty-six counties. This was bound to have consequences for the notion of *Gleichschaltung* (standardisation of institutions) embodied in the Agreement.

Without any doubt, the atmosphere of Anglo-Irish relations changed, and with it went a perceptible easing of the fears and a relaxing of mood among unionists. There could be no illusion now that a new Ireland had come into being. Even the *Irish Times* – that journal which, for all its moral nationalism, seems to inhabit a social space curiously detached from Irish experience – announced after the result: "We have two countries."[74] A remarkable discovery. In fact there are many countries on the island of Ireland, and the least substantial of them all is the New Ireland of the Forum Report. Certainly, the Anglo-Irish Agreement will not conjure it into existence. Even Nicholas Scott took note. In August he reflected upon the change that had come over the politics of the Agreement. "Nobody imagined", he told the *News Letter*, "that when we signed the Anglo-Irish Agreement we were in a 100 metre sprint; we were engaged in a long-distance race."[75] Judiciously, he did not say where we were all running to, but at least for the moment the heat was off unionism. Perhaps the day of prayer had brought results after all.

By the end of the first year of the Agreement, Molyneaux and Paisley could be reasonably satisfied that they had avoided any serious confrontation with the British state. Some pleasure could be taken from the acute embarrassment which the failure of the Divorce Referendum to produce the right result had caused not only the Fitzgerald government but also the British establishment. Nor had there been any weakening of opposition to Hillsborough. Unionist unity was a fact and not an aspiration. The resistance of unionism to its expected division and demoralisation lent a rather exasperated and petulant tone to the pronouncements of British ministers like Scott.

Unionists now afforded themselves the luxury of a more thorough airing of what the idea of equal citizenship ought to mean in concrete constitutional terms. This debate ranged between two poles of political advocacy, devolution and integration. These two terms are not mutually exclusive, for some forms of devolution are compatible with integration. Sometimes, in the course of furious exchanges about the merits of either, the protagonist of one might admit to not really disagreeing in principle with the protagonist of the other. In practice, however, devolutionists and integrationists understood themselves to belong to two different camps – though two camps at one in their mutual hostility to the Agreement. The next two Chapters consider the arguments of those disposed, respectively, towards devolution and integration.

NOTES

1. P. Arthur, "Northern Ireland: The Unfinished Business of Anglo-Irish Relations" in P.J. Drudy (ed.), op. cit., p. 76.
2. *New Statesman*, 10 Jan. 1986.
3. A. Coughlan, op. cit., p. 16.
4. P. Bew and H. Patterson, "The New Stalemate: Unionism and the Anglo-Irish Agreement" in P. Teague (ed.), *Beyond The Rhetoric* (London: Lawrence and Wishart 1987), p. 45.
5. *Time and Tide*, Winter 1986.
6. *The Socialist*, Jan. 1986.
7. *Spectator*, 11 Jan. 1986.
8. P. Keatinge, "Ireland's Foreign Relations in 1985", *Irish Studies in International Affairs*, vol. 2, no. 2 (1986), p. 107.
9. *News Letter*, 26 March 1985.
10. OUP Press Release, 30 March 1985.
11. *Fortnight*, 4 Feb. 1985.
12. Ibid.
13. *News Letter*, 8 June.
14. *Workers' Weekly*, 25 May 1985.
15. Ibid., 10 Aug. 1985.
16. P. Bew and H. Patterson, *The British State and the Ulster Crisis* (London: Verso, 1985), pp. 134–5.
17. The original members of the Working Party were Peter Robinson, Ivan Foster, Sammy Wilson, William Ross, Frank Millar and Peter Smith.
18. *News Letter*, 2 Oct. 1985.
19. Ibid., 14 Nov.
20. *Irish News*, 11 Nov. 1985.
21. A. Coughlan, op. cit., p. 12.
22. *Belfast Telegraph*, 15 Jan. 1986.
23. *News Letter*, 5 Aug. 1985.
24. See A.T.Q. Stewart's thesis concerning the influence of folk memories in his *The Narrow Ground* (Belfast: Pretani Press, 1986).
25. *News Letter*, 16 Nov. 1985.
26. *Fortnight*, Sept. 1987.
27. *Spectator*, 11 Oct. 1986.
28. Ibid., 19 April 1986.
29. *New Society*, 7 March 1986.
30. Fionnuala O'Connor in *Magill*, March 1986.
31. *News Letter*, 25 Feb. 1986.
32. Ibid., 5 March.
33. *Fortnight*, Sept. 1986.
34. *Magill*, March 1986.
35. *Fortnight*, 10 Feb. 1986.
36. R. Wallis and S. Bruce, "Ian Paisley: Defender of the Faith", *Social Studies Review*, vol. 1, no. 4 (March 1986), p. 16.
37. *News Letter*, 11 Nov. 1986.
38. *New Society*, 6 Dec. 1985.
39. OUP Press Release, 20 Feb. 1986.
40. *Workers' Weekly*, 8 March 1986.
41. P. Arthur, "The Anglo-Irish Agreement: Events of 1985–86", *Irish Political Studies*, vol. 2 (1987), p. 103.

42. *Hansard*, 27 Nov. 1985, cols. 919–920.
43. *News Letter*, 4 Sept. 1986.
44. Ibid., 26 Sept. 1986.
45. *Fortnight*, 27 June 1986.
46. *News Letter*, 18 Nov. 1985.
47. Ibid., 6 Dec.
48. Ibid.
49. *Hansard*, 26 Nov. 1985, col. 765.
50. F. Millar, *Why I Say No* (Belfast: Joint Unionist Working Party, 1986).
51. *Hansard*, 26 Nov. 1985, col. 780.
52. OUP Press Release, 2 April 1986.
53. Ibid., 2 Oct. 1986.
54. *Hansard* 27 Nov. 1985, col. 954.
55. Ibid., 26 Nov. 1985, col. 752.
56. B. Clifford, *Parliamentary Sovereignty and Northern Ireland* (Belfast: Athol Books, 1985) p. 1.
57. B. Clifford, *Government Without Opposition* (Belfast: Athol Books, 1986) p. 2.
58. *The Equal Citizen*, no. 2 (7 Dec. 1985).
59. J. Allister, *Alienated But Unbowed* (East Antrim: DUP 1986), p. 62.
60. *Fortnight*, 10 Feb. 1986.
61. 45,000 persons had been summonsed for non-payment of rates by January 1987. See *News Letter*, 16 Jan. 1987.
62. *News Letter*, 25 Nov. 1986.
63. *Belfast Telegraph*, 12 Feb. 1987.
64. OUP Press Release, 26 June 1986.
65. P. Bew and H. Patterson in P. Teague, op. cit., p. 49.
66. OUP Press Release, 14 March 1986.
67. *Workers Weekly*, 8 March 1986.
68. *News Letter*, 25 March 1986.
69. P. Bew and H. Patterson in P. Teague, cit., p. 49.
70. W. Harvey Cox, ''Managing Northern Ireland Intergovernmentally: An Appraisal of the Anglo-Irish Agreement'', *Parliamentary Affairs*, vol. 40, no. 1, (Jan. 1987).
71. *Belfast Telegraph*, 13 Oct. 1986.
72. P. Bew and H. Patterson in P. Teague, op. cit., p. 41.
73. See C. O'Leary, 'The Irish Referendum on Divorce', *Electoral Studies*, vol. 6, no. 1 (Aug. 1987), pp. 69–73.
74. *Irish Times*, 28 June 1986, cited in C. O'Leary, op. cit., p. 73.
75. *News Letter*, 11 Aug. 1986.

UNIVERSITY OF WOLVERHAMPTON
Harrison Learning Centre

ITEMS ISSUED:

Customer ID: WPP60657197

Title: Under siege : Ulster Unionism and the
Anglo-Irish Agreement
ID: 7611404973
Due: 28/11/11 23:59

Total items: 1
Total fines: £8.00
21/11/2011 09:57
Issued: 6
Overdue: 0

Thank you for using Self Service.
Please keep your receipt.

Overdue books are fined at 40p per day for
1 week loans, 10p per day for long loans.

4

THE CASE FOR DEVOLUTION

The case for devolved government in Northern Ireland, which has been propagated by its unionist advocates, involves two intimately related though distinctive arguments. The first is that some form of devolved government for the province is the most effective way to guarantee the Union itself. The second is that in the modern state devolved government is an intrinsically superior form of government to the centralisation of power. These two arguments are intimately related in the unionist mind, because it has hitherto been an axiom that what best guarantees the Union is the form of government which ought to recommend itself to unionists as intrinsically superior. They are logically separate arguments because devolution, in principle, may indeed be a superior form of government in terms of democratic accountability and catering more effectively to local needs; but it might not be the best way of guaranteeing the Union. It could indeed be a way to weaken the links between Northern Ireland and the rest of the United Kingdom. Whatever the abstract virtues of such considerations, the substance of these propositions in unionist discourse cannot be taken in isolation from their historical and constitutional context.

The merits of devolved government for Northern Ireland have had little or nothing to do with principled propositions concerning the nature of good government. Historically, that sort of justification was appended to traditional arguments for the Union advanced by apologists for the Stormont regime, and it has continued as a rule of unionist thought ever since. For many, it remains an unexamined rule, almost a prejudice, rather than a policy. This is not to argue that these advocates of devolution are not sincere in what they say. Their arguments are respectable and deeply rooted in the character of unionist politics. What they have to say must be taken seriously. It is only to argue that the values attributed to devolution must be considered in relation to the function which a devolved government is supposed to perform. As one scholar has put it, the history of the matter was the outcome "not of discussion on the abstract merits or demerits of parliamentary devolution, but of the debate on Irish Home Rule".[1] That is the original circumstance in which the unionist case for devolution must be understood, and it is the one which gives substance to the form. The debate on Irish Home Rule, which devolution was once seen as a means of ending, remains the problem today for which devolution is again being canvassed as a solution. But the terms of the debate have changed, and that is something which an intelligent unionist case for devolution must face up to. That could mean one of two things: either abandoning a primary commitment to devolution, because it can no longer adequately secure the Union, or acknowledging that the Union is no longer what it once was, and accepting a form of devolution consonant with the realities of the new dispensation. We will leave to the end a summary consideration of where the balance of the case for devolution lies.

Therefore, to understand the force and value of the unionist case for devolved government today, we must relate it to the function which devolution in the past has played in Ulster's politics. When we do this, we can discount the second argument about the best forms of government, and concentrate on the first. Devolved government has been a legitimate unionist goal insofar as it has served to maintain rather than subvert the Union. If there had been any suggestion that it would contribute to its subversion rather than its maintenance, then no elaborate theoretical justifications could support it. In the light of those traditional considerations, the purpose of this Chapter is to evaluate the arguments for devolution which have emerged in unionist politics under the impact of the Anglo-Irish Agreement. But first we must briefly survey the history of devolved government in Northern Ireland in terms of its function and principle, since it provides a valuable reference point for a unionist politics to orient itself.

The parliament at Stormont

The Government of Ireland Act, 1920, established a system of government which no one wanted. As Birrell and Murie put it, the institutions of the Northern Ireland polity had been established "not in response to demands within the six north-eastern counties of Ireland for a form of regional self-government, but as part of the British government's general settlement of the Irish question".[2] The majority of Ulster catholics wanted to be part of the Irish Free State. Ulster unionists wanted to maintain without qualification the full extent and authority of the parliament of the United Kingdom. In his classic study of *The Government of Northern Ireland*, R.J. Lawrence concluded that devolution had been a "necessary evil".[3] In what did this necessary evil consist for unionists? A distinctive and abiding feature of unionist argument against Home Rule was that "there was no half-way house between union and separation".[4] This was an article of faith which informed the passionate struggle of Carson and Craig for the Union and nothing but the Union. Articles of political faith can prove most malleable under pressure of circumstances. Forced by the British government to accept a form of devolved government for Ulster, the only option open to unionists was to make the best of it. Making the best of it meant using the powers at hand to prevent separation. As Craig wrote to Lloyd George, the Government of Ireland Act of 1920 had been accepted as "a final settlement and supreme sacrifice in the interests of peace".[5]

It is rare to find politicians reluctant to accept power, yet unionists had no original desire to exercise the responsibilities thrust upon them. In particular, the leaders of unionism had no desire to "dominate" catholics. As Carson argued in the House of Commons, unionists had never asked to govern any catholic but were perfectly satisfied that both protestants and catholics should be governed from Westminster. The strongest foundation for the good government of Ulster was the fact that Westminster was aloof from the religious and racial distinctions of its inhabitants. These were not the words of a power-hungry supremacist; and until the day when governmental authority was theirs, Ulster unionists continued to argue that devolved government within the Union was a constitutional enormity. But, as Powell so aptly expresses the imperative of the time, "when the English are in hot pursuit of their political interests [albeit through the medium of Welsh wizardry], a little thing like the inherent impossibility of what they profess to intend has never been known to stop them."[6] It was left to the resources of Ulster unionism alone to determine whether partition was to be permanent or not, whether Northern Ireland would remain within the Union or succumb to the political "logic" of a united Ireland. The evil necessity in which unionism found itself was therefore not of its own choice. Ultimately it was to make a virtue of that necessity.

The recognition of the reluctance to accept the provisions of the Government of Ireland Act provides an insight into that curious and ambiguous phenomenon of unionism which has been dignified with the name "self-determination". Unionists of late have been disposed to employ this term frequently in their speeches, and to those unfamiliar with the nature of unionist politics it can cause some confusion. Originally, unionists were advocates of a form of self-determination which is the opposite of what is conventionally understood by that term in political discourse. Self-determination is most often advocated by those groups seeking some type of separate development, and is usually a claim to determine one's own form of a government in a way which distinguishes and differentiates a specific communal identity. The institutions of state are to be used to establish this identity and define its boundaries authoritatively. This is precisely what unionist leaders did not want to do. They had no desire whatever to make Northern Ireland into a distinct and differentiated residuum of the Union. The wisdom of unionism was to ensure that the rights and duties of citizenship were equal throughout the United Kingdom. In this respect, unionists wanted to be the same as, and not different from, other British citizens. Their concern for self-determination was not a positive ethnic, religious or nationalist one at all. It was a negative one – in short, that British citizens ought not to be compelled against their will to become part of an economically backward, authoritarian and religiously exclusive Irish state. Because the British government wanted to encourage separate development and a distinctive political identity – it had a positive notion of self-determination for Ulster – intelligent unionism had to re-affirm constantly its purpose of remaining stubbornly indifferent to that future mapped out for it. It is partly for this reason that unionism failed to develop a dynamic political culture, and why it has remained somewhat inarticulate. The present criticism that the anti-Agreement ''Ulster Says No'' campaign is too negative misses the essential point. The basic intelligence of unionist politics is not to be found in constitutional innovation and the scheming which attends such an enterprise. It lies in the prevention of those ''imaginative'' initiatives which threaten the principle of the Union.

Founded on this original premise of what ''self-determination'' within Northern Ireland actually meant for unionism, there developed a style of politics that was both rational and necessary. Brendan Clifford has characterised this style as ''masterful inactivity''. He interprets it in the following way. The system imposed upon unionists in 1920 was designed to exclude the province from the British system of politics. ''For more than forty years'', Clifford argues, ''the disruptive bias of that system was partially counteracted by the approach of the Unionist Party.'' In fact it was the leadership of Ulster unionism which did this by ''minimising political activity in the province''. Masterful inactivity, in other words, was the genius of unionist self-determination. The great triumph of unionist leadership up to the time of Terence O'Neill in the 1960s was to ''prevent Stormont from becoming a state'' – at least a state that had illusions about being self-determined.[7] Therefore the efficient secret of successful devolution in Northern Ireland was political indolence. It was the avoidance of all those statesmanlike values that were later to become so disastrously evident – values like dynamism, imagination and initiative. These may be relevant in an independent state, but are positively contradictory in the conditions of willing subordination which was the nature of devolved government in Northern Ireland. What was important and central to the whole business of devolved government was unionist control of security. This too was a rather negative enterprise, concerned with preventing insurgency and containing political disaffection; it had little to do with a burning desire for self-government.

And it was a fitting epitaph for Stormont that its demise was not precipitated by its inability to carry out a programme of positive reforms. By
1972 it had proved capable, albeit under pressure, of passing
reforming measures. It was abolished because the British government
would no longer entrust it with control of security.

However, masterful inactivity regarding the powers available to the
devolved government was only one side of the coin. The other was a
considered determination to ensure that Northern Ireland kept fully in
step with the standard of public services available in the rest of the
United Kingdom. As R.J. Lawrence succinctly argued, the concern of
the unionist leadership was not political independence but material
improvement. This was fully in tune with the aspiration of unionist
support, catholic as well as protestant. Parity of public service in
health, education and social benefit was the material corollary of equal
citizenship. It was a unionist maxim that this should be acknowledged
as a right and not as charity. This masterful activity to ensure that
Ulster received its proper share of British prosperity also had repercussions for legislative activity at Stormont, for it meant that Stormont
enactments were derivative of the Westminster model. Properly so, for
the intellectual and administrative calibre of the local political élite was
hardly adequate to the task of social improvement on the grand scale.
Writing in 1965, Lawrence summed up well the experience of devolution in Ulster. He stressed that Northern Ireland had evaded rather
than refuted the Unionist thesis that Home Rule was impracticable.
"That thesis rested on the natural assumption that a regional legislature would insist on making full use of its powers. Ulster preferred
close co-operation with Britain. She has been able and willing to pay
the price, in part because of the quality of her leaders, in part because
her people did not want self-government, and in part because they
were deeply divided."[8] Unionist self-determination operated under a
self-denying ordinance.

In short, the historical significance of devolution was to hold Ulster
for the Union. This was a task progressive enough for a political entity
assailed from within and without by those who did not accept its legitimacy, or the right of unionists to oppose the triumphant march of a
narrow and exclusive Gaelic nationalism. Thus there is some truth in
the repeated claim that devolution was a bulwark for the Union, a
necessary security in default of a consistent and responsible policy on
the part of the British state. But it is a truth that had to be vindicated by
the strategy of leaders like Craig in the circumstances of the time. It is
far from being an eternal truth; its validity is historical. An expression
of its temporal necessity is to be found in the statement of the Ulster
Unionist Council in 1936. "Had we refused", the report argued,
"to accept a Parliament for Northern Ireland and remained at

Westminster, there can be little doubt but that now we would be either inside the Free State or fighting desperately against incorporation. Northern Ireland without a Parliament of its own would be a standing temptation to certain British politicians to make another bid for a final settlement with Irish Republicans.'' The Labour government's Ireland Act of 1949 seemed to solve that particular fear and to provide the regime with the guarantee of the Union which it had always sought. In these new conditions, one might have expected the narrow rigidities of Northern Ireland politics to expand and soften.

However, the insidious quality of the Lloyd George settlement was not so easily overcome. The Ireland Act of 1949 ought to have meant that the historic task of Stormont had been achieved. Ulster had won its Home Rule struggle, and the circumstances justifying devolved government existed no longer. Northern Ireland was not now going to be absorbed within a catholic state, but would remain fully within the United Kingdom on the same basis as Scotland and Wales. Belfast would be as British as Birmingham and Carson would have been vindicated. Unfortunately that was not the real thrust of the 1949 Act. British politics usually concerns itself with remedying incoherences in relationships. In this case, the incoherence to be remedied was not that of superfluous devolution within the unitary state, but the inconsistency of the prevailing relationship with southern Ireland, which had declared itself a republic and could therefore no longer be a part of the Commonwealth. The impact on the politics of Northern Ireland was baneful. It strengthened the idea of devolution as an end in itself, and built into it a justification for its most insupportable feature—the sectarian exclusiveness of the Unionist party. It did this by the way it sought to guarantee the Union. The Act declared that Northern Ireland would remain a part of the United Kingdom, and in no event would cease to be so without the consent of the Northern Ireland parliament. This served to make a virtue of unionist unity and to legitimise those practices to which it leant, practices which have since been categorised by the catch-all term "gerrymandering". This was hardly the regime of brutal repression which has become a part of the petrified forest of republican myth, but it was a regime which encouraged sectarianism in both unionism and nationalism. The underwriting of devolved government also encouraged a new generation of unionist politicians to mistake the shadow of political authority for its true source, and confuse the purpose of unionism in a way that Carson and Craig never did.

Ironically, after 1949 the Stormont system had gained sufficient security to encourage its own self-destruction. By the late 1950s and early '60s, unionist governments began to accord themselves a grandeur and a dignity which circumstances did not warrant. In the ambiguity of devolved government there was an understandable temptation among unionist politicians to believe that the material prosperity and social improvements of Northern Ireland were the result of an internally-generated administrative wisdom. This was fuelled by the contrast with the relative backwardness of the Republic. But whatever the reality of society and economy in the south, one thing is clear: Irish governments were alone responsible for their achievements or their lack of them; and could demand the respect which go with sovereignty and independence. Governments in Northern Ireland could not be equated with those in Dublin. They were not fully responsible for raising finance or for making the specific sacrifices which progress demands. Of course they had never wanted these responsibilities in the first place. Therefore the only possible and legitimate unionist response should have been to argue that unionism means participating in the benefits conferred by membership of the United Kingdom, and is not at all concerned with the virtues of independence. Unfortunately Stormont governments tended to forget this.

Birrell and Murie suggest that fatal error of mind which began to afflict unionist politics after forty years of devolved government. They note the seductive illusion of the 1920 settlement; for, while remaining within the United Kingdom, "Northern Ireland thus developed many of the characteristics of an independent state".[9] But, unlike the Republic, they were characteristics with no foundation in reality. Nationalist leaders in Ulster, like Eddie McAteer, were fully justified in their witheringly ironic attacks on the pretension and presumption of the regime. There is something ridiculous about the pomp of cabinet government on the lilliputian scale that passed for administration in Northern Ireland. The ridiculing of the polity was probably a more effective weapon in the nationalist armoury than anything else, for when they rose to the bait to defend their own dignity as important personages in world history, unionist leaders reinforced the whole fantasy of independence. Without realising what they were about, they were subtly altering the understanding of self-determination in a way that endangered the maintenance of the Union. By so doing, they gave a distinctive credibility to the "our wee Ulster" mentality which has always been part of the character of unionism. Hitherto, celebration of "our wee Ulster" had been of political significance only as a means of mobilising support for the Union. On the other hand, standing on the dignity of Stormont had the tendency to transform parochiality into a constitutional preference, a celebration of devolution for its own sake. This served only to muddle the picture in a way that rebounded to the advantage of Irish nationalism. It is clear that, in the wake of the Anglo-Irish Agreement, unionism is still suffering from that muddle.

Beyond Stormont

After Freud, as E.L. Doctorow has told us, neither sex nor dreams could ever be the same again. Similarly, after the demise of Stormont, devolution ought never to have been the same again for unionism. There was some initial exaggeration by leaders like William Craig and his Vanguard supporters of the potential of independence, but this was only the extreme version of the Stormont virus. The generality of unionist politicians hankered after some reconstruction of the old order. But that could never be. What was essential to the meaning of the old order was now denied to unionists. They could not have control of security policy. Indeed their bulwark against republicanism had been swept away at the stroke of a Conservative Prime Minister's pen. Attempts by the British government to reconstruct some form of devolved government for Northern Ireland foundered on justifiable unionist suspicion that the structures proposed – from Whitelaw onwards – were designed not to guarantee the Union but to weaken it; that the rubric of "cross-community support", while laudable in itself, was an insidious means of circumventing majority opposition to Irish unity. Thus, while the unionist parties remained committed to devolved government for Northern Ireland, what devolved government now meant as practical politics was something they did not want at all. This was the basis of intense frustration for all the regional parties and for the British government too. The answer, which seemed to lie in the logic of direct rule from Westminster on the lines originally proposed by Carson in 1920, was the only one which no side was prepared to admit.

It might be said that the frustrations attending the attempt to reconstruct an acceptable form of devolution on a power-sharing basis between unionist and nationalist were the result not of popular resistance but of party intransigence. The evidence for this assertion seems to lie in the statistics of the support for power-sharing devolution in opinion polls. Since *vox populi* is *vox dei*, the assumption frequently is that some demonic wilfulness leads political leaders astray, distracting them from the necessary reconciliation of the "two traditions". But insofar as the traditions to be reconciled are unionism and nationalism, the engagement is simply impossible. These two traditions recognise reconciliation in mutually exclusive ways. Cross-community support, as far as unionists are concerned, means that nationalists ought to accept the Union, work constructively within the institutions of devolved government, and thereby rightfully share in the benefits of equal citizenship. For nationalists the opposite is intended by cross-community support. The purpose of the SDLP is not just to have their tradition recognised – for who can fail to recognise it? – but to frustrate any strengthening of the Union which might postpone the goal of Irish unity. Pollsters' statistics do not record these pre-suppositions, but the general fatalism of the electorate that, although power-sharing is a good idea in principle, it would not work in practice, reflects a shrewd understanding of political realities on the part of respondents. It is this realistic popular assessment which policy-makers have consistently, and with an almost demonic wilfulness, ignored.

It should have come as no surprise to London that the policy it proposed was unrealisable, for evidence was already to hand. In his pioneer study of political attitudes in Northern Ireland *Governing Without Consensus* (a text which, despite everything that has happened since, is still as fresh in its insight as ever), Richard Rose observed that the "discord would be resolved, as far as Protestants are concerned, if only Catholics abandoned their symbolic commitment to a United Ireland".[10] Rose charted faithfully the irreconcilable assumptions which informed unionist and nationalist notions of "consensus". He was careful to stress the limitations that any sensible policy ought to acknowledge. Nothing has changed those assumptions, although the policy of the British and Irish governments, culminating in the Anglo-Irish Agreement, has only served to perpetuate discord by ignoring them. Indeed, it has helped to turn a symbolic nationalist commitment into a destructive and virulent insurgent campaign. What is perhaps surprising in the history of the Troubles has been the willingness of the unionist parties to maintain public faith in devolved government for so long. The Faulknerite unionists were probably too close to the satis-factions of office in the Stormont regime and too accommodating to the will of the British establishment to know any better. Those unionists who opposed the power-sharing Executive were simply enraged that the mould they had come to love had been broken. But thereafter, ten years of fruitless debate about the form of legislative devolution ought to have convinced unionism, from "Neanderthal" to "liberal", that the whole business was probably not worth the candle and involved too many unnecessary risks.

When we consider the dispositions of the two unionist parties on devolution before the Hillsborough démarche, it is possible to detect a distinctive difference of emphasis. The DUP were fully engaged in the search for some formula that would have brought devolved govern-ment back to Northern Ireland. It was the DUP which put its energies into trying to make a success of the Northern Ireland Assembly set up by James Prior in the early 1980s. Paisley's powerful rhetoric and defiant postures ought not to disguise the fact that he was the unionist leader most in tune with the purposes of the British government in this period. The very conciliatory message, if not the very conciliatory words, of the DUP second rank like Peter Robinson and Jim Allister confound the simplistic impression of Paisleyism conveyed by the media. During the time of the Assembly it shared a common political ground with the Alliance party, which has always shown an excessively slavish submission to the dictates of British policy. DUP thinking was outlined in criticisms of the Forum Report, such as *Ulster: The Future Assured*, and its premises were set out by Jim Allister, who was prominent in developing party policy, in his response to the Anglo-Irish Agreement. For successful devolution to take place, Allister argued, "Unionists are required to accept that simple majority rule is unavailable." Nationalists had to accept that "as-of-right power-sharing must be labelled a non-starter." This was the starting point for any rational set of devolutionary proposals. "From this mutually concessiona:y starting point, the search for common ground between both sides' favoured option should cause us to draw together the more promising aspects of several previous proposals." In the view of the DUP, it would be possible to establish all sorts of checks and balances which might provide suitable assurances for the minority without guaranteeing the SDLP a place in government. There was even the possibility, or so Allister claimed, for voluntary coalitions to develop which could provide SDLP members with executive positions.[11] Unfortunately for the DUP, the SDLP refused to co-operate. John Hume had already given up on any "internal settlement" of the Ulster question. Indeed it is questionable whether such an idea had ever entered his head. Now he was looking with some assurance to London and Dublin to do the talking – or the lancing of inconvenient boils – for him.

The OUP had become much more equivocal about devolved government under the leadership of Molyneaux and assisted by the logic of Enoch Powell. On assuming the leadership of the party, Molyneaux had expressed his belief that there could not be devolution for at least five years. The objective of the OUP, he argued, should be to improve and to democratise direct rule.[12] Molyneaux and Powell did understand that devolution was not an end in itself, and that unionism should be about the Union and not cabinet posts in Belfast. Thus the OUP refused to take part directly in the Thatcher government's first attempt to get a devolved settlement, the so-called Atkins Conference in 1980. The party was also a reluctant participant in the Northern Ireland Assembly, and there was much bitterness between it and the DUP, not only over the prospects for devolution, but also over which party should be the standard-bearer of unionism. The leadership of the OUP looked to a more balanced political strategy. This found expression in the discussion document *The Way Forward* of 1984. What that paper recognised was that "there is no immediate prospect of devolved power on a legislative and executive basis." The reason was the one which we have explored already; that the two traditions of nationalism and unionism cannot be accommodated at the regional level and share power. The OUP paper concluded that the present object of those parties "committed to devolution must be to obtain control of such powers as are not necessarily inconsistent with the two communities continuing to maintain their diverse constitutional policies . . . The Ulster Unionist Party feels that this can best be done on the basis of devolving those administrative and functional powers which are enjoyed at local government level in other parts of the United Kingdom."[13] There was also provision made for a Bill of Rights to guarantee the interests of the minority. In principle, then, the OUP had not abandoned devolution, but had relegated it to its proper place. In fact the party was more concerned with consolidating the interests of the Union within the Westminster system and holding the Conservative government to its manifesto commitment of 1979. *The Way Forward* was, in its philosophy, that same manifesto commitment expressed in rather more words. Yet words are never enough. Having stated a good case, the OUP expected the British government to embrace it with jubilation. The leaders did nothing to propagate their ideas or to put effective pressure on the SDLP or the Republic.

Of course this was not the only sort of thinking on the devolution question within the OUP. There remained a sizeable body of opinion that still subscribed to the bulwark theory and was in tune with the aim, if not the methods and personnel, of the DUP. But this was not the authoritative voice of the party. So long as Molyneaux retained control, there would be no salivating after "full-blooded" devolution. As the leader put it in an interview with Padraig O'Malley: "We stand for the maintenance of the Union above and beyond all else and consistent with that, we want a devolved government in a form that will not threaten the Union."[14] Nothing could be more sensible for the foundation of unionist policy or more faithful to its original spirit. Devolution is understood in its true proportion. However, both the DUP and many of his own supporters felt that Molyneaux, under the influence of Powell, was not interested in devolution at all. This caused, and has continued to cause, dissent within the party.

This brief and severely abridged assessment of the differential perceptions of devolution within unionist politics helps partly to explain one feature of the opposition to the Hillsborough accord. Most commentators have recorded that the DUP has become the vanguard of the visible protest against the Agreement. Its councillors seemed the most steadfast in the boycott campaign; DUP activists were prominent in the disturbances at Maryfield and the relentless harassment of NIO ministers; and it was the DUP that was closely involved in the setting up of Ulster Resistance. This is too easily put down to the character of the DUP itself and the elemental fervour of its religious and political motivation. No doubt that is true,but there is another factor that is frequently overlooked. The DUP is totally devoted to the idea of devolved government. (In the early 1970s, Paisley dallied with the idea of integration, but it was one he soon dropped.) With the Agreement in place, the party and its leader have been in a complete impasse. There is no possibility of the party accepting even majority-rule devolved government so long as the Agreement remains. Therefore much of the fury of the DUP is to be understood in relation to that simple failure of policy: it had been led up the Assembly path by the British government and then ignominiously abandoned. There is no other course for the DUP but to commit itself to the smashing of the Agreement, for it has never been able to think beyond the portals of the Stormont buildings. On the other hand, there can be no doubting the OUP's fundamental opposition to the Agreement. But the party had not invested its soul in the Assembly, and has not experienced the same direct sense of loss. The challenge of the Hillsborough accord provoked a reflective as well as an emotional response within the OUP. While both parties were prepared to unite in a common endeavour to change government policy, the OUP displayed a greater willingness to "think" a way out of the crisis. While it was thinking, it was less likely to be marching or shouting.

Before 15 November 1985, all the provincial parties in Northern Ireland had pirouetted around the prospect of devolution according to proposals choreographed by the British government. This had become a long-running political show which bored its sponsor and did nothing but exasperate those taking part in it. The audience, the long-suffering electorate of Northern Ireland, expressed little interest in what was going on. At Hillsborough the British brought in another partner to try to liven things up a bit. The professed intention was to encourage the parties finally to agree to devolved government so that the new joint management would be relieved of the headache of having themselves to keep things in order. Under this new dispensation, the idea of devolution had been transformed once again. Devolution was being presented to unionists under the terms of the Agreement as a means to mitigate a massive political defeat and to help stabilise the situation in Northern Ireland necessary to the smooth implementation of joint sovereignty.

After Hillsborough

It became clear, soon after Mrs Thatcher had recommended the Agreement as a means to reinforce the Union, that the Prime Minister did not comprehend the detail of the treaty she had signed. In an interview in the *Belfast Telegraph* on 17 December 1985, she interpreted the treaty as meaning that only "the people of Northern Ireland can get rid of the Intergovernmental Conference by agreeing to devolved government."[15] The Agreement does not say that at all. It is spelled out in Article 2(*b*) that: "The United Kingdom Government accept that the Irish Government will put forward views and proposals on matters relating to Northern Ireland within the field of activity of the Conference in so far as those matters are not the responsibility of a devolved administration in Northern Ireland." That is clear. Even if a devolved government, of whatever character, was to be set up in Belfast, the scope of the Conference and its Secretariat would be diminished, but neither institution would be dissolved. Mrs Thatcher had relied too much on the advice of those who make a habit of being economical with the truth. Characteristically, the realisation that she did not know what she was talking about did not deflect the Prime Minister from insisting that her government would steadfastly implement the Agreement.

Furthermore, Article 4(*c*) states: "Both Governments recognise that devolution can be achieved only with the co-operation of constitutional representatives within Northern Ireland of both traditions there. The Conference shall be a framework within which the Irish Government may put forward views and proposals on the modalities of bringing about devolution in Northern Ireland, in so far as they relate to the interests of the minority community." Devolution has been changed into a function of the Irish dimension rather than vice-versa. By this article the British government is admitting that it cannot alone determine what is best for both communities in Northern Ireland – which is at odds with the claim that its sovereignty has not been impaired by the Agreement. The unionist reaction to these articles has been universally hostile. As Peter Smith wrote, devolved government "has been made an impossible conundrum by the British government endorsing SDLP requirements which unionists cannot meet. These requirements are not limited to institutionalised power-sharing, but include 'an Irish dimension' (presently, the retention of the Anglo-Irish (Conference)."[16] So it would seem that, far from encouraging both sides to compromise on devolution, the Agreement was specifically designed to humiliate and disorient unionism as a preliminary to its complete capitulation to the bargaining position of the SDLP.

Impossible conundrum or not, and despite the altered circumstances in which the prospects of devolved government would have to be contemplated, it did not take long for some unionist politicians to devote their energies to the resolution of the riddle. Mostly they have felt it to be their duty to find some way out of the crisis which the Agreement had created. But, in feeling so obliged, they are actually accepting that burden of guilt which Hume used to call the unionist "veto". There are at least three central propositions advanced by those advocating devolution which merit some consideration. First, there is the claim that devolution is the only realistic option for unionism. It is the only realistic option because unionism must take account of the will of the British and Irish governments on the one hand and the interests of the nationalist community on the other. Secondly, it is argued that only when unionists propose a reasonable and defensible form of devolved government will the SDLP be forced to make concessions. It is hoped thereby to trade devolution for the Agreement. Thirdly, the idea of devolved government becoming a bulwark for the Union still has currency in unionist circles. It may be a bulwark consisting of rather different political materials, but it remains a bulwark nonetheless. It is necessary to consider each of these claims in turn.

On 19 June 1986, Tom King announced: "This Government does not support and would not be prepared to put forward integration as a policy for Northern Ireland." Ironically, this was said as he made known his decision to close down the now irrelevant Assembly. He went on to argue in familiar fashion: "To try to suggest there are no differences between Northern Ireland and other parts of the United Kingdom is to ignore completely the whole background, history, attitudes and political parties."[17] For someone who had been Northern Ireland Secretary for just over six months, King had obviously acquired a remarkably deep knowledge of Ulster history and society. It was even more remarkable when one considers that no one was talking to him. It was an English political prejudice, though a prejudice which unionist "realists" were prepared to acknowledge as the basis upon which any resolution of the Hillsborough crisis had to be negotiated. Even before King made his speech, Frank Millar had told an OUP audience in Armagh that although he had long been emotionally and intellectually an integrationist, "Mrs Thatcher told us in unequivocal terms that integration simply is not on."[18] The General Secretary of the OUP was to return to the same theme a year later, only this time with a significant difference. As he told the Fermanagh association: "Recognising that the unionist demand for integration might continue to prove unacceptable to London, the Executive Committee identified devolution as the alternative means by which to protect the rights and interests of all the people of Northern Ireland and to restore to the people control of their destiny."[19] This was an authoritative statement by Millar on behalf of the governing body of the OUP. What it clearly indicated was that his own personal pessimism had now permeated the magic circle.

However this may be, the thrust of the argument is clear: whether unionists like it or not, integration is just not possible. And since no one is contemplating independence or even dominion status as serious alternatives, then the only way for unionists to go is along the devolutionary road. At first sight, this is an eminently realistic prognosis. But this is not all there is to the devolution case. The unionist expectation is that their willingness to accede to the intent of devolution will mean the ending of the Hillsborough accord. In the Fermanagh speech, Millar went on to say: "Just as I have no interest in a form of quasi-integration which could exist cheek by jowl with the Anglo-Irish Agreement, likewise I have no interest whatsoever in devolution of the kind envisaged by the Agreement." It is at this point that devolutionist "realism" begins to look a little like wishful thinking. No evidence is provided to show that either London or Dublin has been prepared to underwrite devolution outside the framework of the Agreement. The experience so far has been that neither would contemplate suspension to facilitate devolutionary negotiations – the conundrum stays unresolved. Indeed Millar, who was an influential advocate of the devolutionary case, ended up in a rather contradictory argument. In a special article written for the *News Letter* of 20 April 1987, he posed the question whether Dublin, London or the SDLP really wanted to get devolved government in Northern Ireland. He thought they did not. "It is the demand for integration which offers London its greatest opportunity and the demand for devolution which presents London with its greatest difficulty." If this is truly the situation, then it is hardly likely that the negotiating skills of unionist leaders are going to make the parties to the Agreement do something they have no mind to do. The suspicion then must be that talks on devolution must be part of a strategy to encourage unionists to compromise themselves. Beneath the realism lies a profound overestimation of the capacities and the persuasive powers of provincial politicians.

The other aspect of the political realism propounded by devolutionists is the fact of a divided community. As John McMichael,* chairman of the UDA's Ulster Political Research Group, declared, "this is a divided society with too large a disgruntled minority to be ignored or wished away."[20] The SDLP would not depart, and nor would its nationalism. Therefore, it was only realistic to accommodate that political force within a mutually acceptable constitutional arrangement for Northern Ireland. Generally, the fundamental weakness of the integrationist case is held to be its failure to address the problem of nationalism directly. Devolutionists claim that to commit unionism to an integrationist strategy is to evade the responsibility of working for a lasting and peaceful settlement. Yet in the context of the Anglo-Irish

*Murdered by the IRA in December 1987.

Agreement, the ability of unionism to negotiate a settlement with any dignity or self-respect seems problematic. The logic of devolutionary realism convinced Peter Smith that the price for remaining in the Union was to concede a role for the minority which the minority *itself* believed would adequately safeguard its essential interests. It might well be that such a concession on devolution would be one which unionists themselves could not accept as adequately safeguarding them a "place within the United Kingdom into the foreseeable future".[21] At this point we can detect a certain desperation or fatalism creeping into some of the arguments for devolution – exactly the sort of demoralisation which the Agreement was designed to foster. To adopt in *advance* of any negotiations a simple attitude of "What are they likely to give us?" rather than "What is it we want?", is certainly one form of realism – the realism of those who are convinced that they have already lost. The reasonableness of the devolutionist case rests on another premise – an estimation of the sort of deal which is negotiable with the political representatives of the minority in the SDLP.

There is the feeling among unionist supporters of devolution that the SDLP holds all the cards; and, as McMichael believed, all the jokers as well.[22] It is also firmly believed that the unionist leaders have not taken the opportunity to put pressure on the SDLP to lay those cards on the table. Devolutionists could point, in support of their contention, to King's speech following the result of the by-elections in January 1986. It seemed that the Secretary of State was prepared to put Hume and his colleagues under some pressure to reach an equitable arrangement with unionists. King announced that he looked to the SDLP, now that the unionists had made their symbolic act of defiance, "to become involved in constitutional politics in Northern Ireland in a much more effective way than it has so far". He went on: "I certainly look to the SDLP to play a full part in support for the security forces in the fight against terrorism."[23] Devolutionists have the confidence that the SDLP is vulnerable to a determined unionist push for an internal settlement. For instance, the Honorary Secretary of the Ulster Unionist Council argued that unionists had neglected the SDLP's Achilles heel. Smith's opinion was that "nationalists must be challenged as to what they want – either Dublin speaks for them, or they speak for themselves." In other words, unionists would have to confront the SDLP directly with the alternative of either retaining the Agreement and having no part in the devolved government of Northern Ireland, or agreeing to relinquish the Agreement and becoming power-sharers in a new Ulster. "If the political gauntlet was thrown down to the nationalists and the SDLP as to the consequences of relying totally on the Dublin Government, the reality would emerge that the SDLP is not as Hume-dominated as at first appears."[24] The possibility exists, therefore, of negotiating a way out of the Agreement conundrum with a willing section of constitutional nationalism. At first sight, this would seem to make good sense.

Two points may be made about this assumption. First, it is believed, and it is probably true, that there are those within the SDLP who long for some little political sinecure in a provincial parliament. And there are certainly those who resent the impression that the SDLP is a one-man band. Hume, the "statesman", overshadows the rest. Certainly the rest would like some reward for their supportive role. This does not mean that the Anglo-Irish Agreement, which Hume helped along, is a negotiable commodity with which the lesser fry can obtain for themselves a comfortable public salary. Differences of opinion within the SDLP there may be. A preparedness to go back to the situation before Hillsborough is not in evidence. Rank-and-file activists have the old scent of "an all-Ireland or nothing" in their nostrils once again. The pleasure in politics for the SDLP is not being co-operative in making Northern Ireland a workable political entity; it lies in trying desperately to prove by word and deed that it is not. The second point is that the influence accorded to the SDLP is probably an excessive one. Hume exerts a horrible fascination over some unionists, who attribute to him great powers of political leverage. This may be so in terms of their own capacities; but he is only a persistent and tireless hawker of platitudes. It was not Hume the statesman who, by the force of his vision, won over two sovereign governments to the philosophy of the Agreement. The British and Irish governments have found it mutually convenient to engage in co-operation, and John Hume is ultimately a peripheral and expendable figure in that relationship. Therefore, it is not fully in the gift of the SDLP to negotiate away the Anglo-Irish Agreement even if it wanted to (and there is no sign that it wants to). If the Agreement is scrapped, it will be because either London or Dublin, or both together, have tired of the whole duplicitous game. The DUP position recognises this, for "the destruction of the Accord is a prerequisite to any progress towards our goal. Only then would there be any chance of the SDLP facing realities rather than dreams."[25] Unfortunately for this picture of events, the dream and the reality are back to front. The reality is the Agreement, and the dream is a devolved government. With the Agreement in place, unionists would be negotiating not only with the SDLP but with the British and Irish governments as well; and, given the lack of clear analysis on the part of devolutionists, negotiations would be conducted in a fog of unknowing about the real intentions of the opposing parties and about what devolved government is supposed to be for.

The third claim of the advocates of devolution is one which must overleap the difficulties we have mentioned and assumes that a deal will be made with the SDLP. When this is done, devolved government can once again become a bulwark of the Union. This bulwark must be constructed to resist dangers from three sides. The first danger lies in the schemes of British politicians and officials in London. The second is militant republicanism within Northern Ireland. The third is the mischievous irredentist design of the Republic of Ireland. Of these the last one, perhaps surprisingly, would appear to be the least pressing. It is assumed that what is acceptable in terms of devolved government for the SDLP will be good enough for Dublin, although this admission of the willingness of the Republic to accept an internal settlement alone tends to make nonsense of much traditional unionist fear. As we have argued, this might come close to a developing sentiment in the Republic, but may underestimate the potent ideological dynamic of Irish nationalism in the North. However this may be, it has been the first two dangers which have attracted the greatest attention.

When the Unionist Council in 1936 expressed its suspicions of Westminster, it was careful to qualify them. ''Some'' politicians in London had a mind to reach a settlement with Irish republicans and to prise Northern Ireland out of the Union. Today there is no qualification. The whole of the British establishment want to be rid of the burden of Ulster. Well before the Hillsborough Agreement was signed, Harold McCusker had confided to Padraig O'Malley that he believed the British government wanted ''to get out over a period of time with minimal trouble to themselves'' and to engineer a united Ireland. McCusker's opinion was that ''the thing that can prevent that happening would be for us to get effective control of our own affairs back into our hands again.''[26] After 1985 the edge was sharper, the tone shriller, and the distrust of the English and all their works still more bitter. Even so, McCusker's argument remained the same.[27] Devolution would be the unionist bulwark. That logic was already part of the DUP's intellectual baggage. It pressed the demand for a Northern Ireland parliament and government to withstand the intrigue of Westminster. In Allister's words: ''We must put in structures which are a bulwark against an Anglo-Irish Agreement ever happening again.''[28] Similar arguments could be taken at random from a wealth of anti-Agreement speeches and articles.

There can be no doubting the sincerity with which these views are held, but sincerity need not be good politics. Two points need to be made here. First, unionists have every justification for being suspicious of the intentions and the practices of British governments. Everyone ought to be suspicious of governments. However, resistance to the inimical purposes of Westminster should be rationally grounded. If London's intention is to get Ulster out of the Union, then the devolutionary ''carrot'' is a rather curious one for unionists to take. It is a curious style of politics to fulminate, on the one hand, against the perfidy of British officials, and then, on the other, to demand what those British officials have always wanted. Either devolutionists know something the British government does not; or their policy is illogical. That interpretation would seem to apply whether there was an Anglo-Irish Agreement or not.

The second point relates to the general disposition of some of those arguing for devolution. One way, a Machiavellian way, of breaking the Union is to get unionists to do it themselves. Much of the unionist devolutionary rhetoric reeks of little Ulsterism, an intimation of a form of self-determination that unionism has traditionally tried to defuse. Devolution in these terms may be a means, as Peter Smith has candidly put it, "to permanently safeguard the Protestant community in Northern Ireland". But it is not a policy consistent with the demand for equal citizenship. Nor does it necessarily demand the maintenance of the Union. Even the IRA, if their words are to be believed, are willing to safeguard the interests of the protestant community in their Eire Nua (New Ireland). Again, the unionist sin is emotionalism masquerading as realism; and this emotionalism can be exploited by government in a calculated manner to encourage unionists to venture their *own* schemes for the undoing of the Union.

The crucial point is this. Any idea that in the post-Agreement political conditions devolved government can be a bulwark of the protestant interest against the schemes of the British government is simply wishful thinking. As Robert McCartney elegantly criticised that assumption: "Devolution is no bulwark for the Union if it is vulnerable to something no more lethal than a Prime Minister's pen."[29] Hillsborough only further emphasises Ulster's political dependence. On the one hand, the quest for devolved government is inspired by the belief that a Northern Ireland cabinet could use its powers to resist any moves hostile to the "protestant" interest. This is to ignore all experience, and presupposes a popular will to transform a devolved government into an independent state. As we have shown, there is neither the purpose nor the capacity within unionism to do such a thing. McCartney's attack on the spirit of some devolutionist expectations as inherently separatist is quite accurate. However, this notion of a "protestant" bulwark is doubly unrealistic because there can never be a protestant parliament for a protestant people. Since devolved government is unthinkable without the participation of the SDLP, such a vision of resisting assimilation with the Republic to the point of independence is fantasy. On the other hand, in a more sensible vein perhaps, devolutionists consider that a settlement with the SDLP will enable a cross-community government to deal effectively with the threat of republican terrorism inside Northern Ireland.

In the opinion of the locally prominent Fermanagh Official Unionist councillor, Raymond Ferguson, there could be no defeat of the IRA if unionists relied exclusively on Westminster. First, the British government has neither the will nor the interest to destroy it. Second, it is a fundamental belief of republicanism that Westminster will eventually get sick of the violence and declare its intent to withdraw. The political vacuum within Northern Ireland perpetuates the destruction and death which everyone abhors. The answer is for unionists to come up with proposals giving the minority a full share in the responsibility of government. He concluded that "until militant republicans were faced by a government that dared not let them succeed, violence would continue."[30] Ferguson's argument must be taken seriously, since his constituents have borne the brunt of the IRA's nasty sectarian war and would probably qualify more than most to embody the interests of the protestant community in Northern Ireland. The new bulwark which would protect them from republican sectarianism would be a very different one from the old Stormont. It could only be a partnership government between unionist and constitutional nationalists founded on the common rejection of political violence and having the confidence, the legitimacy and the means to stamp out terrorism, whatever its source. In theory this is an attractive picture for those who have suffered the effects of IRA insurgency. For its realisation it depends upon devolved government having effective control of security.

Would the SDLP be prepared to accept that? Surprisingly, sympathetic noises have been made by individuals in the SDLP which suggest that their co-operation is not impossible. For instance, Austin Currie, a SDLP minister in the power-sharing Executive of 1974, insisted in an interview in the journal *Fortnight* that any devolved administration ought to have maximum control over security matters. The experience of 1974 taught him, so he explained, "the serious limitation on power of not having control over security". He went on: "The settlement I propose is, of course, a political settlement in which the necessity for security underpinning will be minimised. But any administration which cannot enforce its decisions is a eunuch."[31] Sean Farren, another prominent member of the SDLP, echoed Currie's ruminations and believed that Ulster people should have control over their own security in any new administration in the province. This would mean that catholics would be encouraged to join the security forces and play a full role in combatting terrorism.[32] Yet the comments of both men were extremely vague, and Farren's in particular were a sustained essay in ambiguity and evasion. In substance the message remains that in the event of the SDLP getting everything it wants, they will consider encouraging support for the security forces. They would be irrational to suggest otherwise. This is the opposite of the "doomsday" scenario. It is the "deliverance" day scenario. Deliver us the political goods and we will promise to deliver on security. Deliverance day, like doomsday, is always the day after tomorrow. For why should the SDLP give what its opponents want if there is every possibility of getting more by prevarication? That is not the basis for the cross-community government upon which genuine conciliators like Ferguson ground their hopes. Indeed, there is more than a suspicion that such overtures from the SDLP are designed to encourage impatience and dissension within unionism. Despite the theme and the tone of these speculations, constitutional nationalism continues to regard security as a convenient bargaining card and not, like unionism, as a fundamental human right. The hurdle of SDLP commitment to an internal settlement in Northern Ireland, over which one's imagination must leap to envisage devolved government as a bulwark for the Union, has always seemed to be too high. It was precisely that rising hurdle which proponents of an internal settlement were trying to clear.

With stolid persistence, unionists kept returning to the task. Amid all the general sentiments favouring an internal settlement, two specific sets of proposals are worthy of consideration. The first of these is *A Northern Ireland Charter*, drawn up by The Northern Ireland Charter Group and published on 5 March 1986. A revised and augmented version of this document was presented in October the same year as *A Charter for Progress in Northern Ireland*. The second attempt to outline a comprehensive settlement was *Common Sense*, sponsored by the UDA's Ulster Political Research Group and published on 29 January 1987. Both these groups are peripheral to the authoritative centre of Ulster unionism. Although they have little in common, both were willing to play the role of devolutionary ginger groups within unionist politics. Their purpose was to set in motion a movement of opinion in favour of devolved government and to inspire a positive direction in the anti-Agreement campaign which both felt was going nowhere. In their particular expression of the case for a devolved government, both groups illustrate the general claims we have been considering.

The Charter Group proposals

The Charter Group represents the old identity of Ulster unionism. This is important if its distinctive political disposition is to be understood. Two of its sponsors, Harry West and Austin Ardill, were once central figures in unionist politics. West is a former leader of the OUP, and both opposed the power-sharing experiment of 1974. At the time of the Agreement, they were inconsequential in unionist politics, as indeed was the third member of the Group, David McNarry. The Charter Group adopted a "statesmanlike" demeanour, a demeanour that is only possible when one is essentially outside the struggle. On the premise of rising above the destructive quarrels of Ulster politics, the Charter Group was in fact showing that it was out of touch with the temper of unionism. It also showed a precipitate desire to encourage unionists to advance conciliatory proposals. But to have done so within six months of the Hillsborough accord, as the Charter Group proposed, would have undermined the only credible political position unionism could hold, namely that the Agreement was an intolerable and undemocratic imposition, a "great wrong" committed against the citizens of Northern Ireland, and only when it had been removed could legitimate discussions on the future of the province take place. In their search for the definitive constitutional identity of Northern Ireland, the members of the Charter Group seemed oblivious of that simple fact. And, as Disraeli once observed, there is nothing more ridiculous than statesmen in a hurry.

For instance, an article of Charterist faith is that unionism must be positive. West argued that the "unionist protest against the Anglo-Irish Agreement has been greatly weakened by its negative policy. It is tactically preferable to campaign 'for' something rather than 'against' something. A campaign 'for' involves choosing one's ground to fight on."[33] But that is only true if the ground you choose to fight on is to your advantage. To adopt an absolute principle of positive action may be magnificent, but it is not politics. For the ground on to which the Charter Group wanted to move in March 1986 was precisely the ground which the Agreement had prepared for a divided and demoralised unionism. It believed it had scouted the terrain sufficiently since the Group had consulted two equally inconsequential SDLP members, Paddy O'Hanlon and Ben Carraher. Molyneaux's response, both deadpan and dismissive, was that the Charter effort had been a useful "reconnaissance exercise". Hume was more direct. Although he was himself advocating "unconditional talks", he did not believe that unionists had been sufficiently softened up at this point by the security forces his party refuses to support. He said, "This initiative is dead." Such rebuffs have not discouraged the Group.

It is not the detail of what the Charter Group proposes but the configuration of its arguments which demand some analysis. Its statement of the devolutionary case makes a virtue of regional government as an end in itself. It frequently uses the expression "regional autonomy" to define its aim. In January 1987 it published a document entitled *A Tradition We Must Maintain*, and in many ways this title captures the essential priority, not just of the Charter Group, but of many in the devolutionist camp. That tradition is regional self-government first and the Union second, a position which stands the original spirit of unionism on its head. To claim this is not merely to make an argument rest on a turn of phrase. The evidence for it lies in the Northern Ireland Charter itself. In the first section of the Charter – "A New Dimension – A New Northern Ireland" – Article 8 cites five reasons why devolved government is the best form of government for a new Northern Ireland. None of these five reasons mentions what would appear to be the crucial one for traditional unionism; namely, that devolved government is the best guarantee for the Union itself. Yet all five particulars make very clear the extent to which Northern Ireland differs from the rest of the United Kingdom. This is what British policy-makers love to hear, for it confirms their prejudices and indifference. Indeed they may detect in the Charter Group's fascination with the emergence of a new Northern Ireland all the welcome indications of little-Ulster separatism. In the *Charter For Progress* of October 1986, the illusions of prospective autonomy are manifest. In article 6 of the Preamble, mention is made of the "irrevocable cultural political identity of its own" which Northern Ireland has established. It is an entity "to which must be attached institutions of government". Nor can the "geographical existence of Northern Ireland" be swept away by constitutional or political changes. There is much verbiage here that is meaningless, although the distinct trace of a separatist disposition is found in article 8 of the Charter's Principles. This article advocates the registration of a representative flag and emblem consistent with Northern Ireland's "new constitutional position" and the adoption of an anthem "to which all can readily give allegiance". It reveals a concern with the symbols of mini-statehood and ignores the substantive issues dividing unionism and nationalism.

Charter Group terminology accepts the reality of two traditions in Northern Ireland. There is the "British Ulster" tradition, and there is the "Irish" tradition. Significantly, the Charter defines these in political as well as cultural terms. This ignores the central distinction between unionism and nationalism: that unionism is a doctrine concerned with the state, while nationalism is a doctrine concerned with the totality of political-cultural relations. Their failure to comprehend this distinction means that the sponsors of the Charter immediately concede the game to nationalism. They are not, in Harry West's phrase, "choosing the ground" for their idea of the Union (that is, in so far as they still do subscribe to that idea in any recognisable sense), but enter the whole cultural-identity morass of nationalism. What is indefensible in the Charter interpretation is the rigidity of the traditions they acknowledge. For instance, the Irish cultural tradition is understood as part of the cultural tradition of the rest of Ireland, and the British Ulster tradition as part of the culture of the United

Kingdom; but these assertions do not bear close examination. The Charter Group seems to think that apartheid (over and above the separate development which the catholics have demanded) is the absolute cultural norm in Northern Ireland, and to ignore the common cultural diet of the *Daily Mirror, Dallas* and *Eastenders*. Even worse, there is provision for these absurd cultural distinctions to be forever institutionalised in the political relationships of the "new Northern Ireland" – what the Charter calls "a full-blooded devolved legislature at Stormont". Devolutionist realism here becomes sectarianism made into a constitutional principle. It is also contradictory. The dynamic of nationalism cannot rest with half-way-houses like this "New Northern Ireland", especially when the other tradition seems to have accepted its definition of the Irish problem. The Charter vision depends on an *exclusive* "Irish" commitment to Northern Ireland, while at the same time endeavouring to institutionalise the purpose of the "Irish" identity to become part of "the cultural tradition of the rest of Ireland, the major part of which is under a different jurisdiction" (*A Northern Ireland Charter*: Part One, Article 8). No elaborate constitutional ingenuity can resolve that particular conundrum. The wishful-thinking syndrome is not sufficient.

The Charter prospectus for devolution has a definite quality that is almost anti-political, a quality that appeals to the a-political tendency of the unionist middle class who want a quiet life. There is also the Group's solicitude for the tender conscience of the SDLP and its willingness to be conciliatory to the point of servility. The keen attention paid to the necessity to corral the "traditions" into their sectarian territory is designed to maintain the neat predictabilities and aridities of Ulster political life, which the SDLP sees as being much to its advantage. And the reason for this concern to accommodate the priorities of the SDLP, even before unionists sit down to talk with them, is the hope that the SDLP will help to shoulder the responsibility for ending political violence. Charterists have no time for those who would try to set about the task of winning catholics to the Union. Nor, of course, has the SDLP. Ironically, the Charter Group begins to adopt the political attributes of those with whom it wishes to negotiate. On the one hand, like the SDLP, it calls "triumphalist" those who advocate integration and equal British citizenship; on the other, despite its criticism of British government policy, it advocates with vigour the intention of that policy, a policy designed to accentuate differences and to encourage a separatist mentality. The Charter spirit moves in a mysterious way.

The public expressions of Charter members are inspired by a funda-mental determination to build their bulwark against Westminster intrigue (the contradiction of which we have already noted) and republican violence by a deal with the SDLP (which assumes that the SDLP want to, or can, end terrorism to the extent of putting off even further its goal of Irish unity). Indeed there is a naivety about these expectations which is remarkable, given the length of time the Charterists have been involved in Ulster politics. West, for instance, appears to believe that if unionists reach a settlement with the SDLP, not only will direct rule end, but "the Northern Ireland Office, the Secretary of State [and] his ministers" will depart as well.[34] This would qualify for the Benthamite epithet of nonsense on stilts. The NIO will only depart on the day when Northern Ireland has been comfortably assimilated into some permanent constitutional arrangement with the Republic of Ireland. But the deficiencies in the ideas of the Charter Group are not confined to it, but represent a general malaise in the case for "full-blooded" devolution. The Charter Group may be, as one Official Unionist unkindly put it, "the unelectable in pursuit of the unattainable".[35] But what makes their project unattainable lies not in its detail, which is imaginative enough. It seems to be the inability of any sensible form of devolved government to fulfil the unionist priority of guaranteeing the Union, while satisfying the expectations of Irish unity which the Agreement has raised within the SDLP. Unionist devolutionists want their bulwark as a replacement for the Agreement. The SDLP want the Agreement, and a suitable form of devolution, as their route to unity.

"Common Sense"

There is a prejudice in unionism which holds that the working class has nothing intelligent to say about politics. Unionist voters worship respectability and often defer to the claim of formal education rather than to the wisdom of argument. On both counts, the political wing of the Ulster Defence Association is suspect. It is not respectable, nor do its representatives speak with the appropriate accents. However, individuals like John McMichael and those he gathered round him in the UDA did think deeply and originally about the Ulster crisis. *Common Sense*, their brief policy statement, was not the product of the moment but the outcome of a long period of reflection. After Hillsborough, the political activists in the UDA showed a mature understanding of the forces at work, and engaged in a critical consideration of the options open to Ulster unionists. Individuals within the UDA played an important role in sustaining the momentum of the protest against the Agreement. The impact within unionist politics of the Ulster Political Research Group's proposals was immediate, and was used by those who otherwise had no time for the UDA to pressure the unionist leadership along the devolved government path. Therefore

Common Sense has to be understood in terms of, first, the political evolution of the UDA itself and, secondly, the purpose it was designed to fulfil in the anti-Agreement campaign.

Unlike the IRA, the UDA has never been able to establish a credible political organisation or a credible programme. The OUP and the DUP have been recognised as the political organisations which "speak for Ulster". In the mid-1970s the UDA leadership was searching for a creative role in protestant politics. It first flirted with, and then fully committed itself to, the idea of negotiated independence for Northern Ireland. During the 1970s, the UDA leadership had been slowly emancipating itself from its political tutelage; and the experience of the 1977 constitutional stoppage, when the UDA felt it had been betrayed by the unionist parties, was a further spur towards a distinctive political philosophy. The idea of some magical third way between unionism and nationalism exerted a powerful attraction upon the leadership. They were infected with the "Quiet American" virus. This was a welcome development for the British government. The Northern Ireland Office encouraged the UDA along the independence path for two reasons: first, if the largest loyalist paramilitary organisation was talking politics, it would be diverted from political violence, and secondly, the British government is always keen to foster Ulster separatism, not because it has any interest in an independent Northern Ireland, but because the separatist mentality helps to keep Ulster quarantined from the rest of British political life. In 1978, the New Ulster Political Research Group was set up "to develop a constitutional and political policy on behalf of the Ulster Defence Association for presentation to the people of Northern Ireland".[36] What the NUPRG came up with, unsurprisingly, was a programme for an independent Ulster. It outlined this programme in its policy document *Beyond the Religious Divide*, published in March 1979.

The policy document argued that "any proposal which involved London would be rejected by the minority community and any proposal which involved Dublin would be rejected by the majority community." The course of negotiated independence was advanced as the only viable option for all the people of Ulster, because it was the "only proposal which does not have a victor and a loser". The proposed constitution was firmly within the liberal tradition of the separation of powers. There were distinctive and balanced executive, legislative and judicial organs. There was provision for a Bill of Rights which would express the "rational character of the Common Good" and the dignity of individual personality. However, despite its sincerity and effort, the UDA had only given hostages to political fortune. Far from bringing the UDA into the political mainstream, it was left with an irrelevant political "solution" that was only one more in the flotsam and jetsam of good intention. In fact, the UDA had taken the understanding of "self-determination" to lengths which no average protestant could willingly follow. For the organisation was advocating, as a first negotiating step, the breaking of the Union. The "logic" of the independence proposals could not mask that fundamental irrationality. The idea certainly found no support among catholics. The UDA soldiered on with this policy for the next few years, but with a diminishing commitment.

For some time before the Hillsborough accord, the political activists within the UDA had concluded a re-definition of what they meant by independence in a way which completely transformed its meaning. A passing deference to the ideal of negotiated independence was still made, but this was not what their practical political disposition implied. Self-determination understood as a right to independence had become self-determination as a right for unionists to decide the constitutional character of Northern Ireland. The UDA's position was now the traditional unionist one, for it was really a demand that Northern Ireland should remain a part of the United Kingdom. Having adopted this stance, the politics of the UDA was really no different from that of the two main unionist parties. This is why, after 15 November 1985, the leadership did not see itself as a separate political agent, pursuing a distinctive course, but tried to use its influence to act as a ginger group within the broad ranks of unionism. That was the condition and perspective within which *Common Sense* evolved.

Many of the ideas of *Beyond the Religious Divide* were carried over into *Common Sense*, which was published on 29 January 1987. John McMichael, the political brain behind the document, had made it an axiom of any intelligent settlement that there must be seen to be no winners and losers in the constitutional game. The philosophy of the proposal was the same. The radical liberalism of Tom Paine and the principles of the American Declaration of Independence were self-consciously espoused.[37] It is no coincidence that the separation and balance of powers form a substantial part of the UDA's constitutional initiative; only this time the UDA was not interested in negotiated independence but in formulating a workable devolutionary settlement which recognised Ulster's present position within the United Kingdom. *Common Sense* argued that if such a solution was to stand any chance of success, it had to ensure two things: first, "that Ulster 'Protestants' no longer feel compelled to defend the frontier"; and secondly, "that Ulster 'Catholics' support, and play a full role in, society". The details of the proposal are not important. There is the familiar pattern of institutions with a written constitution, devolved government and legislature, proportional representation, "consensus" government, Bill of Rights and supreme court. The constitutional character of all this is summed up in the UDA's felicitous phrase ''co-determination'', a mutually acceptable resolution of two opposing ideas of self-determination within Northern Ireland. Tacked on to the tail of this devolved, partnership government was an appeal for the political parties of Great Britain to organise and campaign in Northern Ireland. This addition was logically at odds with the rest of the proposals, which were founded on the ultimate ''reality'' of two exclusive politico-religious traditions which demanded institutional expression. Bringing the British parties to Northern Ireland was designed to transform that very ''reality'' into a modern one where social and economic divisions would transcend the religio-political ones. This only read like an ill-considered afterthought, an attempt by the UDA to provide something for everyone.

What is of interest is the political calculation which informed the UDA's plan. John McMichael outlined what he called the four cardinal realities of Ulster politics. First, Northern Ireland's position within the United Kingdom was not likely to change in the foreseeable future. Secondly, Ulster had a deeply divided political society. Thirdly, unionists would never accept the Agreement. Fourthly, Ulster catholics had to be fully involved in the affairs of the province.[38] Only the first three could be called ''realities''. The fourth was a hope which the devolutionary proposals of *Common Sense* were designed to fulfil. His understanding of the facts of the situation was no different from that of the Charter Group. The UDA was also concerned that unionism should adopt a positive proposal which could be used as a means to negotiate away the Anglo-Irish Agreement. McMichael and his intimates were increasingly frustrated by what they saw as an ineffective and pusillanimous unionist campaign. Again, the position differed little from that of the Charterists. However the intent of the UDA's proposal within unionism differed in one fundamental respect from that of the Charter Group.

Both proposals hoped to seize the initiative in unionist politics by providing a rallying-point for those who wanted to pressurise Molyneaux and Paisley towards negotiations on devolved government. The UDA's proposal had a further purpose. We mentioned in Chapter 3 the press rumours about paramilitary plans to push aside the politicians in favour of a campaign of violent action. Speculation about plans for independence also helped to fill up the column inches. Unionist politicians too would mutter about the possibility of dark forces waiting in the wings. This could serve two alternative purposes: either to suggest to the British government that concessions ought to be made to reasonable leaders if it wanted to avoid facing the consequences of dealing with the hard men of loyalism; or to avoid calls to enter into talks on devolved government by arguing that a ''partnership'' or ''cross-community'' settlement would be brought down, as in 1974, by concerted paramilitary action. Publishing *Common Sense* was the UDA leadership making it clear that they had no intention of acting as anyone's bogeyman. It was also stating firmly that, on certain conditions, it would not be opposed to an executive role for nationalist politicians in a devolved administration. It was trying to deprive the leaders of the unionist parties of one important reason for political inertia. In an article written for the *News Letter*, McMichael addressed Paisley's criticism that the UDA document was a capitulation to the nationalist demand for power-sharing which the paramilitaries had opposed in the Sunningdale arrangements. Defending the proposals of 1987, he observed: ''As one who actually physically took part in the dismantling of the Sunningdale agreement, I would remind Dr Paisley that the principal objection to that treaty was because of the Council of Ireland clause which allowed the Government of Eire a formal role in the affairs of Northern Ireland. As to the power-sharing executive, it was undemocratically structured and appointed and did not have the consent of a broad enough section of the community.''[39] The purpose was to re-interpret paramilitary history, for the distinction between Executive and Council of Ireland is one that is easy to make in retrospect but was not so clear at the time. It is also to make a distinction that still operates.

Thus in the present crisis the main body of loyalist paramilitaries is just as adamant that it will not tolerate any direct involvement of the government of the Republic in the affairs of Northern Ireland. Hillsborough is no different from Sunningdale. Both were insufferable *diktats*, and have no legitimate standing in a democratic polity. Consensus government, co-operation between the communities on a mutually agreed basis, is something entirely different. The subtitle of *Common Sense* is ''Northern Ireland – An Agreed Process''. The UDA was saying that so long as there was consent from both sides to establish a devolved system to replace the Agreement, no one had anything to fear from loyalist paramilitarism. While the reaction of Molyneaux and Paisley to the proposals was hostile, devolutionists within both parties tried to take the initiative and maintain the momentum which the UDA démarche had created. Favourable reaction came from those who had spent their careers condemning the UDA. Even the Northern Ireland Office and members of the SDLP commended its vision and goodwill – not, one imagines, because of any sympathy with loyalists, but because they wanted to press and embarrass the unionist leadership. In the rather surprising configurations of post-Hillsborough politics, it could be argued that the Northern Ireland Office, the UDA and the SDLP shared a common aim in gingering up unionist politics.

Beyond the internal politics of the unionist campaign, *Common Sense*

had a particular strategic intent. This had to do with a general devolutionist concern with the politics of the SDLP. After a year of "Ulster
Says No", the UDA leadership argued for a positive appeal which
would allow unionism to go on the offensive. If the unionist parties
adopted a generous package of devolutionary measures, then it would
have the initiative. McMichael estimated that the British government
would "heave a sigh of relief and seek to support the unionist case".
This would break up the Hillsborough bloc and test the SDLP for the
first time. The reasoning was thus: "If unionists present a positive and
reasonable package for devolved consensus government, it will put the
Roman Catholic community under severe pressure, as it will be forced
to consider whether the Anglo-Irish Agreement is preferable to a cross-
community settlement for full-blooded devolution in Northern
Ireland, because it can't have both." Trading the Agreement for an
internal settlement, claimed McMichael, would enable John Hume
"to achieve everything he has claimed to want for Roman Catholics
within Northern Ireland".[40] If the SDLP were not interested in reconciliation within Northern Ireland, then that would be made plain to the
British government and to the world. The UDA wanted to put John
Hume on that particular hook and see if he could wriggle off it. The
failure of unionism to confront the SDLP directly was held to be an
opportunity wasted.

However reasonable and clearly thought out the proposals for devolved
government have been – and the UDA attempt was particularly well
thought out – there appears to exist a dramatic gulf between
conception and attainment. This in itself is not a sufficient argument
against trying to negotiate such an arrangement. However, the issue is
not an abstract one but has to do with strategies for the maintenance of
the Union. This Chapter has considered the principles upon which
devolution had been accepted by unionists when the polity of Northern
Ireland was established. Taking these to be the measure of an intelligent unionist policy, the advocacy of devolved government as a
response to the Anglo-Irish Agreement was assessed according to that
historical index. This may seem a rather conservative prejudice, but no
other sensible procedure suggested itself without straying too far into
the realms of fantasy. However, it is possible to argue, as many do, that
the values of the 1920s are no longer valid in the 1980s; that the Union
between Great Britain and Northern Ireland has been given notice of
its termination at Hillsborough and therefore unionists had better
make their dispositions accordingly. That would appear to be the pessimistic message of Peter Smith and, as it would seem, the thrust of
Charter thinking. In an unguarded moment on a local radio broadcast,

Harry West let slip the view that unionists had better get used to the idea of living with the Agreement and deal with the SDLP. It is also the logic of some of those who still talk of independence.

As we argue at the beginning of this Chapter, this could be all that unionism can now expect. There might be no point at all in resurrecting Carson and memories of what might have been. Coming to terms with reality may be hard, but it is better to do it now and save something rather than prevaricate and lose everything. Charterists may have a point, yet when we explore the assumptions of Charter-style thinking, it becomes clear that their so-called "realism" is not as "hard" as they believe. It may have all the substance of a mirage. On the other hand, the DUP, the UDA and some in the OUP might retort that their commitment to devolution is soundly unionist and has nothing to do with the faint-heartedness of the Charter Group. They might have different intentions, certainly, but those intentions are still founded on much the same assumptions. Devolution after the Agreement, whether advocated as the best of a bad job, a tradition to be maintained, as a means to upset the SDLP or whatever, cannot really satisfy the traditional purposes of unionism. If unionists ever do enter into negotiations on "full-blooded" devolution under the shadow of Hillsborough (and that is what seemed on offer), it will merely be a sign that they have accepted a defeat. It often seems that the case for devolution is argued as a way of limiting and containing that defeat. Ultimately, it is suggested, damage limitation may be the wisest course – indeed, the only course – for unionist politics to take.

The dilemma which now confronted unionism was clearly summed up by the Official Unionist, David Trimble. Speaking to the branch of his party in Windsor, a district in South Belfast, he said that if unionists agreed to devolution, then the "attributes of Britishness will be slowly stripped from the province", devolution being quite consistent with the nationalist logic of Hillsborough. Continue to oppose the Agreement with principled determination, and unionists will further alienate and antagonise the people of Great Britain who do not understand their position. But on balance he was assured that the second course was the wise course of action. "We should say that there will be no devolution (except on democratic principles), and insist on the Government's duty to govern us as if we were truly part of the United Kingdom."[41] This had been eminently sensible advice for unionism in the direct aftermath of the Agreement. If some sort of settlement had been rushed into headlong without allowing time for reflection or for the trend of events to be gauged, there could have been no honourable and no freely negotiated settlement. Despite the "tradition" of regional autonomy espoused as central to unionism by the Charter Group, this course of resistance has seemd fully in tune with the general sensibilities of unionist voters. As one of the unsung heroes of the unionist campaign, Belfast Councillor Fred Cobain, argued: "The people of the Shankill are not interested in Stormont. But they are interested in basic British rights."[42] And regardless of all the ingenuity expended on constitutional procedures to perpetuate two, and only two, traditions in Northern Ireland, the majority of people on the Falls would have the same practical concern. Even someone like John Taylor, MP and MEP, long associated with opposition to integrationist moves within the OUP and often seen as a unionist weathervane, substantiates this interpretation. "I was always keen on devolution", confided Taylor, "but I now realise that the chances of obtaining it are almost nil."[43]

Indeed, for most of the younger unionists engaged in the anti-Agreement campaign, Stormont is either a faint memory or like a tale of the Great White Buffalo. A whole generation has grown up with a clearer perspective on a regional parliament. It recognises the incapacity of such an institution to accommodate the pressures of local politics, let alone provide an exclusive focus of loyalty. While the Agreement is in place, few can see devolution as a path to right, justice and democracy. As *Young Unionist* advised, following Powell, "to say No is the most positive and constructive course open to unionism."[44] Defying the Agreement also meant defying the devolutionary provisions which it contains. On that point the DUP and OUP have generally been in harmony. Every denial is also an affirmation. The re-affirmation of the Union after Hillsborough provoked a deeper reflection on the meaning of equal British citizenship, and it is to this factor that we now turn.

NOTES

1. R.J. Lawrence, *The Government of Northern Ireland* (Oxford: Clarendon Press, 1965), p. 1.
2. D.Birrell and A.Murie, *Policy and Government in Northern Ireland: The Lessons of Devolution* (Dublin: Gill and Macmillan, 1980), p. 5.
3. Lawrence, op.cit., p. 166.
4. Ibid., p. 7.
5. Ibid., p. 18.
6. Cited in *News Letter*, Jan. 6, 1988.
7. B.Clifford, *The Road to Nowhere* (Belfast: Athol Books, 1987), pp. 1–2.
8. Lawrence, op. cit., p. 181.
9. Birrell and Murie, op.cit., p. 28.
10. R.Rose, *Governing Without Consensus* (London: Faber and Faber, 1971), p. 470.
11. J.Allister, op. cit., pp. 56–7.
12. OUP Press Release, September 15, 1979.
13. Ulster Unionist Assembly Party, *The Way Forward*, April 1984.

14. P.O'Malley, *The Uncivil Wars* (Belfast: Blackstaff Press, 1983) p. 166.
15. Cited in H.Roberts, op.cit., p. 12.
16. P.Smith *Why Unionists Say No* (Joint Unionist Working Party 1986), p. 34.
17. *News Letter*, 20 June 1986.
18. OUP Press Release, 14 March 1986.
19. OUP Press Release, 30 March 1987.
20. *News Letter*, 25 May 1987.
21. Ibid., 3 Sept. 1986.
22. *Belfast Telegraph*, 1 May 1987.
23. *News Letter*, 25 Jan. 1986.
24. Ibid., 22 June 1987.
25. Allister, op.cit., p. 54.
26. O'Malley, op.cit., p. 153.
27. *News Letter*, Nov. 8, 1986.
28. Ibid., 20 April 1987.
29. Ibid.
30. *News Letter*, 10 Dec. 1987.
31. *Fortnight*, June 1987.
32. *News Letter*, 27 April 1987.
33. *Fortnight*, June 1987.
34. Ibid.
35. Reg Empey, quoted in the *News Letter*, Sept. 12, 1987.
36. *Magill*, Dec. 1978.
37. *Ulster*, April 1987.
38. *Fortnight*, April 1987.
39. *News Letter*, 25 May 1987.
40. Ibid., 25 May 1987.
41. OUP Press Release, 10 March 1986.
42. Quoted in *Young Unionist*, no. 3 (1986).
43. *News Letter*, 3 May 1986.
44. *Young Unionist*, no. 6 (1987).

5

THE CASE FOR INTEGRATION

One commentator tried to characterise the difference between integrationists and devolutionists in terms of the two great historical personages of unionism, and thus as the battle for the mantle of unionist tradition. For those disposed towards integration, "the reference point is Carson – Carson the Parliamentarian resisting Home Rule for any part of Ireland." For devolutionists the reference point is "the pragmatic state-builder Craig" whose "attachment to the Union", it is claimed, "was conditional on what was seen as Britain delivering its part of the bargain."[1] Now there is very little historical substance to this distinction for, as we have tried to show, what separated Carson and Craig had nothing to do with ideas about the Union. It had to do with political circumstance and public responsibility. Craig was not a "state-builder" in so far as that suggests a creative design for the polity of Northern Ireland. That was the last thing on his mind. He was, however, prepared to use the security powers bequeathed to him by Westminster to ensure that Northern Ireland remained part of the Union and to prevent it collapsing, as London had hoped, into some all-Ireland dominion. On the other hand, there is some truth in the suggestion that present-day devolutionists are disposed towards "state-building", for that is what talk about regional autonomy, political bulwarks and new relationships in Ireland seems to imply. Nor should it be surprising that some provincial journalists and political pundits share in and support that singular fantasy. Every Gopher Prairie needs its *Dauntless*. And there is also some truth in the representation of integrationists as the claimants to Carson's mantle, to the true and original spirit of Ulster unionism, what in one manifestation became known as the "real" unionism.

But this journalistic excursion only brushes the surface of the issue. We need to go deeper. To borrow a phrase from Robert Berki, the distinction between devolution and integration in unionist politics is between the idealism of nostalgia and the idealism of imagination. "Idealism", according to Berki, "is born of the endeavour to comprehend political reality in *unitary* terms, in a series of straightforward and precise propositions." The essence of idealism is to understand the world as something simple, to focus on "some part of a total situation". For the philosopher this is inadequate since it provides only comfort to the believer or "a plausible set of justifications for pre-existing prejudices".[2] It leads to dualism, the two sides of the single coin of reality. But what is inadequate for the philosopher is what is fundamental for the politician. The one-sidedness of idealism is the very quality of commitment, of that passionate faith which is necessary to achieve any political objective. As Hegel wrote (and this is relevant to the Irish experience), the tragedy of history is not the struggle between right and wrong but the struggle between right and right. What Berki reveals is that all political advocacy is by its nature both partly right and partly wrong. Political judgement means assessing, in the circumstances, that which is more appropriate to the attainment of one's goal.

In Berki's understanding, this dualism has shown itself in a broad differentiation in political thought between a "nostalgic", or conservative, vision which focuses upon a set of past experiences as the inspiration for present action; and an "imaginative", or radical vision, which focuses upon an idea, a creative engagement to achieve that which has not yet been. This distinction may be subject to all sorts of qualifications, yet as a means to order and investigate the complexities of political reality it is a suggestive intellectual achievement. And although the categories have to be contorted somewhat to be applied intelligently to Northern Ireland, a relevant interpretation would seem to be this. The case for devolution is the expression of a nostalgic idealism for the experience of regional government in Northern Ireland. It is a tradition to be maintained and not an ideal to be attained. Devolution has the contours of substance because it is a mode of government which is part of the history of the province. What was a pragmatic and contingent political act in 1920 has been transformed into a permanent necessity. That is a characteristic of conservative thinking, the turning of chance into necessity. The parliament buildings at Stormont are the physical expression and symbol of this belief. The case for integration lives in the frustrated ideal of anti-Home Rule unionism and the vitality of its hoped-for achievement. It is an imaginative idealism, and in this it is no different from any other political radicalism, for instance socialism, which is both past disappointment and future expectation. The case for integration can therefore be more critical of the historical practice of unionist politics. Since its ideal has never been fully realised, political history is the failure of individuals and of governments to live up to that ideal. Lifted above the particulars of Ulster history, the idea appears to take on a life of its own. It projects a bright vision of what should be; and that vision is in no way dimmed by what Laurence Sterne called the "sad vicissitude of things", the tyrannies of political circumstance by which others guide their actions.

Both devolution and integration can lay claim to part of the unionist tradition, and the character of contemporary unionism – or,to use

Berki's term, the political "realism" of modern unionism involves both of them. As analytical expressions, the terms "nostalgia" and "imagination" do not suggest either recommendation or condemnation. Indeed, there is no exact fit of the two expressions to either commitment, although the bias *within unionism*, in terms of those who advocate these alternatives, is weighty enough. Full integration of Northern Ireland into the political system of the United Kingdom has no appeal within the DUP, which, for all its concern with the religious sunlight, is happiest with the familiar shadows in the cave of Ulster politics. But integration has significant support within the major party of unionism, the OUP, which, for all its cautious conservatism, is more open to the influence of intellectual argument. It also exerts a powerful attraction on those who belong to neither unionist party but who support the Union. After Hillsborough this latter group injected much needed intelligent argument into the weary predictabilities of conventional unionist politics. In particular, when ranged alongside the most impressive of modern unionist politicians, Robert McCartney, a potent and exciting new force was established, which certainly owed more to radical imagination than to conservative nostalgia.

For devolutionists, the strength of the case for integration is also its major weakness. Its strength lies in the imaginative inspiration of the option which has never been tried. Its purity of principle and its impeccable Carsonite heritage give it both a virtue and a legitimacy which make all else seem tainted and compromised. Integration is a simple claim and, in what it denies, expresses what it confirms. Devolutionists must endeavour to come up with the most elaborate constitutional schemes and ingenious mechanisms to give credibility to their proposition that recognising and permanently institutionalising sectarianism within Northern Ireland can secure consensus and peace. Those who advocate integration do not. Opposition to the Anglo-Irish Agreement does not enjoin them to come up with some constitutional blueprint. The essence of the integrationist case is that it is when – and only when – Northern Ireland is governed in the same way as the rest of the United Kingdom will the conditions for peace and reconciliation ever exist. What makes this idea even more attractive as a basis for opposition is that the Hillsborough accord is designed to prevent precisely that parity of status. The integrationist analysis goes to the heart of the matter; its thesis is the very antithesis of the Agreement, and therefore fully engages Hillsborough's political intent. The radical idealism of unionism is inspired all the more since the integrationist case is the one that infuriates the SDLP, outrages the irredentist backwoodsmen in Irish politics, and discomfits the British government.

Its weakness, according to the opponents of integration, lies in those very factors. First, it has not been tried because it cannot be tried. The idea is unrealistic; and even if it might have worked in Carson's day, it is just not practical politics today. It is not an idea whose time has come but an idea whose time has gone. Secondly, it ignores the nationalism of the minority and, rather than confront this, takes refuge in a beautiful illusion. Integrationists try to transcend the Ulster crisis instead of resolving it, and in this are no better than the most dogmatic republican. Finally, comprehension of the Machiavellian purpose of the Agreement does not necessarily recommend an equal and opposite reaction. Politics is the art of the possible and the advocacy of the sensible. Devolutionists believe that the integrationist case is neither possible nor sensible. Nothing better illustrates the difference between the conservatism of the devolutionist and the radicalism of the integrationist than that final criticism. For as every good radical knows, the purpose of political reflection is not just to understand the world but to change it. The thrust of the integrationist case is that Ulster does not have to submit to those "realities" imposed upon it by the British and Irish governments. It is possible to challenge them and to change them. It is possible to make one's own realities. As this Chapter unfolds, we shall examine the substance of the devolutionist charges on all these points.

Some have questioned the utility of the term "integration" as a definition of a coherent tendency within unionism. For Jim Davidson, in an influential pamphlet in the integration-devolution debate, integration is, in general usage, "a word without meaning"; it is a "verbal puzzle" which contributes to a general confusion, namely that "futile, meaningless debate which goes on in Northern Ireland between 'devolution' and 'integration'."[3] However, when one looks closer at Davidson's argument he does not reject integration as "a word without meaning". His pamphlet really says that integration, properly understood, is not necessarily incompatible with some forms of devolution, which is a very different contention. What he demands is a particular form of integration first; and only then is it sensible, in his opinion, for people to entertain the notion of devolution. This is made even clearer in a later pamphlet when Davidson openly qualifies his former position. Integration now has meaning "when you specify what kind of integration you are talking about." Therefore, far from being meaningless, integration is a word which has a number of meanings, *one* of which Davidson believes to be a priority.[4] It is not just the general use of the term but also its specific allocation which has raised some academic doubt. In a penetrating article on the arguments within unionism post-Hillsborough, Paul Bew and Henry Patterson were reluctant to apply the integrationist label to that broad strand of opinion within unionism opposed to the push for full-blooded devolution. They preferred to label that particular disposition "minimalist".[5] This interpretation is essentially correct; and, since it has for long been the authoritative if understated strategy of the OUP leadership, the term captures well its caution and concern for balance. Nonetheless it is the bias or leaning, however minimal, that is important. As we shall try to show, that leaning is quite definitely towards some genuine form of integration, and is recognised as such by those who support it and also by those who oppose it.

Despite all these very proper reservations about the term – a sign of a new intensity of political interest which is not prepared to wallow in the usual cliches about unionism – there does seem to be enough in common between the various articulations to accord integrationists a recognisable identity. At least they are more concerned to re-establish a sound foundation for Northern Ireland as a fully integral part of the United Kingdom; for it is an axiom of integrationist belief that what is truly without meaning is the constant assertion by British ministers that Northern Ireland *is* an integral part of the state. The Hillsborough Agreement did not create this article of faith, but merely confirmed it. It is believed that only when Northern Ireland is integrated into the British state, "one and indivisibly", can attention be devoted to the question of the relevant form of devolution, if any, which the province requires. Integrate first and devolution can look after itself. Integrate, and all else falls into place. The will of the majority will be respected; the rights of the minority guaranteed under the rule of law; terrorism, which feeds on constitutional uncertainty, will be defeated; and the prospect will open up of an effective and mutually beneficial relationship with the Republic of Ireland. What devolutionists see as an evasion of the "realities" of the situation is in fact an alternative way of interpreting those same realities.

The idiom of integrationists is the idiom of equal citizenship, the expression both of unionism's historical Covenant and its unfulfilled ideal. It has a particular resonance in the wake of the Agreement, this "time of threatened calamity" when the true cause becomes clear once again, the cause of that "cherished position of equal citizenship within the United Kingdom". Only, this time it is a position to be attained rather than retained, although it still has the proper and inspiring ring about it. Equal citizenship was to be the "Good Cry" which would bring together all the Tadpoles and Tapers of unionist politics into a united campaign; a "Good Cry" which might regain for unionism that which it has lacked since the beginning of the present crisis – the moral high ground. *Workers' Weekly* summed up the situation succinctly. It argued that unionism has a "primary and sympathetic demand" and a "secondary and less sympathetic one" in its dealings with the British government. The first is the demand for equal citizenship and the second the demand that the Agreement be scrapped. If unionism were to mobilise effectively all its resources to campaign for the former, then the latter would naturally follow.[6] If equal citizenship was to be more than mere cant, it had to embody some intelligible political project. What was involved in the demand for equal citizenship?

Distilling from the various lists of demands made in the name of equal citizenship, the following four principles may be said to constitute the sum of the integrationist case. First, Northern Ireland legislation at Westminster ought to be debated in the manner appropriate to that of Scotland and Wales. There should be a Northern Ireland Grand Committee and a rapid end to the system of Orders in Council. Secondly, there ought to be a proper reform of local government which would abolish the so-called "Macrory Gap". This was the gap in democratic accountability for the provision of public services due to the absence of an upper tier of local government comparable with that in the rest of the United Kingdom. Thirdly, no major constitutional changes ought to be imposed upon the citizens of Northern Ireland without a referendum to test their support. Finally, the citizens of Northern Ireland ought to have the right to join, and to vote for or against, the political parties which form the government of the United Kingdom. Together these principles form a package designed to achieve the legislative, the administrative, the constitutional and the electoral integration of Northern Ireland within the United Kingdom *state*. Its achievement would represent a major reversal of policy by the United Kingdom *government*. That has always been the vital distinction made by unionists. Only those ensnared by the simplicities of the conditional loyalty thesis continue to fail to comprehend its significance.

Of course, within the scope of these demands there was from the start the clear possibility for difference of emphasis and priority. It was certainly the case that some of these demands were more easily obtainable than others, although their value as a means to enhance the quality of the Union, while the Agreement remained in place, was open to serious question. Just as some forms of devolution were perfectly compatible with the Agreement, so too were aspects of integration. Thus, on the one hand, weighing the attractions of a partial normalisation of the treatment of Northern Ireland business within the House of Commons against the political incubus of the Agreement was to be the delicate task of those like Molyneaux and Powell who favoured a cautious, "minimalist" approach. On the other, the Campaign for Equal Citizenship, which achieved such specific prominence within unionist politics after Hillsborough, developed the argument that the first three demands were really predicated on the achievement of the fourth, and pushed for a "maximalist" strategy. The dramatic nature of the public commitment of the CEC, compared with the delphic utterances of the OUP leader, antagonised many of the worthies of unionism who had no interest at all in having the British parties organise and compete in Northern Ireland and who thought that demand to be an exotic growth within unionist politics; indeed, thought it to be subversive of the unionist interest. Insofar as that "interest" was a sectarian one, they were right. The purpose of this Chapter is to assess the contributions of these different actors to the case for integration.

The minimalist position

On 26 April, addressing the Executive Committee of his party, Molyneaux proclaimed: "We are the party of devolution." His next sentence was: "We are the party of *The Way Forward*."[7] That qualification was extremely important, for, as mentioned in the previous Chapter, the sort of devolution envisaged by *The Way Forward* was not the full-blooded variety. The document was self-consciously minimalist, concluding that while the party's "proposal may be considered by some to be too modest . . . it has watched while grander and more ambitious schemes have failed." What it advocated was not a return to devolved government of the kind pursued since 1972 but a democratic reform of local government fully in line with the Conservative Manifesto of 1979. And that Manifesto commitment was recognised as being an integrationist one, although it did not take long for the Conservative government to renege on that "commitment". Molyneaux had outlined his thinking about devolved government with or without an Irish dimension in a rather revealing article written in December 1984, when unionists were confident that the threat posed by the New Ireland Forum had been laid to rest. "Conditioned as I am by British parliamentary thinking", he wrote, "I have an instinctive reservation about any attempt to bring political parties together to produce all-party agreement, for it is not the way of democracy." That was a comment on the Forum itself, but it could be applied with even greater relevance to the proposition of a power-sharing government in Northern Ireland. Molyneaux's argument was that it is impossible to design any workable governmental structure which can accommodate "those who want to stay in the United Kingdom and those who would feel compelled to work from day one to get Ulster out of the UK and into the Republic".[8] The only answer was to secure Northern Ireland's constitutional position as an integral part of the United Kingdom and to democratise the procedures for local administration. Nationalist aspiration to a united Ireland would not be denied. On the other hand, the pursuit of that aspiration ought not to frustrate the possibility of making some limited progress towards a more adequate popular control of public services.

Long before the Agreement was signed, therefore, the leader of the OUP had fashioned a policy which treated gently the different tendencies within his party. Devolution could still be acknowledged, though in terms of administrative accountability rather than regional autonomy. This was to be compatible with a grander design to normalise the political relationship of Northern Ireland with the rest of the United Kingdom by way of legislative integration. This policy, like the character and style of Molyneaux himself, was not an inspirational one. Its success depended on *sotto governo* or under government, a considered ambiguity; that is, an ambiguity subtle enough to prevent an open split within the party, an ambiguity effective enough to attain the purpose it partly conceals. The reason for this approach was due not only to the requirements of party management but also to the assumed imperatives of party competition. Molyneaux was well aware of the Paisleyite challenge, and was reluctant to make any public undertaking that could be exploited to the electoral disadvantage of his own party. It may have been a great miscalculation. At any rate it was not a very heroic judgment. Officials in the old Austro-Hungarian empire used to pursue a policy of "simmering". When they calculated that any decision would antagonise one group more than it would please another, even if that decision were the right decision, they allowed the problem to simmer. Judicious equivocation and prevarication became an end in itself. The Molyneaux style has been somewhat similar, since his concern for the harmonious balance of the unionist patrimony has been more important than making speculative political investments, than taking risks. The OUP leader has operated on the principle of Levin's third law: stand for something and somebody around will feel persecuted.

Alex Kane, a long-standing advocate of the integrationist case within the OUP, reviewed the years between Molyneaux's accession to the leadership and the Agreement. He argued that between 1979 and early 1982 "a section of the Official Unionist Party realised that the devolution battle had been lost and that the best policy was to push for full-blooded integration." The leadership was sympathetic, and recognised the rationality of the thesis. However, "they allowed themselves to be swayed by the naive delusions of their grassroots supporters and by a ballot-box fear of blustering Paisleyism." Kane's conclusion was that by "their refusal to lead rather than be led they may have lost the Union itself."[9] He does not name the "leadership", but one assumes that he means Molyneaux and the majority of his parliamentary colleagues at Westminster. The criticism, if perhaps not the conclusion, is measured and reasonably accurate. In the pre-Hills-borough period that style of leadership might have been frustrating to integrationists, but at least they could see that the parliamentary party was inching towards a similar objective. After Hillsborough it seemed a completely redundant and intolerably complacent strategy. Integration could not come by stealth, but could only be seized by an intelligent mobilisation of opinion. Minimalism no longer measured up to the challenge of the times. Some people were certain to feel persecuted, and that their views were being ignored. The task of integrationists was to make sure it was not their views which would be ignored.

To impress some urgency upon the party, Kane was instrumental in setting up the "UK Group". It included notable figures within the OUP like Cecil Walker, MP, and Fred Cobain, leader of the party in Belfast City Council. On June 23, it published the policy document *No Longer a Place Apart*, which advocated the central principles of the case for equal citizenship. It stated that the "task of Ulster unionism today is to create a framework in which every Ulsterman and Ulsterwoman, regardless of political or religious belief, can consider themselves equal British citizens." This could only be done within the Union, a polity which had demonstrated its capacity to recognise diversity and distinction within the bounds of a unitary state. By contrast, the reality of the Republican state, the idea which it embodied, was incompatible with such diversity. Devolved government was also inadequate to achieve this end. It would only maintain diversity within Northern Ireland at the level of irreconcilable conflict, at the level of a perpetual sectarianism. Only integration, the document argued, "truly offers civil and religious liberty for all in Northern Ireland." Kane explained the integration argument in more detail in an article in the *News Letter*. He wrote that while integration may not be the first choice of any group, it is the "only choice, which, in practice, is inoffensive to every other group". (The same used to be said about that *ersatz* form of equal citizenship, direct rule.) Integration, rather than devolution, would be a means of alleviating the real fears of catholics and protestants and of creating the proper atmosphere for the ending of political violence. "Unionists have nothing to fear from it, for it safeguards their citizenship and their kingdom. Roman Catholics have nothing to fear from it for it safeguards them from the paranoid whims of unionist leaders and structures."[10] The UK Group was restrained in its criticism of the leadership. Having made its declaration, it did little to follow it up; it suffered from that unionist affliction of lacking the energy for sustained ideological advocacy.

Another party lobby for integration was the Young Unionist Council. In its policy document *The New Agenda*, published in the spring of 1986, the Young Unionists tried to develop the "positive features of the Unionist vision". It was a call for the leadership to campaign for "democratic equal citizenship". Devolution was dismissed as a naturally weak form of government, "which does not help to sustain the Union but which will continually cast a question-mark over the existence of the Union." The programme of *The New Agenda* concluded that the solution to the crisis "must address itself to the issue of inequality of rights – the inequality which treats Ulster differently from the rest of the Kingdom, which marginalises Ulster in the institutions of government and which banishes Ulster people from its party political system".[11] This Young Unionist document reveals the lack of interest in devolution within the new influential and thoughtful generation of unionist activists. It also reveals very clearly and intelligently the proposition advanced in Chapter 1. Unionism has little to do with the idea of national identity and everything to do with the idea of the state. That was really the principle of the message contained in the Young Unionist document. The proposal of the Young Unionists was an attempt to encourage Molyneaux to commit himself to a forward policy, to make fully explicit the rejection of devolution.

However, the circumstances after the Agreement introduced a new element of caution and restraint which compounded the hesitancy of the former period. Molyneaux and those around him were conscious of the need to maintain unionist unity. Now, unionist unity was not only an intra-party but also an inter-party affair. The pact with the DUP had to be maintained above all else. This became a shibboleth. It could only be done by avoiding grand initiatives and concentrating on that which united, namely, opposition to the Anglo-Irish Agreement. For Bew and Patterson, Molyneaux exhibited the Kutuzov syndrome – "immobile but tenacious".[12] It entailed trying to neutralise and marginalise those, such as McCartney, who tried to commit the OUP to an openly integrationist line, and likewise devolu-tionists, such as David McNarry, who were equally troublesome. It meant resorting to all sorts of rhetorical devices to avoid divulging what unionism ought to do. In this case the phrase "equal citizenship" became a mere emollient. The OUP leader was well aware of the criticism levelled against him by those who wanted a more positive approach. Speaking to the Queen's University Unionist Association in March 1987, Molyneaux generalised the criticisms within and without unionist politics to imply a strategy of subversion. "The garrison is being told", he said, "it will run short of rations; that defeat is inevitable and that they had better come to terms; and most pedestrian of all, that under no circumstances must the garrison trust its commander who quite unreasonably refuses to reveal his war aims to all – the enemy included.''[13] There is nothing so effective as to suggest a conspiracy, in particular a conspiracy to reveal those secret plans which are going to win the war. Two weeks later, at the Ulster Unionist Council, Molyneaux rounded on those ''self-appointed'' groups within unionist politics which claimed to have the answer to Ulster's agony. Their squabbling, argued Molyneaux, was ''the sure recipe for prolonging the life of the accord''.[14] Unionism must proceed cautiously and avoid gesturism. Above all else, unity must be maintained.

The OUP leader has been reasonably successful so far in this; over the first three years of the accord he has persevered with the original strategy. That remarkable consistency gave all the appearance of a directionless policy, an end in itself rather than a means to dismantle the Agreement. The general criticism was that unionist unity has had a corrosively negative effect upon the spirit and vivacity of the anti-Agreement campaign. Unity became a substitute for action. There is some truth in this. We argued in Chapter 3 that Molyneaux's purpose was to prevent the campaign going off the rails in a way that would damage unionism's remaining credibility. As we argued, this is an intelligent purpose. On the other hand, the notion of what unionist unity consists of has been a less than comprehensive one. Neither Molyneaux nor Paisley has been keen on a free market in ideas. The OUP-DUP pact for the General Election of 1987 was a definite ideological cartel. But it is not entirely accurate to claim that unionists ''know what they don't want, but not a clue what they do want, nor how to get it''.[15] It would seem that Molyneaux does know what he wants, has been consistent – if publicly evasive – in its pursuit, and has a thoroughly pragmatic assessment of the possibilities of integration. Mrs Thatcher had already made known what was on offer at the meeting in Downing Street on February 25, 1986. Administrative and legislative integration in some form is a possibility; the stumbling-block is the Agreement. Molyneaux can only wait and hope for it to collapse from within. In the mean time unionists must do nothing foolish or precipitate. They must continue to re-build goodwill within Westminster. His strategy represents parliamentary unionism in its most formalised and cautious expression.[16] That is precisely what Molyneaux meant when he spoke of his British parliamentary conditioning.

Such a conditioning he shared with Enoch Powell, who had been the most prominent intellectual influence for integration within the leadership of the OUP. He has had the freedom to say what Molyneaux was restrained from saying, and he has said it with a familiar directness. There are a number of interlocking components to the Powellian argument for integration. First, there is a critique of devolution. Logically, Powell argues, devolution is incompatible with a unitary parliamentary state. When it comes to a debate about the future of Scotland or Wales, British politicians, Labour as well as Conservative, recognise that. The logic of devolution is the logic of federalism. A federal United Kingdom "does not and will not exist". Devolution in Great Britain is understood to mean the break up of the Union. Yet when British politicians and officials advocate devolved government for Northern Ireland their intention is precisely to break up the Union. The purpose is to put in place the relevant constitutional mechanisms to smooth the way to a united Ireland. This was the intention of Lloyd George, and it remains the intention today. The considerations which apply to Scotland and Wales – "internal" political considerations – are not those applied to Northern Ireland. The government has only a conditional and a partial loyalty to the Union of Great Britain *and* Northern Ireland.[17] Secondly, devolution is impossible given the conditions placed upon a settlement by the British and Irish governments. One cannot institutionalise the irreconcilable. You cannot split the difference between unionism and nationalism. "To present proposals or devise political initiatives which purport to combine these opposites, or to satisfy equally those whose political purposes are incompatible is either nonsense or deceit."[18] Thirdly, it *is* deceit. There is a conspiracy on the part of the Foreign Office and the Northern Ireland Office (which is mainly staffed by ex-FO civil servants) to remove Northern Ireland from the Union. This has nothing at all to do with the cause of justice and good government. It has to do with definite "external" political considerations – the strategic interests of NATO and the United States. "If America wants a united Ireland for political and strategic reasons, Her Majesty's Government will set about arranging it, even if the price is treachery to British citizens and national humiliation."[19] Finally, the logical conclusion is that unionists must not be seduced by the petty baubles of devolved government and play into the hands of those who want to undermine the Union. Unionists "must affirm their right to continue as British citizens represented like all others in the Parliament of the United Kingdom and entitled to the same rights and status as all the rest."[20]

Powell's parliamentary skills, and the affection with which he is held within certain circles of the Conservative Party, constituted an important factor in the way the OUP strategy developed. It was easy to mistake respect for Powell among government figures like Ian Gow for real influence, and to concentrate on winning friends and influencing people at Westminster. Indeed, for the best part of six years of Conservative government things did appear to be going well for the integrationist cause. It was noted by a number of commentators that Northern Ireland was slowly becoming administratively integrated into the mainstream British system.[21] No wonder, then, that the Agreement came like a bolt from the blue and shattered the magnificent illusion. It was also revealed how easy it is for respect to turn to ridicule when it is in the interests of backbenchers to bay with the government pack and when it suits journalists to join in the hunt.

Ferdinand Mount, another of Mrs Thatcher's one-time advisers, engaged in some silly journalism in the *Spectator*. His purpose was to dismiss Powell as brilliant but stupid, and to link his name with such political giants as Hobbes, Rousseau, Hitler, Gorbachov and Paisley.[22] James Naughtie, the political correspondent of the *Guardian*, did his bit by dismissing Powell as a "Westminster irrelevance, a crackling record stuck in its groove, driving everyone mad and threatening never to end". Even the Tory Right, he claimed, had had enough of their former guru.[23] Powell himself was dismissed as a mad genius and his arguments were scorned. The attack on Powell points to a prevailing feature of the media's grasp of political affairs in Northern Ireland. That critical judgement usually applied to affairs of state is sadly missing. The very people who were shocked by the invasion of Grenada and denounced the bombing of Libya were also those who argued that Powell must be off his head to suggest that there could be any relationship between the Agreement and American policy.[24] British newspapers, so conscious of their importance as a barrier to overweening power and despotic government, so critical of illiberal demagogues like Powell, were urging the government to ignore the majority, disregard inconveniences like rights of citizenship, and get the business settled in Northern Ireland. Like Hume, they were all for lancing boils. An intelligent case for unionism like Powell's was too inconvenient to confront.

During the Home Rule crisis the fate of Ulster concentrated the mind of a whole political generation in Britain and confronted it with a challenge of political principle which was taken to be profoundly significant. The principle is the same today, but the cause of Ulster is an esoteric one. Even Oxford, legendary home of lost causes, has no interest, if Anthony Kenny's threadbare justification of government policy is anything to go by.[25] Even so, one group did emerge after 15 November 1985 to "increase knowledge and understanding within and without the United Kingdom of the need to maintain the Union of Great Britain and Northern Ireland". That group is the Friends of the Union. Its task is to seek membership "from those who have a commitment to the integrity of the United Kingdom" and "who seek to establish full and equal standards of citizenship for the people of Northern Ireland within the United Kingdom". By the autumn of 1986 it could claim a membership of 650.[26] The most prominent and active figures within the Friends were Ian Gow and Sir John Biggs-

Davison. A number of other Conservative MPs are members, including some who voted for the Agreement in the House of Commons. The Friends of the Union has published a number of short pamphlets of mixed quality which advocate the integrationist case. Gow has propagated equal citizenship as the most hopeful way forward when it becomes clear that the Agreement cannot work.[27] Biggs-Davison attacked the idea that catholics favour a united Ireland and that integration in any way threatens the interests or ethos of Ulster catholics. "They would not be threatened by integration. But the lesson of Stormont is that catholics are safer under Westminster."[28] The disposition of the Friends complements the parliamentary strategy of Molyneaux. It is measured, moderate and concerned, above all, with political propriety.

The Friends of the Union drew some hostile fire from a number of quarters. It has been a petty stock-in-trade of journalists hostile to unionism to dismiss support for the Union within British politics. This is usually done not by addressing the arguments but by referring to those who propose them.[29] For instance, when unionists appeared to be winning support within the Conservative Party in the first term of the Thatcher government, David McKittrick, who has since made a name for "objective" journalism, labelled these sympathisers as the "Neanderthal right" on the "extreme wing" of the party. They were anti-EEC, anti-trade union and pro-monetarism, and therefore what they had to say about Northern Ireland was not worth listening to.[30] The Friends have been treated with similar disdain by the press for being unsympathetic to what passes for statesmanship in Anglo-Irish relations. Like Gow's resignation from government because of the Agreement, the Friends are taken to represent a noble and honourable gesture but an ultimately futile one.

Not surprisingly, the Friends have been criticised by factions in Northern Ireland. From one side, David McNarry of the Charter Group denounced the "so-called friends" who were being manipulated by a "small and insignificant band of English Tory parliamentarians". According to McNarry, their purpose has been to frustrate the possibility of regional autonomy and to encourage a form of administrative integration which would enable the British government to impose what it liked on. "the hard-pressed unionist community."[31] From the other side, the equal citizenship campaigners within *Workers' Weekly* perceived a plot, a plot which "consists in this: that the sole purpose of the Friends of the Union is to feed the delusions of Jim Molyneaux that the Conservative Party will eventually do right by him."[32] Certainly, the Friends are opposed to regional autonomy – they are unionists not quasi-separatists – but there is no evidence at all that they are part of a plot either to further paralyse the political will of Molyneaux or to undermine resistance to the Agreement. The Friends of the Union represent something which is very Conservative and very British. It is a form of political criticism which politely begs to differ from the policy of the leader. When this has to do with issues close to the Tory heart, like public schools, rural bus services or mortgage tax relief, it can be immensely effective. When it confronts an issue like the Agreement, it is equally politely ignored.

One organisation which has been rarely polite in its criticisms, and one which certainly cannot be ignored, is the Campaign for Equal Citizenship. The CEC does not have the monopoly of the term equal citizenship, though it has been the most active and energetic in the propagation of the idea. It has been a rare phenomenon in the recent history of support for the Union, and as such repays extensive consideration.

The Campaign for Equal Citizenship

As a practical political force, the Campaign for Equal Citizenship represented the conjuncture of circumstance, idea and personalities in the crucial period between 1985 and 1988. The circumstance was the impact of the Anglo-Irish Agreement. It has often been said that CEC meetings, which after 1985 were attracting large and attentive audiences, could have been held before the Agreement in a telephone booth. The truth of that would be acknowledged by CEC activists themselves. However the same could be said of any political movement from the Labour Party and Taff Vale to the Bolsheviks and a sealed train. The important thing for the CEC is that it believes itself to be in the van of what the French would call an *idée en marche*. No expression captures more accurately the "idealism of imagination" which informed, and continues to inform, the commitment of CEC members. The idea is straightforward. Because Northern Ireland is excluded from the British system of party competition it is condemned to sectarianism. It is abnormal only because the citizens of the province cannot participate in that which produces political normality in the rest of the United Kingdom. Put simply: "The aim of the Campaign for Equal Citizenship is to secure for the people of Northern Ireland – all the people of Northern Ireland – the right to vote for their government."[33] The personalities involved were the barrister and OUP politician Robert McCartney, who was able to engage the dynamism of the CEC with the impressive force of his public personality; those like Brendan Clifford, David Morrison and others clustered around the old British and Irish Communist Organisation, who provided much of the intellectual impulse to the Campaign; and some, like Jeff Dudgeon, who had been engaged in isolated and progressive causes. This was a creative, though also a volatile, mixture. The energies which combined with such dramatic effectiveness in the General Election of June 1987 were, in the autumn of that year, to engage in a harsh and acrimonious dispute, ostensibly over tactics. The circumstances we have already considered. It is necessary therefore to trace the development and coherence of the idea of electoral integration and the impact of the McCartney campaign upon unionist politics.

The intellectual inspiration for the Campaign for Equal Citizenship did not come from within traditional unionist politics at all. It had its roots in the Civil Rights protests of the late 1960s and still cleaves to the original demand – British Rights for British Citizens. As Brendan Clifford argued, it had nothing to do with the usual concerns of the parties of Ulster unionism. "The implication of the Civil Rights slogans of 1968–9 was a programme of normalising Ulster as a region of the UK. It was a programme to end the self-ghettoisation chosen by the Catholic commmity in the 1920s, and thereby to make possible the ending of Protestant provincial government, and the establishment of normal British politics and of equal rights for all British citizens." As the Troubles developed that project was abandoned by catholic politicians and the solution to catholic grievance became the old nationalist one – a united Ireland or nothing.[34] The tragedy, as Clifford understands it, is that nationalist leaders have been quite happy that catholics should have nothing rather than accept the alternative which was canvassed in the late sixties. However, that alternative vision lived on in the efforts of individuals and in the principles of groups like the British and Irish Communist Organisation and the Campaign for Labour Representation in Northern Ireland. The motivation has been to break the cramped sectarian mould of Ulster politics, to transcend the narrow ground of provincial party competition, and to participate fully in the life of the British state.

That consistent purpose, despite differences of emphasis, has been a source of much confusion over the role of the CEC. On the one hand, the CEC had to take a position on every controversy in Ulster politics, and had to be intimately involved with its personalities, its factions and its pettiness. The Campaign only has a meaning within the peculiarity of the Ulster situation. Within the limited range of possibilities which this situation presented, the CEC had no choice but to be partisan. Since it is opposed to the claims of Irish nationalism, to the idea of regional autonomy and to the Anglo-Irish Agreement, it had to associate itself to some degree with the arguments of those unionist politicians advocating integration. On the other hand, the CEC represents an idea which is much greater than the particulars of unionist politics. That idea is transcendent; put simply, the idea of the Union is more important than the integrity of any unionist party or faction. It is more important than even the survival of any unionist organisation. The CEC was a radical organisation in a very conservative environment. Therefore it was forced to be *in* but not truly *of* the politics of traditional Ulster unionism – a point revealed by the sort of activist who was attracted to the CEC ranks. There was a fund of liberal unionists, but most significant was the appeal to those who saw the Campaign as a way to support the Union without having to support either of the two main unionist parties. That irritated quite a few people, who like straight answers to such questions as ''Whose side are you on?'' It frustrated and maddened those activists in all the local parties who have grown up with the firm landmarks of provincial sectarianism. The Campaign has certainly confused the local press and TV pundits, with the notable exception of the *News Letter*. They could not grasp the association of a rational case for the Union and civil rights because the first is supposed to be protestant and the second catholic. The impact of the CEC on local political life has been (like Verlaine on Rimbaud) to disorder the senses. In the state of dismay after Hillsborough, that imaginative engagement had a broad appeal to unionist sensibilities. It was also ambiguous enough for those ill-disposed towards it to generate all sorts of accusations, most of them unfounded. A number of points need to be considered to draw out the character of CEC arguments, their conformity to and divergence from unionist concerns. First, there is an understanding of the nature of the British state. Secondly, there is an understanding of the state in the Republic. Thirdly, there is a theory of party politics. Finally, there is an expectation of the impact of electoral integration upon the politics and society of Northern Ireland.

For McCartney, current support for the Union ''can only be postulated in terms of liberty.'' The United Kingdom, with all its faults, is a pluralist state. The idea of freedom under the law is the principle of state. It is an inclusive principle and has nothing to do with the naturalistic simplicities and exclusiveness of nationhood. Of course British politicians still talk of the British nation. But that is usually rhetorical excess or a fault of terminology. The maturity of the British state, if not always the maturity of British politicians, lies in the philosophy of right, the doctrine of liberty, which lies at its heart. Before the establishment of the CEC, McCartney was already expounding one of its central theses. In the United Kingdom, he argued, ''catholic millions and their Irish co-religionists who have chosen to live there find no oppression, nor in real terms do they suffer any social or political disadvantage.'' He went on: ''Indeed, it is the present determination of the government of the United Kingdom to ensure the fundamental rights of the minority which creates the political tension between that government and the forces of irrational and sectarian unionism which see the Union merely as a convenient constitutional device for maintaining a non-catholic ascendancy. The true and essential Union is not an exclusive Union of loyalists or protestants, but a union between peoples who believe in liberal democracy and civil and religious liberty for all in the fullest sense of a pluralist society."[35] There was a partisan cutting edge to this exposition. McCartney, in his OUP capacity, was striking a heavy blow at the fundamentalism of the Paisleyites. But the principled thrust is clear. It is the Carsonite axiom that the good government of all in Northern Ireland depends upon the impartiality of the principle of right which the British state embodies. Neither unionist majoritarianism nor nationalist unity can achieve it. Both are tainted with the partisan passions of contending faction, corrupted by their own history.

A similar understanding was to be found outside unionist party ranks in the columns of *Workers' Weekly*, the journal which tried to keep unionist politicians up to the mark on the issue of equal citizenship as the Hillsborough crisis unfolded. It argued that the signing of the Agreement had been the greatest possible betrayal of the cause of political relaxation in Northern Ireland. It was a devastating setback to those who had been attempting to foster cross-community links. "A great reconciling compromise was in the process of being forged under Direct Rule," it claimed. On the one hand, the "chances of achieving a United Ireland were receding fast, which kept the Protestants happy." On the other hand, "Protestant Ascendancy had gone, never to return and if Direct Rule had a bias, it was in favour of Catholics. And this was acceptable to the great majority of Catholics."[36] The notion that the "status quo is not an option", which was propagated assiduously by nationalists and their sympathisers before the Agreement, was reality stood on its head. Direct rule, reformed and democratised, was the only acceptable and popularly sustainable option.

Thus the image of the liberalising atmosphere of British political life is strong within the CEC. In his submission to the OUP policy committee, McCartney succinctly summed up the case for integration as the means to the emancipation and spiritual enlargement of provincial politics. "The main function of the Union", he proposed, "is to guarantee, apart from the material benefits of being part of a relatively rich country, that Northern Ireland will continue to be associated with the political freedoms and democracy of the United Kingdom, which afford a wide scope for conflicting opinions and ideas and a broad tolerance for the views of others."[37] As we noted in Chapter 1, this belief has always been a traditional aspect of the character of unionism. The value of civil and religious liberty for all citizens within the Union has long been inscribed on its banner. However, as we also observed in Chapter 4, the long experience of devolved government had almost detached the idea of liberty from the idea of the Union, giving unionism the flavour of a self-determinism at odds with its true interest. That true interest McCartney and supporters were later to call "real" unionism, in the name of which they were prepared to challenge the whole unionist establishment. What has annoyed devolutionists like the Charter Group and other worthies of unionism is that the celebration of that principle of liberty of the British state implies less than total veneration for the achievements of the Stormont regime. They have argued that the CEC, like unionism's arch-enemy Charles Haughey, thinks of Northern Ireland as a failed political entity.

This clearly illustrates the point made above, that the CEC was compelled to be in, but not fully of, unionist politics. Fidelity to the idea of the Union forced the CEC, beyond the received wisdom and fundamental sensibilities of unionist discourse, to say things that are "not said" and to challenge beliefs which are never challenged. Yet it is absurd to argue that either the CEC in general or McCartney in particular took the same view as Haughey. The Fianna Fail leader believes that Northern Ireland is a failed political entity, and will remain so for as long as the six counties are kept under British rule. Republican dogma is clear on that point, although it is unlikely that Haughey the political leader would be willing to accept the logical consequence of that dogma in the near future. The CEC argues that Northern Ireland is a failed political entity (if success is equated with peace, stability and reconciliation) precisely because it is isolated and excluded from the political life of the rest of the British state. Therefore the charge is wide of the mark. The aim was not to undermine the "entity" of Northern Ireland, but to remind unionists that that entity had neither independent existence nor exclusive value apart from the wider life of the Union, of the British state. That was not a betrayal of the idea of the Union. It is a fact of life.

The reverence for the principle of right which the United Kingdom is held to embody explains the genuine outrage at the way in which Northern Ireland is governed. It is treated, according to supporters of equal citizenship, like a colonial dependency. The Anglo-Irish Agreement itself is one manifestation of that status. In *Government Without Opposition*, Brendan Clifford argued that the British system of government "is a very good system to belong to". But it is a "bad system to be governed by, in a post-colonial era, if you are not effectively represented within it." Since the substance of the CEC case is that Northern Ireland is not effectively represented in the affairs of state, then the present arrangement is an intolerable infringement of the very principles of good government which the average citizen of the

United Kingdom takes for granted. "Northern Ireland has government of a kind which England abhors. It has bi-partisan government. It has government without opposition."[38] It is, as he called it elsewhere, "parliamentary despotism". However, at one point Clifford's argument appears to contradict the thesis of impartiality which McCartney outlined above. He says that "the only wise statesmen above the conflict are dictators". It is only in Northern Ireland that British politicians have the possibility to act like dictators and "their foolishness is one of the many crosses we have to bear as a result of being excluded from the political system of the democratic state by which we are governed."[39] Thus there appeared to be two contradictory suggestions in the case which equal citizenship supporters were advancing: that because it is "aloof entirely from these racial and religious distinctions" (Carson), Westminster ensures good government; and that because of this aloofness under direct rule, Northern Ireland suffers from a colonial dictatorship (which is what devolutionists and the SDLP also argue). This is saved from contradiction by the assumptions made about the extension of the British party system to Northern Ireland which we consider in detail below.

If support for the Union is postulated in terms of liberty, opposition to Irish unity is postulated in terms of authority. "The growth of the nationalist movement in Ireland with an inherent anti-liberal and irrational content coincided with the emergence of an authoritarian Church as the de facto state religion." The "authority of the State and the Church was to overwhelm the individual." McCartney's conclusion is clear. The liberties of British Ulster, which are those of catholic and protestant alike, however attenuated they may be by the antagonistic workings of direct rule, are incompatible with the pervasive authoritarianism of the Republican state. "The very success of this authority was to be one of the greatest single obstructions to the nation's irredentist claim to incorporate the territory and people of Northern Ireland into a united Ireland."[40] Clifford, who comes from the Republic of Ireland, makes more or less the same point. In his opinion, the political leaders of Eire opted for "an intransigent and offensive Catholic nationalism" which the country has maintained to the present. Therefore the people of the Republic have "no reasonable grounds for complaint about partition."[41] If there had ever been any real desire to create the conditions for rapprochement between north and south then the answer lay in the hands of the citizens of the Republic themselves. One quite justifiable retort to that sort of argument would be to simply say that it takes two to compromise and that unionists have been equally intransigent. But the relationship has never been one of "equality". It is the Republic which makes a claim on Northern Ireland and not vice-versa. It must be its responsibility, since it has publicly eschewed the use of force, to make an effort to gain unionist consent. This it has never honestly sought to do, for it was never popular to do so. Even the most benign interpretation of the Republic's intent was shattered by the result of the Divorce Referendum in June 1987. Its citizens showed their preference for traditional catholic nationalism and its cultural exclusiveness. This they are quite entitled to do. While they may continue to complain about partition, it is no more than irrational emotionalism, for they show no real interest in bringing it to an end.

Neither the people nor the political leaders in the Republic want any social change predicated on the partition issue. In Clifford's view, any reasonable person should understand why. Quoting Pearse, he thinks it inconceivable that "amidst the bulks of actual things" the Republican state will transform itself to suit the interests of British policy or even the best intentions of certain Irish nationalists. For what is being proposed (and it was originally implied by the setting up of the New Ireland Forum) is that "the Catholic-nationalist movement which formed the Southern state should go into voluntary liquidation, that the state should be thrown into the melting pot, and that a new, liberal, multi-national, secular, welfare state should be put on offer to Unionists." Anyone with a passing knowledge of Southern politics, argues Clifford, would know the impossibility of such an eventuality.[42] The only inaccuracy in Clifford's assessment is that it is not only for unionists that such a new Ireland would need to be on offer, but also for northern catholics. In the words of Conor Lynch, "the Catholics of Northern Ireland have far more civil rights than anyone in the Republic." Outlining a catalogue of abuses from the jailing of homosexuals and striking trade unionists to limited contraception and the unconstitutionality of divorce and abortion, Lynch concludes: "The Southern State has come on a bit since it was barred from the United Nations for its fascist sympathies – but it hasn't come on all that much."[43] The backward, reactionary, authoritarian and intolerant condition of Irish politics and society portrayed in CEC literature set off perfectly the liberal ideal of equal British citizenship. The CEC shared this revulsion for the Republic, of course, with traditional Ulster unionism. However it differed significantly from it in the following respect. The essential political concern of the CEC analysis was and is with the predicament of the Ulster catholics rather than that of the Ulster protestants. Given their assessment of the nature of southern politics and society and their understanding of the superiority of the Union, the equal citizenship thesis holds the nationalism of Ulster catholics to be fundamentally irrational. Hence the need for a new political oulet.

The central thesis of the CEC argument concerned party politics.

The application of that thesis to the condition of Northern Ireland results in the claim that: first, the exclusion of the province from the party system of the state of which it is a part is an intolerable denial of basic democratic rights; secondly, that sectarianism and extremism can only be ended if the citizens of Northern Ireland have the opportunity to participate in those British parties which have the possibility of forming a government. As Conor Cruise O'Brien might say, this is a "very theoretical theory", a veritable idealism of the imagination. What is unusual, given the abhorrence of unionist voters for abstract thought, is the extent to which the argument of the Campaign gained credibility. Some commentators have tried to dismiss the intellectual appeal of the argument for ordinary voters by asserting that, in the absence of positive leadership from Molyneaux and Paisley, anything new and exciting was bound to attract adherents.[44] There seems little evidence for this contention. It is true that McCartney himself attracted support as a politician capable of presenting an intelligent case for the Union, whatever the arguments for electoral integration. But this is not to argue that people do not understand those arguments. What does the party politics thesis assert?

The *sine qua non* of a healthy pluralist democracy is representative and responsible government. In complex polities like the United Kingdom, this can only be achieved by a system of effective party competition. The essence of British parliamentary democracy is to be found in the history and practice of party politics. As Hugh Roberts indicates, it is through the operation of the political system of the state that "the government is constituted, interests represented, policies debated, laws made and consent for them secured."[45] Party competition, the life-blood of that political system, serves a twofold function. It permits alternative ideas and policies to be canvassed and publicly scrutinised. It also ensures a sensitivity to the opinion of the electorate, for its votes ultimately determine which party forms the government. Party provides the organisational means whereby different social interests may be mobilised to achieve political power, and the conventions of party politics regulate their conflict.

In this particular guise, party politics are often looked upon as a necessary evil. They are popularly contrasted with statesmanship and there is the deep-laid feeling that party is somehow at odds with the idea of the national interest. For instance, one often hears the complaint that MPs are "playing party politics" when they should be taking cognisance of what is best for the country as a whole. Indeed, the accusation against Stanley Baldwin – that he put his party before his country – was, ironically, one of the most effective *party* political points to be made against the Conservatives in the first half of the twentieth century. In other words, party is divisive and partial and at odds with the general good. Obviously there is something to this popular prejudice. The distinction between the common good and the particular good is an element of classical political analysis which can be grasped readily by the average person. However, such criticism of party politics may be understood otherwise, as an inheritance of pre-democratic times, a longing for unity and authority as a relief from the responsibilities of diversity and freedom. It is a desire for certainty which the narrow-minded philistine can share with the most sophisticated aesthete, which can bring together a General Franco and a George Santayana. What both dispositions share is a distaste for the nature of modern democratic politics, a distaste which is still current in liberal democracies no matter how securely founded they may appear to be. Political parties and pluralism are inseparable. Party is essential to our conception of British democratic practice and it is impossible, in any real sense, to try to distinguish between statesmanship and party interest.

The reason for this is quite simple. It is an inadequate and one-sided interpretation of party competition in Britain which focuses only on division. For, while parties exist to challenge and criticise, and to compete with each other for power, they also contribute to the integration of the electorate into the common life of the state. In terms of their own particular policy programme and ideological appeal, the Labour Party or the Conservative Party bind together very diverse interests from very different regions throughout the United Kingdom. And despite latter-day electoral trends towards the concentration of party support according to region, the general rule still holds good. Conservative candidates may win seats with ease in the south-east of England and Labour candidates may carry all before them in Scotland. None the less, there remain active Labour parties in the Home Counties and there is still such a breed as the Scottish Conservative. The notion of a great north-south divide in Britain has been severely exaggerated. Significantly, party competition throughout the United Kingdom achieves a more general integration in political life. For the issues – to use a Bennite phrase – are the same issues, with the allowance for some constituency peculiarities, throughout the United Kingdom. The cunning reason of the system is this: even when party politics are divisive, they are so in a way which involves the electorate in a public debate about *common* problems. However vicariously, citizens become caught up in the general life of the state. Parties presuppose that an intelligible unity of political life and parties help to maintain that unity. In one of the best books on the subject, Richard Rose has shown how, even at the height of the success of Scottish and Welsh nationalism in the 1970s, the mass of the electorate in Scotland and Wales still voted for the major parties of the Union.[46] In Westminster devolution was recognised to be a matter of universal political concern and not, as with Northern Ireland, something the provincials ought to sort out among themselves. The integrity of the British polity can only be understood in terms of the diversity embodied within the system of party competition.

From all this the electors of Northern Ireland are excluded. Provincial parties foster divisions but do not provide for that integration which transforms division into purposeful and constructive politics. Trapped within their political ghetto, Ulster people have little chance of overcoming the conditions of extremism. They are like demented flies buzzing around inside a small sealed room with no hope of release. This is not because of choice but because of the refusal of the national parties to organise there. This fact, according to Roberts, has been consistently overlooked in academic analyses of the Ulster crisis. In some cases it has been deliberately concealed. The people of Northern Ireland have no great wish to be "abnormal"; "they have not chosen to exclude themselves but have been excluded by the actions of the major British parties", and "their continuing exclusion is today sustained by deliberate decision of the leaders of those parties."[47] The CEC believed there to be a conspiracy to deny Northern Ireland access to the party political system which determines the government and policy of the state of which it is a part. This is not merely a technical anomaly. It is an offence against democracy, a denial of a fundamental civil right, and completely at odds with the spirit of British public life. This state of affairs can only be preserved by hiding the truth from the British people, in whose democratic instincts the CEC retains a firm belief. As a civil right the "case for electoral integration is irrefutable. No reputable argument can be made against it. All its opponents can do is try to prevent it from being heard."[48] Therefore, for the initial CEC campaign to succeed, there had to be activity on two fronts: first, the conspiracy of silence had to be broken and a challenge thrown down to the national parties on the issue of civil rights; and secondly, unionist politics had to be won over to this distinctive political priority within the rubric of equal citizenship. This was an ambivalent strategy. For instance, success in winning over the OUP to the cause of equal citizenship (however unlikely) was bound to raise doubts as to the extent to which equal citizenship was a genuine civil rights issue rather than a tactical unionist ploy. This ambivalence was the seed of future disputes within CEC ranks, even though those who were subsequently to claim absolute fidelity to civil rights were also those who were most active in the pursuit of "real unionism".

However things were to turn out, the task which was set was an enormous one, although the rewards for Northern Ireland would be immense. National parties would have an electoral stake in the province and would therefore be compelled to be sensitive to the will of the electorate. It would prevent, so the CEC believed, the unrepresentative and irresponsible forms of government which have been imposed on the Ulster people. Participation in national party politics would release the compressed energies of those confined to the "political prison" of provinciality. The "scope and the excitement if the British Parties were to organise" in Northern Ireland has been the imaginative inspiration for equal citizenship supporters. "The political life of the province could be transformed."[49] As Clifford put it, the long-suffering outcasts of the United Kingdom would be "not only acting as full and spirited British citizens"; they could "initiate a process of cross-fertilisation between the two national communities in the province – a process which is made impossible by the absence of British party politics."[50]

As a democratic claim the CEC argument is hard to refute. There is no principled or theoretical justification for the deliberate exclusion of Ulster people from the party politics of the rest of the United Kingdom. What makes it even more insupportable and anomalous is the fact that many Ulster trade unionists pay a union political levy, part of which goes to the Labour Party from which they are barred as individual members and for which they cannot vote. Similarly, an Ulster resident may contribute to the coffers of the Conservative Party, but is prevented from joining. People from Scotland, Wales and England who settle in Northern Ireland and who were formerly active in party politics find themselves non-persons. This, according to the CEC, makes an absurdity of the idea of a unitary state. Unfortunately, the resolution of this anomaly has less to do with the acknowledgement of the principle at issue, although the main parties do their best to avoid addressing it. It has to do with the practical interests of the parties concerned. The CEC was rightly aggrieved that Northern Ireland citizens cannot take part in and influence the policy of those parties which have the authority to govern them. And given the premises of the party system thesis, Northern Ireland can only have unrepresentative and irresponsible government.

But the British parties have other concerns. They neither see electoral advantage nor political interest in the challenge. Indeed they are afraid that rather than "real" British politics transforming the Ulster crisis, the Ulster crisis will contaminate their own present immunity from religious sectarianism. No matter how often the CEC may cite the cases of Liverpool and Glasgow as examples of the transformational properties of socio-economic as opposed to provincial sectarian politics, British politicians remain uninterested. They are happy to resort to the old excuse that Northern Ireland is different. Of course the CEC's argument is that one of the major reasons why it is different is because the major parties do not organise there. The response of British politicians is not addressed to the challenge but is actually part of the problem. When it suits them, they can be masters of circular reasoning. This may not be logical or honourable but reflects precisely what Roberts, following Bagehot, understands to be the practical genius of British political life: "sound stupidity". He suggests that for once in their history British politicians ought to behave like the French and become enamoured of a major issue of constitutional principle.[51] Similarly, McCartney has often quoted Victor Hugo to the effect that nothing can stop the march of an idea whose time has come – in this case the idea of equal citizenship. As Laurence Sterne wrote: "They order these things better in France." And so they do, for reason and logic are important to the French mind. There is no doubt that a claim such as the CEC's would have engaged the ferocious commitment – for and against – of the French intelligentsia. At least it would have been taken seriously. The appalling truth is that, if there is such a thing as a British intelligentsia, it suffers from the same disease as the political establishment; an imperviousness to novel ideas and a conceited complacency which passes for wisdom. That was the real resistance to the message of the CEC. It is a fundamental resistance which is only slowly beginning to weaken as the Agreement philosophy begins to reveal its inherent absurdities.

Finally, the impact on Northern Ireland of national party competition is estimated to be profound. But for an argument which nationalist opponents have dismissed as unreconstructed protestant supremacism, the main concern of the CEC has been not with the possibilities this opens up for protestants but with the political outlet it would provide for the catholic community. It is taken for granted that unionists will feel at home in the national parties. It is the catholic community which is identified as suffering from a corrosive form of political irrationality. It is held to be well aware that its material interests, at least, lie in making the best of its British citizenship; but it has inherited a political tradition which prevents it from doing so. If to participate in "British" politics can only be associated with participation in the OUP or the DUP, then the answer from catholics can only be negative – and justifiably so. No self-respecting catholic, of whatever political colour would or could associate with either the Orange Order or the Free Presbyterian Church. Just as no self-respecting protestant would or could have anything to do with the Hibernicism of the SDLP. But while all protestants know that they do not want a united Ireland and vote accordingly, the reverse is not the case with catholics. Many catholics do not want a united Ireland either, but because of the provincial party system are condemned to vote SDLP. It is this presumed state of affairs which the CEC has been committed to transform by campaigning for the British parties to organise and compete in Northern Ireland.

One immediate difficulty with that particular argument might be the Alliance Party. Does it not already provide an escape from sectarianism and allow catholics to support the Union, albeit quietly, without going all the way to voting for the unionist parties? To nail that particular contention, the CEC has devoted some energy to refuting the Alliance pretension to be the natural party of non-sectarian politics. According to McCartney, the Alliance Party ''offers only limited scope for non-sectarian politics and indeed its only reason for being is that Northern Ireland's citizens are treated unequally from those in Great Britain.'' It can never amount to more than ''a hose pipe playing on an Orange and Green volcano that is constantly threatening to erupt''.[52] The formal critique has been that far from transcending sectarianism and effecting a radical transformation of Ulster politics, the Alliance is a part of that sectarian system and feeds off it. Rather than being a modern and secular party, the Alliance is a parochial ''ecumenical'' organisation and fatally compromised by that which it rejects.

Whatever the truth of that argument, it did not deflect the CEC from its intention of creating new conditions whereby catholics could be won over to British politics. Therefore the remarks of the SDLP's Denis Haughey about the purpose of the CEC betray a complete misunderstanding. His charge was that support for equal citizenship was a ''thoroughly dishonest attempt to further the aims of extreme unionism'' and to ''deny the political and national rights of the minority in Northern Ireland forever''.[53] Clifford has outlined the real aim. If Ireland were to be united, he argues, northern catholics would be forced to do what southern catholics are forced to do today for want of a welfare state like that which exists in Northern Ireland: emigrate to Great Britain. ''This is the dilemma of the Northern Catholic community. It is compelled to be nationalist in politics.'' The absence of the British parties confines catholics ''in a communal politics which can only express itself in the traditional communal routine of nationalism. But this is a case in which *'the movement is everything, the final aim is nothing'*.''[54] It was ''Fenians'' like Clifford who recognised this and wanted to change it. His view is no different today from what it was in the late 1960s. ''A large part, perhaps more than one-half, of the catholic community is now ready to become unionist in effect, provided it is enabled to become unionist in its own way, and without any grand proclamation.'' There is ''only one way in which this can happen: through the British party political system''.[55] McCartney's advocacy of the case for integration has been similarly concerned to win over the pro-Union section of the minority. That is one of the reasons for the CEC taking the particular course it has done. Traditional unionist politics has little time for the potential for political change within the catholic community. And of course, the very thing the SDLP does not want is for catholics to have the opportunity to play a full and constructive part in British politics. Hence Haughey's outburst, the natural reflex of the sectarian. Only in the "logic" of modern nationalism does the possibility of citizens having the choice of a greater range of political alternatives become the denial of a right. The CEC position in no way denies anyone their rights, national or whatever. What it does do is provide those who would otherwise feel obliged to shackle themselves to Haughey's simplicities the opportunity to break free.

Indeed it could be argued, as unionist opponents of equal citizenship have argued, that the extension of British party organisation to Northern Ireland could work to the advantage of nationalism. It could do this in two ways: first, if the national parties competed in Ulster elections they could divide the unionist vote; and secondly, membership of any of the British parties would be to lend support to a political consensus in favour of ultimate Irish unity. One might imagine that, if it was not so narrowly sectarian in outlook, the SDLP might actually *welcome* an infusion of "normal" British politics into Northern Ireland. That it does not is an indication of its true single-mindedness, its concern only with achieving those conditions in which the "healing process" takes place according to a republican prescription. Nor does it care for the accountability of British government so long as that government is using its power to weaken the Union. By contrast, accountability *as a civil right* has been central to the whole CEC project. The underlying assumption of its strategy is that when Ulster citizens become elegible to join the parties of state, they can influence directly the policy of those parties – and do so in a way that recognises the determination of the vast majority of them to remain fully within the United Kingdom. To get the national parties to organise in the province would be a first sign that they acknowledged that there were principles of accountability and civil rights to respond to.

An opinion poll carried out by Coopers and Lybrand in May 1987 appeared to give substance to the claims which people like Clifford for a long time, and the CEC more recently, had been saying. Asked to select "the best form of government for Northern Ireland", only 22 per cent of catholics were prepared to opt for a united Ireland, and this was 9 per cent of the total poll. One CEC publication happily gave the lie to Haughey: "It has always been suggested that the CEC objective of full participation in the politics of the UK is opposed by Catholics in general. We have always known that this is not true." It cited the Coopers and Lybrand poll in justification. More than that, the poll revealed that 65 per cent of protestants and 59 per cent of catholics agreed that the British political parties should put forward candidates for election in Northern Ireland. ''No other political organisation in Northern Ireland has a comparable level of cross-community support for its political objective,'' the pamphlet proclaimed. It reinforced the belief that electoral integration is the way to overcome the sectarian conflict in the province.[56] Of course, every organisation will cite the opinion poll which is to its advantage. However, what is most unusual about the Coopers and Lybrand poll is this. Hitherto the ''correct'' or moderate answer to give to a question about proposed forms of government for Northern Ireland has always been to support provincial power-sharing. The measure of the impact of the CEC, whether one believes the poll or not, or whether one accepts CEC logic, is the positive popular perception of the message which it has been assiduously advancing.

The propositions advanced by the CEC are of some intellectual sophistication, and its vision is a radical one which transcends the commonplace of local politics. It was a vision which was to convince and attract one of the most intelligent and articulate of the unionist politicians to emerge in the 1980s. Robert McCartney got involved with unionist politics, along with colleagues like Peter Smith, whose career was to take a very different path after the Agreement, to introduce a rational cutting edge to arguments for the Union. McCartney's style was also distinctively combative, and therefore unusual within the rather respectable confines of the OUP. Indeed, he sprang to immediate prominence when, exasperated by the Big Man's bluster, he seized the microphone from Paisley at a Belfast City Hall rally in November 1981 and began an address about rational unionism. This has been a strong part of McCartney's appeal – a man able to ''speak out'' and put into words the inarticulate feelings of the honest Ulster unionist. Under the CEC banner, McCartney was able to present an intelligent and intelligible vision around which working-class and middle-class people of either denomination could gather. The articulate quality of the message and its aggressive spirit were just as important as the message itself.

That strength, however, has also been McCartney's weakness. His pugnacity offended many influential figures in unionist politics. Similarly, his abrasiveness and inability to suffer fools gladly have made him enemies in those places where many fools reside – especially in the Northern Ireland Office and the provincial parties. He also faced hostility from a very different source. There is that anti-intellectual streak in Ulster politics which hates people to be too clever or to do too well for themselves. Some of the hostility towards McCartney came from that irrational sentiment which avers that the working–class boy from the Shankill Road has got a little above himself. So despite his impeccable credentials for carrying forward the unionist cause – a Queen's Counsel with a forceful personality and good connections – McCartney was probably destined to play the role of a critical outsider. The politics of the CEC complemented his own political disenchantment with the old and apparently tired identity of unionism. Any serious politician must have a belief in his own powers and in the virtue of his endeavour: this McCartney certainly has. He made a revealing personal statement to the English journalist Richard Ford: "I offer an end to sectarian politics, a policy that will strengthen the union, and the service of someone who is reasonably articulate, and will have the professional expertise to argue the unionist case for them."[57] Thus the man and the message were closely linked. McCartney's personality was sure to help the CEC make a public impact.

The first public blooding for the cause of equal citizenship came when Boyd Black, a university lecturer, contested the Fulham (London) by-election on 10 April 1986 on the platform of "Democratic Rights for Northern Ireland". He received a derisory 98 votes. For Paul Arthur this indicated the "enormity of the task" facing the CEC.[58] That is self-evident. Yet not only the vote was significant in Fulham. The Boyd Black campaign brought together the very diverse and unusual political talents which were to constitute the distinctive character of the CEC. McCartney committed himself publicly to Black's candidacy, declaring that integration "is the most acceptable political solution for the majority of people in Northern Ireland."[59] On the issue of democratic rights for Northern Ireland, the unionist QC could share common ground with Sean McGouran, secretary of Ulster's Gay Rights Association; Eammon O'Kane, chairman of the Campaign for Labour Representation; and Harry McAllister, secretary of Larne Trades Council. The Fulham campaign also drew in people of no public position, like John Cobain, whose energies were to be essential in helping the CEC achieve a wider popular appeal. Fulham strengthened that alliance rather than discouraging it, and it was after the experience of the English by-election that the spirit and the momentum of the CEC began to make itself felt in local politics. McCartney's adherence was vital, for he helped to get effective media coverage for the Campaign. He carried the message into the tail-end of the Northern Ireland Assembly, and pushed the integration case within the OUP's policy committee. He claimed to be "astounded" by the number of OUP members who expressed support for integration and therefore were potentially open to the arguments advanced by the CEC.[60] McCartney's push for an integrationist initiative and his public support of the CEC cause were bound to open up divisions within the OUP and between the OUP and the DUP. This was the last thing that Molyneaux or Paisley wanted. McCartney had to be stopped, for he seemed to have struck a dangerously popular note.

At the first public meeting of the CEC, held on 14 May 1986, 100 people turned up. The first public rally, held in Belfast's Ulster Hall on 3 July, attracted 700 who heard McCartney deliver a rousing demand for equality of citizenship. His belief was that the OUP was ripe for political transformation: "I am convinced that if a meeting of the Ulster Unionist Council were held tomorrow, the integration option would be carried by four to one."[61] Throughout the summer and autumn of 1986, the equal citizenship arguments were canvassed within the OUP, while the CEC itself devoted its energies to spreading its message to a wider public. Meanwhile, the OUP leadership were planning to upset the McCartney bandwagon. For this they had all the advantage of elective authority, and in addition one important argument. There was always something quixotic in the CEC belief that it could win over the OUP to the idea of electoral integration, for the more convinced McCartney became of the truth of that thesis the less convinced he became of the worth of the OUP itself. This enabled the leadership to isolate him not just as a maverick, but as a renegade. In the Lundy-culture of unionism that is a deadly charge. But it went beyond personalities and tactics to the strategic implications of the CEC position. Its logic, as Clifford freely admitted, was that unionist politics "seeks its own dissolution by demanding a right of entry by the people of the province into the parties of state".[62] To propose that conclusion as the result of strict logical deduction is one thing; to believe that an organisation like the OUP, having acknowledged it, could then set about its own dissolution is another. It was an impossible proposition and contradicted the iron law of political self-preservation, the inherited wisdom of unionism in the twentieth century.

At the OUP conference on 8 November 1986, the forces of conservative minimalism were mobilised against McCartney's initiative. In a session closed to the press, the leadership opposed the motion he had sponsored, which would have committed the party to campaign for integration and equal citizenship. What defeated him was the fear of unionist disunity. Avoiding a sound critique of the McCartney motion, an amendment, proposed by OUP MPs and delivered by Enoch Powell, proclaimed the necessity of maintaining unionist unity in the present crisis and argued that nothing should distract unionists from their opposition to the Anglo-Irish Agreement. The merit of equal citizenship was not an issue. Its timing as a proposal for party policy was held to be wrong. By such procedural and technical manoeuvering, the motion was lost. The amendment was carried by 199 votes to 143, the principle of unionist unity by 256 votes to 104.

Afterwards, McCartney claimed that he had come within an ace of imposing on the largest unionist party a policy of integration and equal citizenship.[63] Still, it is winning which is important and, as Richard Nixon was fond of saying, much more fun. It was always unlikely that, given the signals coming from Molyneaux and his colleagues, the Conference would have rejected the authoritative suggestion of its leader. It was a suggestion, not a definite instruction, for the latter would have required the presentation of an alternative. Whether the OUP leadership have ever read Heaney or not, they know the utility of the injunction: whatever you say, say nothing. Saying nothing but No, rather than fracture unionist unity, became the guiding purpose of the OUP. The immediate objective had been secured. McCartney had had his come-uppance.

The shibboleth of unionist unity was used again to expel McCartney, along with his constituency association, from the party altogether. In mid-February, the idea was floated that all sitting unionist MPs should be unopposed in a future General Election, and it was approved by the OUP Executive on February 27. Such a ruling was a particular challenge to McCartney and the CEC. A General Election campaign would be the perfect public testing ground for the demands of equal citizenship. It would provide the opportunity to achieve success on both those fronts on which it must campaign. It could win a vital victory within unionism. It could also begin to publicise effectively the equal citizenship case with the national tribune which McCartney's seat in the House of Commons would provide for them. There was also a sense of urgency which is well captured by a comment in *Workers' Weekly*: "We now have to make up in double quick time for the 10 years or so in which the Unionists failed to make the case for equal citizenship."[64] An election campaign could accelerate their success. To risk expulsion was a risk worth taking.

The expulsion duly took place on 19 May. The pretext was not that McCartney's North Down association had defied the "no contest" edict. It was McCartney's conduct, which was held to be detrimental to the interests of the party. But there is little doubt that if it had not been for the electoral challenge to the authority of the leadership, Molyneaux's instinct would have been to ridicule and dismiss the CEC President's pretensions. This he had already done in his address to the Ulster Unionist Council on 28 March.[65] But his candidacy was another matter. It was now time to be rid of the troublesome barrister. The main charge was that the presidency of the CEC was incompatible with the constitution and rules of the OUP, in that the aim of the CEC was to invite mainland parties to organise in Northern Ireland "as rivals to, in competition with or in substitution for" the OUP. As we have argued, this was the ace card in the leadership's hand. The CEC's idea of the Union *is* at odds with the particular concrete interests of the OUP as an organisation. As we have also seen, Molyneaux does not actually dissent from that idea, but he is not prepared to damage the concrete political interests of the party he leads to achieve it. It would be hard for him to do otherwise. It was simply a strategic blunder of the CEC not to have acknowledged that reality soon enough. Wrangling within the OUP diverted public attention from the clarity of the message and gave many hostages to fortune.

The June election campaign illustrated the profound ambiguity of the CEC's "Real Unionism". Fighting in the safe unionist territory of North Down, there was little opportunity to make any significant inroads into the nationalist vote, or to test, even provisionally, the rather ambitious claims of the CEC. McCartney's own election literature (against his better judgement) incorporated the Union Jack; and while the message repeated the claim that only "real" politics, the choice to join and to vote for the major British parties, could transform the situation in Northern Ireland, its concerns were mainstream unionist concerns – defeating the IRA, effective security, keeping Dublin out of Ulster's affairs, and British citizenship. It was McCartney's personality and his ability to make the idea of the Union intelligible and defensible which made his campaign so unusual. The rationality of the Union rather than the theoretical correctness of "electoral" integration was the source of his popular appeal. The vision of the Ulster Hall rally came up against that fact of political life. That is not to argue that the McCartney message or electoral integration are not attractive to many catholics. But the experience of North Down had to be absorbed. What that experience intimated was to help divide the CEC some months later.

During the General Election campaign, the full resources of the unionist parties were brought to bear on the defeat of McCartney in North Down. It was an irrational act even in terms of the unionist unity with which it was justified. North Down is a safe unionist seat. Concentration of effort against McCartney only distracted unionists from the need to defend or to regain the marginals in South Down and Newry and Armagh. As it was, the McCartney camp fought a strong campaign with the help of enthusiastic volunteers from all over the province and from Great Britian. Co-ordinated by Robert Lyle and Laurence Kennedy, McCartney's equal citizenship campaign, under the banner of "real unionism", came within another ace of winning the seat from the Popular Unionist Jim Kilfedder. The Real Unionist was 4,000 votes short of one of the largest upsets in unionist politics since the Agreement. The third largest swing in the United Kingdom had been in North Down. McCartney's 14,500 votes constituted a moral victory over the unionist establishment. As McGimpsey notes, the vote enabled the CEC "to claim the intellectual and moral high ground of unionism".[66] But, moral victory or not, it was still a political defeat. It has been enough for the unionist leadership that they seemed to have been successful in halting the forward march of equal citizenship. That was consistent with the current philosophy of immobilism.

The Anglo-Irish Agreement has helped to concentrate the unionist mind, and the arguments of integrationists have been thereby strengthened. Devolution is tarnished by its association with the purposes of the Hillsborough accord and its dependence on the goodwill of the SDLP for its success. The first factor makes it appear a form of capitulation; the second, a form of masochism. Integration has the merit of accurately expressing the concern of most people for the social and economic benefits of the Union and translating this into a powerful moral claim for equality of treatment. At the same time, it challenges the machiavellianism of the Agreement in a simple and direct way and gives opposition to it a rational and intellectual justification. Those with a sense of historical irony may say: "Too late! Too late!" Like conservatives in 1789, unionists in 1985 were "alarmed into reflection". But the spirit of the Agreement, they may argue, like the spirit of the Revolution, cannot be extinguished. Unionist recognition of the reason in integration has only come at the dusk of the Union. Devolutionists share that alarm, although their conclusion is different – that integrationist arguments are an obstacle to, and a distraction from, the real business of securing a lasting settlement in Northern Ireland on a proper basis. It matters little if this distraction is maximalist or minimalist. A new deal for unionists has to be struck. The sort of Union for which integrationists argue is, like romantic Ireland, dead and gone and in its grave. That is a view they share with the Irish and British governments and with the SDLP. As we noted in the previous Chapter, the profound difficulty of devolutionist "realism" is that their concern to negotiate a new deal for unionism might hasten the end of what is left of the Union – and this is precisely what integrationists do believe will be the consequence of devolutionist logic. Nor is there any evidence that there is a burning desire for devolution among protestants and catholics. In response to that suspicion of devolved government, the CEC position has been the idea of the Union at its fullest and most impatient intensity. Molyneaux's position, up till now, has been to work for greater integration by stealth under the cover of unionist unity. He has revealed a dogged intent, amid suspicion and indifference, slowly to shift the ominous bulk of the Agreement.

NOTES

1. Robin Wilson in *Fortnight*, Sept. 1986.
2. R.Berki, *On Political Realism* (London: J.M. Dent, 1981), pp. 193–4.
3. J.Davidson, *Integration – A Word Without Meaning* (Belfast: Athol Books, n.d.), pp. 1–3.
4. J.Davidson, *Electoral Integration* (Belfast: Athol Books, n.d.), p. 2.
5. *Fortnight*, Nov. 1987.
6. *Workers' Weekly*, 5 Oct. 1986.
7. OUP Press Release, 26 April 1985.
8. *Fortnight*, 17 Dec. 1984.
9. *News Letter*, 7 Jan. 1986.
10. *News Letter*, 30 June 1986.
11. Ulster Young Unionist Council, *The New Agenda*, April 1986, pp. 1–13.
12. *Fortnight*, Nov. 1987.
13. OUP Press Release, 13 March 1987.
14. OUP Press Release, 28 March 1987.
15. *Workers' Weekly*, 27 Sept. 1986.
16. In reply to a letter from Peter Brooke of the CEC outlining the four demands of equal citizenship, Molyneaux did not dissent from those aims. He merely restated the order in which they could be achieved: (1) normal legislation for Northern Ireland on the Westminster model; (2) reform of local government; (3) a referendum on constitutional issues; (4) organisation of the British parties in Ulster. Letter, James Molyneaux to Peter Brooke, 10 June 1986.
17. *News Letter*, 6 Jan. 1988.
18. Ibid., 9 Jan. 1987.
19. Ibid., 4 Aug. 1986.
20. Ibid., 26 Sept. 1986.
21. See P.Bew and H.Patterson, *The British State and the Ulster Crisis* (Verso, 1985) pp. 140–50.
22. *Spectator*, 23 Nov. 1985. See also Ibid., 7 Dec. 1985.
23. *Fortnight*, Nov. 1986.
24. See A.Guelke, "The American Connection to the Northern Ireland Conflict", *Irish Studies in International Affairs*, vol. 1, no. 4 (1984).
25. A.Kenny, *The Road to Hillsborough* (Oxford: Pergamon Press, 1986).
26. *News Letter*, 2 Sept. 1986.
27. Ian Gow, *Ulster After the Agreement* (Belfast: Friends of the Union, n.d.) pp. 4–5.
28. Sir John Biggs-Davison, *Ulster Catholics and the Union* (Belfast: Friends of the Union, n.d.), p. 8.
29. See, for example, John Whale, *Magill*, May 1979.
30. *Fortnight*, April 1983.
31. *News Letter*, 3 April 1987.
32. *Workers' Weekly*, 5 April, 1987.
33. CEC, *Northern Ireland Says Yes to Equal Citizenship* (Belfast: CEC, 1987), p. 1.
34. B.Clifford, *Parliamentary Despotism* (Belfast: Athol Books, 1986), p. 17.
35. R.McCartney, "Liberty and Authority in Ireland", *Field Day*, Pamphlet no. 7 (1985), pp. 25–6.
36. *Workers' Weekly*, 10 May 1986.
37. R.McCartney, *The Case for Integration* (mimeo, 1986).
38. B.Clifford, *Government Without Opposition* (Athol Books, 1986), pp. 4–5.
39. Ibid., p. 5.
40. McCartney, op.cit., p. 5.
41. *Young Unionist*, no. 4 (1986).

42. B.Clifford, *Parliamentary Despotism*, op.cit., p. 17.
43. *The Socialist*, Jan. 1986.
44. See P.Bell's letter to the *News Letter* 17 Dec. 1987.
45. H.Roberts, "Sound Stupidity: The British Party System and the Northern Ireland Question", *Government and Opposition*, vol. 22, no. 3 (Summer 1987), p. 328.
46. R.Rose, *Understanding the United Kingdom* (London: Macmillan, 1980).
47. Roberts, op.cit., p. 315.
48. J.Davidson, Electoral Integration, op.cit., p. 3.
49. R.McCartney, "We Have a Vision", speech at the Ulster Hall, 3 July 1986, p. 10.
50. B.Clifford, *Parliamentary Sovereignty and Northern Ireland* (Belfast: Athol Books, 1985), p. 13.
51. Roberts, op.cit., p. 335.
52. *We Have a Vision*, p. 12. See also *News Letter*, 27 May 1987.
53. *News Letter*, 21 March, 1987.
54. B.Clifford, *The Unionist Family* (Belfast: Athol Books, 1987), p. 16.
55. *Young Unionist*, no. 4 (1986).
56. *Northern Ireland Says Yes to Equal Citizenship*, pp. 2–4.
57. *Times*, 3 June, 1987.
58. P.Arthur, "The Anglo-Irish Agreement: The Events of 1985–86", *Irish Political Studies*, vol. 2 (1987), p. 103.
59. *News Letter*, 28 March 1986.
60. *News Letter*, 9 May 1986.
61. *News Letter*, 5 July 1986.
62. B.Clifford, *The Road to Nowhere* (Belfast: Athol Books, 1987), p. 16.
63. *News Letter*, 10 Nov. 1986.
64. *Workers' Weekly*, 9 Aug. 1986.
65. *News Letter*, 30 March 1987.
66. *Fortnight*, Sept. 1987.

6

THE TASK FORCE REPORT AND AFTER

Unity and solidarity had become the touchstone of unionist policy. They had also become the substitute for an intelligent and coordinated strategy against the Agreement. Unity, or so it was claimed, was the only "good weapon" which unionism had – or needed. One was reminded of Ernst Junger's observation, in his parable of political disintegration, that every good weapon is supposed to have its "magic qualities; by merely looking at it we feel ourselves wonderfully strengthened." The comfort of such suppositions is that one will never perish entirely. Even in the face of defeat, the magical qualities of true character, in this case the spiritual inheritance of free-born Ulster people, will snatch the ultimate victory. Unionist unity would be the weapon with which the Agreement would be eventually smashed. But, as Junger warned, such good weapons may be illusory. In politics, as in war, "an outerwork will remain intact when the keep has long since fallen."[1] The posture of the unionist leadership in the early months of 1987 could have been taken for the defiance of those manning the outerwork who knew in their hearts that the keep had long since fallen. John Hume never lost an opportunity to tell them that the game was up. In their own very different ways the governments in London and Dublin were saying the same thing. If only unionists would hoist the white flag and come out with their hands up, then favourable terms of surrender could be negotiated. So it was not without a certain prescience that the historian A.T.Q. Stewart had likened the unionist position, when the Agreement had just been signed, to that faced by defenders of the Alamo.

No doubt the demonstrations of mass opposition to the Agreement which Molyneaux and Paisley were consistently able to achieve – at the City Hall, in the by-election "referendum" and the petition to the Queen – did wonderfully strengthen their resolve and had a certain magical though temporary quality. But holding the fort was not the same thing as getting rid of the Agreement. Hence the widespread feeling that the unionist leadership had no coherent strategy but were hoping for something to turn up. Macawberism in politics may invite abuse, but there are circumstances in which it may be a wise course to adopt. If one calculates that any move is sure to lead to even greater ensnarement, if one believes that the terms of debate are so clearly stacked against one, then it would seem prudent to hold out and wait for something to turn up. Only pure faith can assume that all circumstances may be turned to advantage. We argued in Chapter 3 that there has been a definite tactical rationality in what has been called Molyneaux's "steady course", especially when supporters of the Agreement were doing their utmost to rush unionists into saying something other than "No". Everyone knew that such solicitation was code for "submit to the logic of Hillsborough without preconditions". Therefore the restrained and proper conduct of the "Ulster Says No" campaign redounds to the credit of the unionist leadership. One has only to compare the cost in life and property of the refusal of nationalists to acknowledge their membership of the state to understand the extent of that unionist achievement. And it had been done in the face of great provocation. But there were clear limits to such an approach. Unionists could continue indefinitely to show their hostility to the Agreement. But without any sign of success, there was every possibility of their becoming confused and dispirited. Without a vision of how to use it, the good weapon of unity could only rust in its scabbard.

Therefore, it was really an abdication of political responsibility when, in response to questions about what unionists would do now that their petition to the Queen had been ignored, Harold McCusker told reporters: "There are one million disaffected unionists in Northern Ireland. I don't think they need organising."[2] What the diversity of opinion within unionism *did* need was "organising". It needed organising not in the manner of undifferentiated activism so beloved of the Ulster Clubs, but around a positive idea of the Union. At this level of political strategy, the unionist leadership was at a loss, and their lack of a constructive vision of the Union which could galvanise unionist voters merely contributed to the intensity of the devolution versus integration debate. It also contributed to the unease within the OUP and the DUP that the massed ranks inside the unionist keep were losing faith. One major aspect of that general sense of insecurity was the fact that very few were privy to what was actually going on, not only in the whispering chambers of the Anglo-Irish Conference, but also in the minds of unionist leaders. Unionist unity seemed enclosed in a policy of political secrecy. Everyone was aware that, at some point, communications would have to be re-established with the British government. Few were aware of exactly what unionists would be talking about and to what purpose. To address this unease or, what is probably a more accurate description, to blunt these criticisms, Molyneaux and Paisley decided to establish the Unionist Task Force on 23 February 1987. The Task Force was, like a Wilsonian Royal Commission, a means to buy some time. But, before its report was completed, Mrs Thatcher had called a General Election. This was good news for the two party leaders.

It was good news not because of the possibility of unionists holding the balance of power in a hung parliament. By May 1987 that slight possibility of exogenous salvation had all but disappeared. The Conservative Party was riding high in the polls at around 42 per cent. Despite a flurry of panic during the campaign itself, the Conservative polling figures never budged far from a winning margin over all its opponents. It never looked remotely conceivable that Mrs Thatcher's majority would vanish altogether. Rather, the good news lay in the possibilities which the post-election period would open up for renewed contacts with the government. At the very least, there would be a ready excuse for unionist MPs to build their bridges back to Westminster. When that had been done "in good faith", then there was every opportunity for exploratory "talks" with the government to begin. And there was the hope that, this time, the response would be more generous than just the offer of a more "sensitive" operation of the accord. This Chapter traces the development of this phase of unionist politics from the General Election and the Task Force Report to the early summer of 1988 as the third anniversary and first review of the Anglo-Irish Agreement approached.

The General Election, 1987

The OUP executive in February, and the DUP executive in April, had decided on the policy of a "free run" for all sitting unionist MPs. The justification for these decisions was once again that of "unionist unity". Molyneaux, as leader of the OUP in pre-Agreement days, had once engaged in a tough party battle with the DUP for electoral predominance in Northern Ireland. After 15 November 1985, he suffered an acute relapse of his disunity phobia. The old ghosts of the early 1970s came back to haunt his judgement. He sought refuge in the comforting security of communal solidarity. The OUP leader declared that he "was not prepared to preside over a process of drift which almost destroyed unionism some fourteen years ago". This was quite a remarkable assertion, given the common understanding, both within unionist circles and without, that the Anglo-Irish Agreement had been in part the product of unionist drift for the previous fourteen years. Referring to the Sunningdale episode, it was Molyneaux's opinion that the imposition of that arrangement had been due to "indiscipline in the unionist ranks". This time around, he argued, unionists "must refuse to cooperate in our own destruction".[3] Paisley had announced in similar fashion that no deviation from the electoral pact would be tolerated. "The vital unity so important to Ulster in this hour of crisis will not be allowed to be broken."[4] Now these are impressively authoritative directions. To transgress the injunction of unity, it is claimed, is to seriously weaken the whole fabric of Ulster's Britishness and to threaten its survival. Of course this claim is not without its reasonableness and not without a certain historical validity. For a people under siege, unity is a powerful rallying cry.

However, we must pause here and consider the issue which such statements by the two party leaders were addressing. For there is unity and there is unity. The free-run electoral pact asserted that, no matter what the individual constituency circumstances, there ought to be no competition for votes within the unionist "family". The General Election of 1987 was not really to be an election at all; rather it was to be another referendum on the Anglo-Irish Agreement. The duty required of unionist voters was to turn out once more and register their continued opposition to government policy. By doing so they would strengthen the hand of unionists in the new parliament. The vote would also be taken as a vote of support for the way in which the protest campaign had been conducted hitherto. That was the true prospectus intimated in all the talk of unionist unity. But a cardinal principle of the politics of referenda and plebiscites is to maximise the turn-out. Indeed, unionist leaders ought to have learnt the lesson of the by-election campaign of the previous year in which their opponents made overmuch of the fact that unionists had been unable to reach the 500,000 vote target they had set themselves. The unqualified ruling on electoral competition made no distinction between safe and marginal unionist seats. The "free run" dispensation therefore made no allowance for the factor of the "free ride". Even a passing acquaintance with the lessons of psychological, psephological and sociological research would have enlightened unionist strategists regarding the contradiction of their own position.

Put very simply, the "free-ride" syndrome has to do with one's perception of individual responsibilities. If one can be sure that one will enjoy the benefits of collective action without necessarily incurring any of the costs of individual sacrifice, there is a very human tendency to "free ride" or "free load". The "free ride" problem has been one of the major theoretical concerns of philosophical anarchists and economic libertarians. Translated into the very practical concerns of unionist politics in 1987, the problem was one of encouraging voters in traditionally safe constituencies to bother turning out to the polls. The temptation to "free ride" would be greatly increased if, in effect, there was no election campaign being conducted in those constituencies. With the result a foregone conclusion, the less than "political" individual could rest assured that others would do the required job of returning the unionist candidate. Moreover, if they had any reason to dislike the sitting MP, there was an even greater incentive to stay at home. Thus, those who opposed the electoral pact had a powerful case. It was a powerful case because it was consistent with the professed strategic intention of the party leaders. If the maximisation of the unionist vote was the purpose of the campaign, then it was illogical to deny inter-party competition in safe seats. In principle there was no antithesis between acknowledging the need for unity and permitting a healthy campaign between the parties in unionist strongholds. As it turned out, the principle of unity appeared secondary to the desire of sitting MPs for the easy option. It also avoided a debate about purpose. As election day approached, it became plain that the criticisms of the leadership's tactics were justified. In an opinion poll carried out by Ulster Marketing Surveys on behalf of the two parties, the results of which were published in the *News Letter* on 5 June (probably to jog the conscience of the electorate), it was revealed that less than 70 per cent of potential unionist supporters were certain to vote. As the newspaper editorialised, it would open old sores between and within the two parties if there was a failure to take full advantage of the clear run. But there was a much broader issue involved in these tactical electoral considerations, which has to do with the very nature of unionist unity.

The unionist leaders spoke and acted as if unionist unity was something which was self-evident, clearly defined and over which there could be no argument. Those who disagreed with the policy of unity, it was suggested, were either putting personal ambition before the common good; or they were bent on the confusion of communal purpose. Yet things were not so clear-cut. The very arguments employed to condemn those who opposed the free run policy could equally be used against the unionist MPs; in particular, that they were concerned to defend their own established positions and reputations, on the basis not of reasoned argument and evidence of success but of unfounded scaremongering. Or, as it was more bluntly put, they were seeking a ''blank cheque'' without any demonstration that they could deliver the goods. Unionist unity in this understanding had nothing to do with the comprehensive mobilisation of popular opinion, nor had it to do with embracing the broad interests of pro-Union support. It was concerned to maintain the exclusive authority of the existing public representatives and their prevailing course of action, irrespective of developing arguments within unionism since the signing of the Agreement. Hence the thrust of criticism from the Charter Group, the CEC and some within the DUP was that the sort of unionist unity proposed by the electoral pact was one designed to suffocate debate; that it was not a vital but a sterile unity. On that point, at least, these critics of the leadership could share common cause.

The effect of the free run accord was also *ad hominem*. In the previous Chapter, we examined the intent of the OUP to silence Robert McCartney and to marginalise his equal citizenship campaign. We also noted how wasteful of talent and energy that attempt was. The party was effectively trying to kill the enthusiasm of an idea. But it was also determined to "get" McCartney. This attitude may be likened to the Victorian attitude to children. Within the unionist "family" precocious intellectuals must generally be seen and not heard, and when it comes to a General Election, they must not be seen either. As we observed further, McCartney had too much integrity meekly to accept the status accorded to him. The irony of the whole North Down episode was that the weight and authority of the OUP and DUP establishment was brought to bear in favour of the sitting MP, Jim Kilfedder, who was a member of neither party and had himself broken from the OUP ranks in 1979. The electoral pact frustrated the career of another articulate, but politically very different, unionist. Jim Allister of the DUP had been cultivating support for quite some time in the East Antrim constituency of the OUP MP Roy Beggs, whom Allister had run very close in the General Election of 1983. Allister's booklet on the Agreement, *Alienated but Unbowed*, set out not only the DUP's case for its resistance and a prospectus for devolved government after its demise. It was also an attack on Beggs in particular and the short-comings of the OUP in general. Allister, like McCartney, could rightly feel aggrieved that the inner ranks of authority had closed against him. He was forced to accept the injunction, and resigned altogether from political life. The point at issue here is not that either McCartney's equal citizenship or Allister's "vibrant, fearless" activism were intrinsically superior to the alternative on offer. It is that the leadership tried to ensure that, even where there was no chance of a unionist losing a seat, the electorate would not be allowed to exercise a choice. It was a politics of exclusion, not of inclusion, and the notion of unionist unity was thereby debased. That the appeal to unity only compounded the secrecy and timidity which informed policy formulations at the leadership level was fully confirmed by the publication of the Joint Unionist Manifesto on 21 May.

The two-page manifesto bore the title *To Put Right a Great Wrong*. It made no mention of the deliberations of the Task Force, but concentrated on the generalities of the Agreement and the prospects for its replacement. Having outlined the familiar arguments about the injustice of what was done at Hillsborough, the manifesto stated that the elected MPs would "urgently seek to ascertain whether the new Government is prepared to create the circumstances and conditions necessary to encourage successful negotiations, including the suspension of the working of the Agreement and of the Maryfield Secretariat". That was to be the first step. The next was to assess whether "an alternative to and a replacement of" the Agreement could be negotiated. These two steps did not involve the Westminster unionists in any formal substantive talks. At the most, they would only entail a limited engagement to establish "talks about talks". If the tentative process of rapprochement were to fail at either stage, then unionists would have no alternative, as the manifesto continued, to pursuing their campaign of opposition more energetically, "embracing every form of legitimate political protest". This sounded like pure bravado. The likelihood of the unionist leaders encouraging a protest campaign beyond the circumscribed parameters in which it was already being conducted was remote. As we mentioned in Chapter 3, such restraint was fully in harmony with the general character of the unionist electorate.

The SDLP could gloat that the Agreement had abolished the unionist "veto" on "political progress" – by which it meant that the British and Irish governments had established a formal understanding which was congenial to its own purpose of circumventing the over-whelming opposition in Ulster, catholic as well as protestant, to a united Ireland. It could gloat because it believed that the unionist parties had nothing with which to bargain in order to redress the situation. What were unionists to offer? Righting the great wrong of the Agreement need not necessarily mean that unionists would have to offer anything. Victims of injustice are rarely called upon to make restitution to the perpetrators of injustice. However, since that had been the attitude and sustaining spirit of nationalism in Ulster since partition, and is a proposition which underlies its continued political intransigence, it was hardly an appropriate position for unionists to stick at. It was clear that unionists wanted a new settlement. All the manifesto had to say on this point was that both leaders "are offering the consent of the Unionist community in exchange for a fair, equitable and reasonable alternative to a Pact that has left a trail of death and destruction and a legacy of division and instability". It was for this broad mandate that sitting MPs sought popular support.

Despite the drama of the times for Ulster unionism, the election itself, apart from McCartney's CEC campaign in North Down, was a dull affair. The result was far from being a grand triumph for the leadership position. First, the election-as-referendum proved a disappointment. The sitting MPs and parliamentary candidates who came under the umbrella of the electoral pact polled 380,282 votes or 52 per cent of the total. This was over 50,000 less than the last, pre-Agreement, General Election in 1983. Even Peter Robinson's rock solid support in East Belfast fell with the pro-Agreement Alliance pushing their vote over the 10,000 mark. Only by adding the votes for McCartney and the North Belfast Popular Unionist, George Seaw-right, could Molyneaux and Paisley claim to have amassed a 400,000 anti-Agreement total. The turnout too was down on 1983 except, as Sidney Elliott observes, "in the two constituencies where unionist pact candidates had opposition – North Belfast and North Down".[5] On this point the critics of the free run tactic had been fully vindicated. Second, not only did the unionist vote fall from its 1983 level. They also lost another seat to the SDLP. Enoch Powell lost to Eddie McGrady in South Down by a margin of 731 votes. As the old adage goes: to make one mistake is unfortunate, to make two seems like incompetence. This was an appropriate judgement of the unionist campaign. The election post-mortem by sympathisers and critics alike concluded that the whole affair had been rather badly managed. An election fought on the basis of promoting unionist unity against the Agreement and keeping hold of all fourteen seats resulted in a drop in votes and the loss of one seat.

Once again, the SDLP seemed to have put one over on the unionists. And since it is still the policy of both governments to underpin its fortunes, Hume, Mallon and McGrady could feel satisfaction with their achievement. However, as Elliott's analysis shows, the SDLP had not delivered the goods in terms of vanquishing the Sinn Fein threat. The change between 1985 and 1987 was that "the SDLP has committed enormous resources and some hostages to fortune in order to reduce the SF nationalist share from 40 to 35 per cent".[6] But that is a view of greater salience to the impartial observer, or perhaps the British government and the British media, than to Irish nationalists. It was far from being an immediate problem for the SDLP that the Sinn Fein vote remained relatively buoyant. An appropriate level of republican violence and an appropriate indication of nationalist alienation has always been functional to the party's strategy. It has allowed Hume to have the Anglo-Irish Agreement and to press for even greater concessions to encourage continuation of the "healing process". The agenda of the SDLP is not now to destroy Sinn Fein or the IRA. It is to use them for increased leverage to "shoehorn" unionists out of the United Kingdom.

Throughout the period of the election, a spectre haunted the conduct of unionist arguments: that of the report of the Task Force: There were all sorts of rumours as to what the report contained. There was one suggestion that it favoured a federal Ireland within which Ulster protestants would have a large degree of autonomy and retain control of their own affairs. It was also rumoured that the Task Force had thrown the weight of the recommendations behind some form of "power-sharing". Although the main outlines of the report were available to the party leaders before the calling of the General Election, it was decided to use the campaign as an excuse to delay consideration of its proposals. Indeed it remained uncertain whether the final report would be published at all. Word was put about that since the Task Force had been personally commissioned by Molyneaux and Paisley and was solely responsible to them, then its findings were confidential. There was no obligation upon the two men to "go public". But if they did decide to publish they could determine which parts of the report should see the light of day. However, such were the expectations within unionism about the recommendations of the Task Force that total suppression would have been inconceivable, whatever the leadership's predilection for secrecy. Too many hopes and fears were wrapped up in the exercise.

Nevertheless, it was notable that, despite all the interest – or perhaps precisely because of that interest – neither Molyneaux nor Paisley looked forward to publication with any great enthusiasm. Molyneaux seemed to play down its importance by arguing that there had been a lot of confusion about the role the Task Force had been asked to perform. In particular, he argued, it had not been its "job to put up proposals and options on the precise form [of] any future administration" in Northern Ireland.[7] Paisley too had delivered unprovoked blasts against power-sharing. From these press statements one could detect a clear desire to anticipate and defuse some of the interpretations which Molyneaux and Paisley expected would be put on the report. They were well aware that whatever fine distinctions might be found relating to precise terms of reference, it was likely that the Task Force Report would be seized upon to pressure them into one form of action or another. Their reluctant attitude towards publication of its contents is quite understandable; for the Report might stand as a semi-official index against which conduct of policy might be judged. As the considered wisdom of unionism's second echelon, it might also provide the standard around which a challenge to the leadership could rally. It could actually come to be a positive standard of unionist propriety to challenge the negative shibboleth of unity. In other words, the two leaders, by commissioning the report, might have created the very conditions for disunity which it has been their consistent purpose to avoid. In the end they agreed to make publicly available only an abridged version of the Task Force Report. This was finally released on 2 July 1987.

The Task Force Report

The joint unionist Task Force, composed of two Official Unionists, Frank Millar and Harold McCusker, and one Democratic Unionist, Peter Robinson, had been commissioned on 23 February to consult as widely as possible with pro-Union opinion in order, first, to "secure support for the continuing campaign against the Anglo-Irish Agreement", and secondly, to "ascertain what consensus, if any, exists about alternatives to the Agreement".[8] We have already mentioned the general unease within unionism which had encouraged such reflection and consultation at this time. One sensed that the anti-Agreement protest – especially in the local authorities – was running out of steam. There was also pressure from leading worthies of the protestant churches that unionism had to come up with a positive alternative. These two pressures, assiduously aided by the efforts of the Northern Ireland Office, coincided to produce the intimately related terms of reference of the Task Force. One may suggest another influence on the timing and character of the Task Force review. The publication of the UDA's *Common Sense* in January 1987 had, as its authors intended, seized some of the initiative from the main unionist parties. *Common Sense*, much more than the Charter Group proposals, had immediately established a certain status as the constructive expression of protestant politics. Part of the rationale of the Task Force therefore was to regain the initiative which had been conceded to the UDA and return political attention to the OUP and the DUP where the unionist leaders felt it ought to belong. With this in mind, it is understandable that the central concern of the final published report, *An End to Drift*, based on extensive consultations over a twelve-week period, should have "focused on the search for an alternative to the Agreement". As the authors of the report went on to observe, this concentration registered accurately "the determination of most of those we met that protest can be no substitute for politics". That "in itself", they argued, was a major finding of the report. Such obvious statements established the dominant tone. The Task Force argued by implication, criticised by suggestion, and recommended by innuendo. It said much about the political inarticulateness of contemporary unionism.

The eight-page document only referred in passing to the campaign against the Agreement. The criticisms of the way it had been conducted were not published. Instead the report merely recorded that what censure there was reflected a conviction on the part of some "that they have and know a better way". The views received expressed an "across the board desire to make the anti-Agreement movement more effective". But what was not said was the crucial point: namely, that the "desire" within unionism to make the anti-Agreement campaign more effective has never corresponded with the willingness of the unionist electorate to adopt the necessary measures. The cautious restraint and condemnation of violent excess which has characterised the civil protest since 1985 has been a rational course, given the very limited options open to unionist politics. Even though the activists within the Ulster Clubs and the DUP display a penchant for heroic and combative rhetoric, they are well aware that there is little popular support for "heroic" or "combative" action. But the report was fully

justified in its censure of the British media for their failure to acknowledge the general moderation of unionist protest and their unwillingness to recognise that there might be issues of civil liberty at stake.

McCusker, Robinson and Millar set out three factors of present
circumstances which would act as reference-points for their considerations. First, it was agreed that as far as the terms of Hillsborough were
concerned, the Agreement could not be "devolved away". Devolution, if it were to be agreed, could only be part of a wider settlement.
Secondly, the Agreement established "unrealistic" limits on the
powers which might be devolved. And finally – this was really the crux
of the matter, given these devolutionary assumptions – unionists
"could not contemplate participation in any form of devolved government whose work and functions would be supervised and overseen by
the Anglo-Irish Conference." This was not a particularly illuminating
set of propositions. They said nothing which had not been said *ad
nauseam* over the previous two years. The real opportunity of the Task
Force had been to educate unionist opinion, but it had not done so.
Instead, it simply repeated without reflection all the old clichés of a
limited political discourse. For instance, the authors made passing
reference to "independence" and "the right to self-determination".
What these terms meant, or could come to mean, did not seem to
exercise the minds of the Task Force. Instead they were allowed to
stand as unexamined propositions and therefore to continue to contribute to unionism's woolly thinking. The authors were critical of those
who assumed that unionist politicians must "inevitably be bested in
any negotiations". Unfortunately, the degree of political sophistication revealed in *An End to Drift* merely confirmed the worst suspicions
of those critics. What conclusions did the Task Force Report arrive at?

First, while they recognised that the policy of total integration (again
undefined) continued to attract substantial support within the unionist
community, the authors argued that this was unattainable.
"Devolved-government therefore is our objective and whilst we hope
this will prove attainable within the context of the United Kingdom",
unionists, they warned, "would be wise and prudent to anticipate that
it might not." This proposition requires some examination. Devolved
government for Northern Ireland within the United Kingdom is an
intelligible objective. But what is one to make of the Task Force's
qualification? Does it really suggest that if unionists enter into negotiations with the objective of securing devolved government within the
United Kingdom, they must also be prepared to consider the possibility of devolved government outside the United Kingdom? If that is
not faulty wording or thinking, is one to be infer that it is a nod in the
direction of a federal Ireland. For how could Ulster have *devolved*
government outside the United Kingdom except "within the context"

of another state? And what other state could that be except the Republic of Ireland? Having suggested that contingency (let's be generous and say unwittingly), it is announced in bold type that "having sworn never to accept the Agreement as a basis for continued membership of the United Kingdom, we must ascertain what alternative terms for the Union can be found." That is a statement so obvious that one can only wonder what unionist leaders had been doing since November 1985. But if this is read in the light of the caveat on devolution, a rather disturbing frame of mind is revealed. For were the Task Force trio to be trusted not to be inveigled away from considerations of alternative forms of the Union to considerations of alternative forms *to* the Union? They did, after all, seem prepared to concede the case in advance.

A second proposal was the setting up of a Unionist Convention "to construct and lead a renewed campaign to manifest the absence of consent for the arrangements by which Northern Ireland is presently governed". This was nothing new, and was an idea which had been around in various forms since the anti-Agreement protest had got under way. There was a reasonable basis to this suggestion because, if the campaign against the Agreement was to have any sustained impact, it had to involve as wide a spread of unionist opinion as possible. A Convention would be one way of embracing the diversity of unionism in a quasi-authoritative body and creating the conditions for popular involvement and mobilisation. It might also formally legitimise, as the authors recognised, the conduct of renewed discussions with the British government. Such a Convention would inevitably impart some direction to the protest campaign and weaken the current position of Molyneaux and Paisley. Again, a case could be made for saying that that would be a good thing; that a more open and collegiate leadership would be necessary to cement support in the difficult days of negotiation to come. On the other hand, arguments for a unionist Convention were informed by attitudes which were far from reasonable. For instance the Ulster Clubs had regarded a similar coordinating body as a means not only of conducting a more effective anti-Agreement campaign but also of establishing a potential structure for an independent Ulster. A Convention inspired by the values of little Ulsterism could be a major concession to separatist sentiment. To encourage that sort of politics would play directly into the hands of those responsible for the Hillsborough accord.

The third recommendation was another attempt to circumscribe the independence of the two leaders in any future discussions with the British government. The Task Force argued that a "panel" ought to be appointed to "establish whether a base for formal negotiations exists or can be established". To preserve and protect the position of the leaders, it was recommended that "the said panel be appointed *only* to consult and report." The idea of a panel could be taken to reflect an awareness within both the OUP and the DUP that there was a need for wider consultation. Indeed, the Task Force itself was partly the result of this same concern. It could be argued that the position of the two leaders in any future discussions with the government would be strengthened if it was clear that they were representing a broadly agreed position. There was also the argument that a panel would help to share the burden of discussions and relieve the pressure and responsibility which both men would otherwise have to carry alone. Yet the suggestion of a panel had less to do with an understanding of the effective mechanics of negotiation; rather, it had much to do with what those negotiations should seek to achieve and an estimation of the potential of Molyneaux and Paisley to deliver the required goods. As one anonymous, but pessimistic, unionist informed *Fortnight*, "One wants devolution on terms that aren't possible. And one is not committed to devolution at all."[9] In other words, for the devolutionist purpose of the Task Force to be realised, there had to be some way of circumventing the position of the two leaders. The panel was designed to do that by diluting their mandate. But what sort of devolution was to be the objective?

The Task Force was well aware of the fundamental objections to mentioning power-sharing as a legitimate unionist goal. (That this was not an example of unionist bigotry we have already seen in Chapter 4.) Nor did it mention it explicitly in the text. But it was clearly intimated that unionism would have to think along those lines. As the report stated, it would be necessary that "in earnest of your desire to find a reasonable alternative you should signal that *no matter* could or should be precluded from any negotiations." The spirit of the great unmentionable was detectable in those words since, as the argument went on, both unionist parties had already "abandoned pure majority rule as the price for Devolution". As we also mentioned in Chapter 4, the whole commitment to a devolutionary settlement, which was portrayed by its proponents as the only realistic option, was far from being self-evidently the proper course for unionists to follow. Once again, the Task Force did not attempt to make a case for devolution. It could not do so effectively because its whole approach was muddled and incoherent. Out of that muddle and incoherence emerged its concluding vacuous proposal.

It was proposed that a Special Commission be appointed to advise upon an alternative constitutional arrangement to Northern Ireland's membership of the United Kingdom. The reasoning went as follows. If unionist negotiators in any future talks on a devolved settlement were to have any political leverage at all, they would have to make it plain in advance that failure to reach a satisfactory conclusion would mean that they would have no alternative but to "seek an entirely new base for Northern Ireland *outside* the present constitutional context". What this new base would be, the authors were not prepared to say. They were convinced, none the less, that "whatever the intentions of the Governments in London and Dublin, membership of the United Kingdom or membership of an Irish Republic are *not* the only options available to the people of Northern Ireland." This was a case of bluff designed to cover a lack of clear thought – a fittingly empty conclusion to a report which was a waste of time and effort. The Task Force Report revealed, as perhaps nothing hitherto had done so clearly, the intellectual weakness, the fundamental absence of deep political reflection, within unionism's aspiring new identity. The threadbare platitudes of the Task Force Report were not only unhelpful but also an embarrassment. Unsurprisingly, an equally unreflective media welcomed it as a significant contribution to new thinking within unionism. It was nothing of the sort. It was an escape from serious and constructive thought.

The response of Molyneaux and Paisley was careful and considered. In their statement they simply stressed those points which confirmed their own position, and diplomatically ignored those which did not. On balance this was the proper thing to do; any other reply would have encouraged the Task Force authors to expect more than they deserved. Thus the two leaders welcomed "the fact that the report affirms the policy to which unionism is committed by us, a policy overwhelmingly mandated in the recent election". To head off any possibility of the Task Force establishing a challenging legitimacy, Molyneaux and Paisley introduced the factor of the ballot-box. Both repeated the manifesto promise to initiate exploratory talks about a replacement for the Agreement, but made no mention of the suggestions for a Convention, a panel or a Commission. They had every justification for avoiding comment on those proposals. For if the report was the sum and pinnacle of unionist political thought then the two leaders could legitimately feel that they could do better themselves. At least Molyneaux seems to have a clear idea of the Union. He may have difficulty delivering immediate results, but there is little likelihood of his falling into the dangerous errors of the Task Force. Politely McCusker, Millar and Robinson were thanked for the "time, energy and skill which they brought to this difficult assignment",[10] beyond which neither leader had anything to add. They were quite relieved to put the whole business aside. And they could afford to do this because, whatever genuine worries there might be about the conduct of unionist policy, the constitutional inanities of the Task Force Report only detracted from them. The Task Force had wasted its opportunity.

As Mervyn Pauley, one of the best informed and most perceptive of journalists writing on unionism, observed a month after the report's publication, the members of the Task Force were "in something of a quandary as to their place in the wider scheme of things".[11] And so they might be because there was no possible way, as things stood, for their proposals to be realised. Rightly, the Task Force Report had been consigned to the dustbin for it had added nothing positive to contemporary unionism. Millar resigned his position as General Secretary of the OUP on 11 September 1987 and decided to leave local politics altogether. Later that month, Peter Robinson resigned as deputy leader of the DUP. This was part of a broader attrition of well-known devolutionists, which included the leader of the Alliance Party John Cushnahan. The reception by the unionist leaders of *An End to Drift* certainly meant that there was no possibility of any full-blooded devolved government in the foreseeable future. The way forward was not to be on the basis of the ill-considered grand (and empty) devolutionary gestures suggested by the Task Force but on the basis of the cautious prospectus outlined in *To Put Right a Great Wrong*. What is more, the initial moves were to be under the exclusive direction and control of Molyneaux and Paisley. The steady course was to be resumed.

Talks about talks

The Task Force Report had made the distinction between "discussions and formal negotiations". The joint unionist manifesto had drawn a similar distinction between ascertaining whether there could be movement on the British government's part towards creating the "circumstances and conditions necessary to encourage successful negotiations" and those negotiations themselves. Shortly after the General Election, there were indications that discussing or ascertaining (or whatever one called it) was about to begin. Sensitive steps were taken by both sides. Molyneaux let it be known that the two parties would favourably consider the opportunity for "dialogue" with the government. From the Queen's Speech opening the new Parliament, it was clear that the government was prepared to play down the Agreement and give unionists an excuse to follow where their instincts were leading them. The DUP press officer (also a former Lord Mayor of Belfast), Sammy Wilson, a politician whose anti-Agreement credentials were beyond question, took the evidence of the Queen's Speech and the removal of Nicholas Scott from the Northern Ireland Office as a sign of a positive change of attitude on the part of the Conservative government. He argued that now was the time for unionists to "enter into low-level discussions". He believed that the initial discussions should be with civil servants. His considered view was that there would be no difficulty about these taking place while the Agreement was still being implemented.[12] And although discussions might be held under the Agreement, there was no obligation at all on the part of unionists to relax their hostility to it. Wilson's proposition was to prove convenient to both the unionists and the government. That there was little opposition to the move reflected the opinion which had come across clearly on the doorsteps during the election campaign. Unionist voters had not come to accept the Agreement; but they were increasingly concerned about their isolation and alienation within the British state. They wanted their leaders to do something to relieve the situation without having to capitulate to the Agreement's betrayal of their citizenship.

The first step in the process of "talks about talks" was taken on 14 July in London when Molyneaux and Paisley met Sir Kenneth Bloomfield, head of the Northern Ireland Civil Service, and Sir Robert Andrew, permanent secretary at the Northern Ireland Office. The meeting, which lasted twenty minutes, was designed to set an agenda for future meetings. Nevertheless, it was the first formal encounter between the unionist leaders and representatives of the government since the Downing Street talks with Mrs Thatcher in February 1986.[13] The presence of Bloomfield was intended to ease matters. This was not only because he is an Ulsterman and well respected by local politicians, but more significantly he had not been involved in the negotiations which led up to the signing of the Agreement. What was to be on the agenda for these meetings? In a press statement issued before the encounter with the civil servants the two leaders declared: "The debate at the moment is concerning the willingness on the part of Her Majesty's Government to declare that it is prepared to seek a new agreement." The purpose of the talks was to discover "whether the willingness exists or can be established". The signs were, they claimed, "that the response will be helpful".[14] For its part, the government was happy that the talking had begun, whatever the attendant qualifications. Its aim, according to a Northern Ireland Office source who confided to *Fortnight*, was "to get to a position where everyone is on board".[15] Both these views were rather optimistic; but what else could they say?

The talks about talks appeared to be a straightforward matter. Unionists would only enter into proper negotiations for a settlement to the Hillsborough crisis if the government agreed to "the suspension of the working of the Agreement and of the Maryfield Secretariat" (*To Put Right a Great Wrong*). That did not seem a question needing much exploration. The government was either prepared to do it or it was not. Since there was no indication that it was, it looked as if unionists would have to take no for an answer. There could be little room for manoeuvre if nothing was to be raised beyond that "single narrow issue". Yet, while politicians might find it convenient to make absolute distinctions between the terms of reference and the conditions of discussion, such nuances were unlikely in practice to be maintained for long. In an interview in August, Molyneaux remained adamant that things would only be taken step by step. He was not prepared at that stage to mention "alternatives", because if "we start giving alternatives to the Government and if it doesn't do exactly what we want it to do, those alternatives can appear more like a threat". One detects in those words the reason for Molyneaux's embarrassment with the Task Force Report. Not only was he not prepared to explore (correctly) alternatives to the Union, but he was not even prepared at this stage to make public his considered views on alternatives to the Agreement within the Union. Nor did he consider it wise to produce then what commentators called a "shopping list". He argued that it "would be premature to present a shopping list, and unwise to display your bargaining points at the beginning of a negotiating situation".[16]

Molyneaux's evasiveness caused intense irritation to those devolutionists within his party who believed that time was not on the side of unionist politics. The Charter Group, for instance, set up a hostile barracking from the fringe, and blamed Molyneaux for wasting an important opportunity to seize the initiative and present exciting new proposals for "cross-community" devolved government with "real autonomy". Reduced to its essentials, their criticism was that he did not want to carry forward the talks to the point of negotiations because he did not want devolution at all. It proved relatively easy for Molyneaux to discredit Charterists like McNarry simply because of the intemperance of their attack, its personal nature and the inordinate haste with which they were prepared to capitulate to what the government chose to call "realistic". However, what they had to say was not without some foundation. Peter Smith criticised what he called his party's "not a millimetre" thinking and pointed to "obduracy at certain levels in the party". But he was prepared to admit, which the Charter Group was not, that his belief in "an internal devolutionist settlement, outside the Anglo-Irish Agreement" was a view not shared "by the majority or even a significant minority in the party".[17] Therefore, Molyneaux's refusal to present gratuitous proposals for an internal settlement has been justified not only in terms of negotiating tactics. It has also been fully in accord with the sentiments of the majority of the OUP. Moreover the DUP has been firmly against engaging in full negotiations for a devolved settlement parallel to the continued implementation of the Agreement. Paisley and his supporters recognised it as the trap it is.

Another criticism of the leadership's approach to the talks about talks was to be found in the columns of the UDA's magazine *Ulster*. Like the Charter Group, the UDA had a particular vision of a settlement which the unionist leaders ought to advance. *Common Sense*, it believed, provided the basis for a proper, consensual alternative to the Agreement. Yet with a certain humility not to be found in other devolutionist circles, the UDA was prepared to admit the possibility that Molyneaux and Paisley might come up with something better. It was not the detail of the alternative, or the balance between autonomy and integration, with which certain members of the UDA were concerned. They were agitated rather by the secrecy and exclusiveness of the talks and in particular by the failure of the two leaders to build up in advance a popular constituency for whatever proposals they should eventually agree upon. "One would have thought", argued *Ulster*, "that in the present circumstances the leaders would seek to enthuse their people rather than keeping them in the dark . . . one would have assumed that the 'leadership' would have learned the need to sell our cry for freedom and democracy to the world." Quite the contrary, the UDA believed. Rather than "establish exactly what the Unionist people want – and then muster the troops to fight for it – the 'leadership' avoided strategy (anyone's strategy) preferring to operate off the cuff like the Lone Ranger and Tonto."[18] Because the leaders had neglected those central arts of political life – communication and mobilisation – the UDA argued that unionism has continued to accept retreat and rearguard actions as a way of life. It was incapable of using its own resources to turn the tables on its opponents.

For instance, without a commonly agreed position on an alternative to the Agreement, Molyneaux and Paisley have been the subject of pressure not only from the British government but also from within their own community. They have come under pressure from the protestant churches to make some sort of positive movement towards finding a way out of the current impasse. Increasingly, so the UDA's argument went, even within their own protestant heartlands, unionist leaders had been coming to appear as the villains of the piece. Because they had failed to mobilise the people behind them, they were playing directly into the hands of the government, which welcomed the secrecy and uncertainty of the talks because of the confusion they sowed in unionist ranks, thus maintaining the momentum of demoralisation. This could be reversed if both men were prepared to set out a clear and unambiguous alternative. The focus of pressure would then shift from unionism to the supporters of the Agreement. "A much more sensible approach would be to issue proposals and let our enemies worry about justifying their position". In other words, rather than providing unionists with the opportunity to take the initiative, the conduct of the talks about talks had meant that unionism got the worst of all worlds.

The UDA was expressing a proper concern regarding the balance of political advantages since the General Election, and was not merely repeating the usual undifferentiated exhortation to action which had been a common feature of its criticism hitherto. Like its attack on the "Ulster Says No" campaign, the UDA could rightly say that the talks about talks were going nowhere. Once again Molyneaux and Paisley could reply that it was best to be cautious when the Union was at stake; that it would be a dereliction of their duty to make the grand gesture which might fail and leave unionism even more exposed than before. The talks about talks, therefore, represented the pursuit of the limited objectives of the anti-Agreement campaign by other means. Unionist leaders are well acquainted with the politics of siege.

Unity, stamina, persistence, perseverance, optimism of the will – all those virtues which were held necessary for the conduct of Ulster's resistance to the Agreement came to the aid of the leaders in their justification of the conduct of the talks about talks. Vindication of the talks lay not in what had issued from them but in the encouraging fact that they were still going on. Even after Tom King, the Northern Ireland Secretary, began to attend the formal discussions with Molyneaux and Paisley in the autumn, there was still no admission that anything other than the "single issue" had been broached. On 4 December, Paisley stated that if the talks reached a successful conclusion, "it will be on the single issue we have been mandated to discuss." He dismissed outright the suggestion that the way in which things were being dragged out implied that the engagement was a waste of time. Instead he argued that the "fact that the talks have been going on for this length of time should not be a reason for criticism. It shows we are putting the Government up against the wall, as it were, and using all our skills to get a straightforward response". He and Molyneaux had to be seen "to be prepared to argue our case and not be intransigent".[19] Keeping the talks going without dramatic alternatives or initiatives appeared to have become an end in itself. As the New Year approached, unionists were evidently hoping that the crisis in Anglo-Irish relations which had blown up over extradition and judicial reform would erode even further the crumbling credibility of the Agreement (see below). In that event, unionists could take advantage of the moment to advance their claims for an alternative.

But the calculation that the contradictions of the Agreement compounded by Charles Haughey's unremitting anti-Britishness would shatter present arrangements was a misplaced one. Despite the clear evidence that the Accord had not and could not temper the Republic's irresponsible atavistic nationalism, the British establishment remained reluctant to admit its incapacity to achieve the avowed objectives of Hillsborough. The farce had to continue and, according to the logic of farce, it was to be the unionists who had to make the required adjustments in the talks about talks. The convenient fiction of maintaining a discreet separation between discussions to discover a willingness to consider an alternative to the Agreement, and discussions of what that alternative might be, finally collapsed. The process had imperceptibly but surely moved on to a new stage. It had now become permissible to mention ''alternatives'' in the same breath as ''talks''.

Molyneaux had already intimated before the New Year what he intended that alternative to be. It was to be no visionary proposal for regional autonomy backed up by threats of life outside the Union. It was to be based on proposals put forward in correspondence between the OUP and DUP leaders and Mrs Thatcher in August and September 1985 – that is, *before* the Hillsborough accord had been signed. In that correspondence Molyneaux and Paisley had accepted the need for a cooperative and formalised relationship between Dublin and London. But they had opposed any form of Anglo-Irish Secretariat which would give the Republic's government a direct influence in the internal affairs of Northern Ireland. That distinction has been fundamental to the whole strategy of unionist opposition to the present Agreement. The correspondence had also made it plain that unionists could not be fobbed off with an internal deal on devolved government if it had to co-exist with joint Dublin rule; for that would be asking them to act as accomplices in their own humiliation. Other than those reservations (which only in the bizarre world of post-Agreement politics appear ''large'' reservations), unionists would be prepared to consider any new devolved structure which provided proper protection for minority interests – except, that is, a devolved government which entailed ''as of right'' power-sharing at executive level.[20] That last qualification only seems incorrigibly triumphalist if it is assumed that devolved structures must resemble the 1973 model. Of course it is quite possible to imagine something where cabinet-level power-sharing would not be a relevant concept. When he was asked why the government should consider favourably today proposals which it had rejected before, Molyneaux's reply was simple. He argued that the government had not rejected them but ignored them. It had set its purpose on the Agreement, and the unionist proposals at that time had been ''hideously inconvenient''. With his characteristic faith in the wisdom of British MPs, he believed that there had been a remarkable transformation of opinion within the House of Commons since November 1985.[21] The time was ripe, he believed, to exploit their supposed growing disenchantment with the Hillsborough settlement.

To help finalise the proposals which would be put to the Secretary of State, one concession was made to the recommendations of the Task

Force. It was agreed in January 1988 to set up a ten-man advisory panel (5 OUP and 5 DUP) to help fill in the details of the framework outlined in that pre-Agreement correspondence. Included in the panel were two members of the Task Force, Harold McCusker 'and Peter Robinson (who had once again taken up his post as deputy leader of the DUP). In a three-hour meeting with Tom King at Stormont Castle on 26 January 1988, Molyneaux and Paisley claimed that they were not talking about a suspension of the Agreement but about considerations for a replacement of it. As they revealed in a letter written to King on 12 April, they had at the January meeting ''outlined various ideas for a new British-Irish agreement as a replacement for the Anglo-Irish agreement, which replacement could attract widespread support, and which would succeed where the 1985 accord had failed''.[22] Beyond these teasing hints and careful words, what else did the unionist leaders have in mind?

An idea which had been around in OUP circles for some time before the January meeting was the idea of a Northern Ireland regional council. In popular jargon, this had been up-graded to an Ulster "super council". It was little different from the proposed form of administrative devolution which had been outlined in *The Way Forward*. Agreement on a regional council to oversee the administration of local services – excepting security – would be accompanied by an end to the system of Orders-in-Council at Westminster. Northern Ireland business in the House of Commons would be dealt with in a similar fashion to that of Scotland and Wales. This provided a possibility that, so long as the right words were used, there was enough in such an alternative to bridge the gap between devolution and integration. If it were to form the basis of negotiations, along with a unionist acceptance of a modified Anglo-Irish agreement which was not seen as infringing British sovereignty in Northern Ireland, it might provide real substance to unionist unity, giving something to integrationists and devolutionists alike. It would certainly not be enough for the "regional autonomists"; but then their notion of arriving at some sort of equitable arrangement with the SDLP seemed, by early 1988, quite unrealistic. There had been an attempt on their part to influence opinion in the course of the new talks through the establishment of a Campaign for a Regional Parliament. The CRP transformed itself into the less provocative Campaign for a Devolved Parliament. Despite the reasonableness of its objectives, it was cutting against the grain of SDLP intentions, ignoring the continuing catholic support for Sinn Fein and the mischievous republican priorities of Haughey.[23] The glossy professionalism of its pamphlet, and even the sincerity of its presentation, could not hide the staleness of its thinking.

There was no clear indication that a regional council *was* the form of alternative that Molyneaux and Paisley had put forward as part of their attempt to redefine the relationships between Belfast, London and Dublin. Neither of the two leaders, nor the Secretary of State, was prepared to say. After January there was little communication between the Northern Ireland Office and the unionists and precious little between unionists and their electorate. Both sides were marking time and have continued to do so. Indeed Tom King, the Secretary of State, gave the impression, consistent with his well-known contempt for unionist politics, that he had not even bothered to listen to what Moly-neaux and Paisley had had to say, or even to read their joint submission. That would seem the only explanation for his statement, nine months into discussion, that he was still waiting for unionists to put forward proposals. However the outcome of the meetings was overshadowed by events elsewhere. The focus of political attention had shifted away from unionism. First, Anglo-Irish relations – notwith-standing the wondrous claims which had been made regarding the supreme value of the Agreement for sorting out such diffi-culties – reached their lowest ebb for many years. Megaphone diplomacy was alive and well in the Anglo-Irish Conference. Secondly, the SDLP revealed clearly another of the grand idiocies of the Agree-ment. Having justified Hillsborough as the only way to enable consti-tutional nationalism to defeat the men of violence and provide a breathing space for the "healing process" within Northern Ireland to begin, the British government were forced to watch John Hume engaging in talks with those same men of violence to put further screws on the unionists. The enormity of the exercise, justified as always by sweet and pious words, did not go unobserved. Both these develop-ments need to be considered to assess the options open to unionism.

Anglo-Irish antagonisms

In the area of Anglo-Irish relations, especially in the course of develop-ments in the 1980s, an illusion had been fostered which had boosted the collective ego of the political establishment in the Republic of Ireland – both politicians and the officials who advise them. The idea had taken root that, where negotiating was concerned, they were at least the equals of the political class in London. This was extremely flattering and something which London was keen to perpetuate. Ministers in the Republic were encouraged to think that they could hold their own with the perfidious Brits. They were extremely surprised that in the detailed negotiations leading up to the signing of the Agreement the British had been so accommodating, so sensitive to their views. And since London had been so spiritless in defence of British sovereignty, the notion developed that there was nothing, certainly not the will of the government in London, standing in the way of the smooth attainment of nationalist objectives in Northern Ireland. Once unionist resistance was out of the way – and that was expected to be quite soon – the path would be opened up for Dublin to dictate the pace of the organic fusion of the two parts of Ireland. This could only be done by the Republic acting as the sectarian advocate of the SDLP. It could only be done according to the ideological assumptions clearly set out in the articles of the Agreement; namely that Irish nationalism would embrace the interests of catholics, its true people in Ulster. No longer would it even pretend to care about Ulster protestants. All it required was that the British authorities should cow protestants into submission so that they would cause no trouble in the new Ireland.

While things may not have gone entirely according to plan within Northern Ireland because of the stubborn character of unionist resistance, there was much optimism none the less that at the level of inter-governmental relations the commanding heights of the issue were still under control. The tacit understandings of the negotiating period, in particular the understanding conveyed by the British that they would do nothing to hinder progress towards Irish unity, informed the proceedings of the Conference. Unfortunately for the self-esteem of the Dublin establishment, it had come to confuse the mutual interests of London and Dublin with the particular interests of Irish nationalism. What was forgotten was that while the British government was prepared to accommodate the wishes of the Republic when that suited a common purpose, it would feel no such obligation when concession appeared to entail raising political difficulties *beyond* the confines of the unionist electorate. London looked to Hillsborough for progress in security, containment and a framework for eventual disengagement. What it did not want from the Conference was pressure concerning issues which it felt would reflect adversely on characteristics of British government in Northern Ireland, both historic and current. After all, the whole international purpose of the Agreement had been to relieve Britain of those particular thorns in its side. Nor did London want the obligations of the Agreement to encourage Irish interference in British politics outside Northern Ireland. However, it was only a matter of time before Dublin would push for a concession which London believed neither politic nor in its interest to grant. When that point came it would be revealed how superficial was the much lauded great historic reconciliation between a state which is profoundly anti-British and a state which really accords little significance to its partner.

The first crisis arose over interpretation of Article 8 of the Agreement. Article 8 is concerned with "public confidence in the administration of justice". To that end it set out as part of the remit of the Conference to consider how to give "substantial expression to this aim''. To be reviewed "*inter alia*" was the idea of mixed courts in "both jurisdictions" to try certain offences. Article 8 also established that the Conference would be concerned with "policy aspects of extradition". London was interested in extradition, and the only substantial commitment made by the Republic since 15 November 1985 had been its agreement to pass an Extradition Act which would facilitate the return of terrorist suspects to British jurisdiction. Now although extradition and the administration of justice in Northern Ireland were mentioned in the same article, the Agreement made no explicit link between them. And since the signatories at Hillsborough claimed that there was no hidden agenda, one might have assumed that things were cut and dried. Dublin, of course, had no interest in mixed courts operating in its jurisdiction. But it had an interest in rooting nationalist priorities in the administration of justice in Ulster. Politicians in the Republic had come to feel assured that the British had no objection to the one-way traffic of Anglo-Irish relations. They expected that reform of the judicial system in Ulster would be no different. As it slowly dawned on them that this was not so, the reaction was at first petulant, but later bordered on the hysterical. The "statemanship" shown by the Republic in the first year of the Agreement quickly degenerated into the dependent peevishness which had been Dublin's traditional attitude towards the British government. Over the issue of settling changes in the process of justice in Northern Ireland, the prevailing feeling was that those nasty people in the big house next door had reverted to their old habit of snubbing the peasants.

What Dublin and the SDLP wanted was reform of the "Diplock" non-jury court from a single-judge to a three-judge system. The existing system had been instituted to avoid intimidation of jurors and the perversion of justice. Ironically, given the controversies which have attended its existence, the original suspicion had been that juries would be biased in favour of protestant paramilitaries. Later the "Diplock courts" became the object of an orchestrated nationalist propaganda campaign designed to undermine the capacity of the legal order in Northern Ireland. Sinn Fein and the SDLP were both party to this. When the Agreement had been signed, movement on this issue was important for Hume; it would help to protect his party's flank from the Sinn Fein challenge. A great success could be claimed for nationalism. It might also encourage Sinn Fein voters to believe that Hume could create the conditions for a united Ireland because Dublin and he himself had the British government squared. There was no longer any need to go on shooting protestants and blowing them up. Let the processes of the Agreement defeat the unionists instead. Thus the issue of the three-judge courts had nothing to do with the idea of justice. It had to do with discrediting the existing system of justice and its historical role in the prosecution of terrorist offenders. What the SDLP wanted was, in effect, an admission that courts in Northern Ireland – and by implication the British legal system in general – had been incapable of giving justice to Irish nationalists. What the SDLP also wanted, and had a realistic expectation that it would get given the assumptions of British policy, was, as Roy Bradford noted, a "sectarian balance" in the administration of justice.[24] For the Irish government, sectarian "balance" was a first step towards the long-term goal of absorbing the system of justice in Northern Ireland into its own.

Here the expectations of the Agreement came up against the resistance of the British legal profession and the hostility of the then Lord Chancellor, Lord Hailsham. The judicial system was clearly being used as a scapegoat for the political failures of the British and Irish governments. There was no evidence to substantiate the claims that the Diplock courts meted out injustice and that this had to do with the quality or integrity of the judges themselves. Application of the thesis of nationalist alienation never made contact with the notion of political responsibility. Even if the legal system had been crucified on the open and implied charges of the three-judge court lobby, no assurance was ever given by Dublin or the SDLP that this would in any significant way address the problem of nationalist "alienation". As it transpired, the idea of three-judge courts had nothing at all to do with the merit of the case. It had to do with particular trade-offs which had helped to smooth the passage of the Agreement negotiations. The polite expression which politicians in the Republic coined to describe these trade-offs was "linkage". Linkage politics were the secret protocols of Hillsborough. Ironically, it was Garret Fitzgerald, whom the British media had portrayed as a paragon of openness, embodying the true spirit of the new Ireland, who exposed the deal.

At a meeting of the British-Irish Association at Cambridge in September 1987, Fitzgerald complained that the British government had reneged on a promise to exchange the Diplock court system for the Republic's introduction of extradition. This interpretation of events was endorsed by Dick Spring, Deputy Prime Minister in Fitzgerald's coalition government. As far as Spring was concerned, there had been a clear undertaking that the Northern Ireland courts would be "reformed" in exchange for extradition; "the two things had been unequivocally linked.[25] This linkage was denied by the British government. Tom King's position was that he was not "presently persuaded" that there was a case for change. Nor did he believe that increasing "public confidence in the administration of justice" was a function of judicial reform alone. The British government pointed to other changes as evidence of its commitment to the spirit of Article 8, changes such as the ending of the "supergrass" system (the conviction of terrorists suspects on the evidence of informers, who in return were granted immunity from prosecution) and the reduction in delays between arrest and trial. But since these reforms benefited protestants as well as catholics, they were therefore insufficient to satisfy the sectarian intent of Dublin and the SDLP. A consensus emerged within constitutional nationalism north and south of the border that the Extradition Act, due for ratification in December, should be delayed or postponed altogether. The feeling was that unionists had not been humiliated enough or the British government humbled enough. When Gerry Adams, the President of Sinn Fein, called this whole debate "symbolic", he spoke a greater truth than he knew.[26] It symbolised the perfidy of both sides to the Agreement. It symbolised the intent of the SDLP, despite all the talk of healing wounds and new Irelands, to fix sectarian principles at the very heart of justice. It symbolised the design of the Republic, despite all its concern for an end to viole ice, to use that violence as a lever to prise greater concessions from the British. It was only the massacre at the Remembrance Day commemoration at Enniskillen in November which finally forced Haughey to push through the Extradition Act. In the form in which it was eventually agreed to by the Dail, it is doubtful if the Extradition Act is any aid to the British in their fight against IRA terrorism. Mrs Thatcher was stung to claim that its provisions gave Britain "least-favoured status". That it should take Mrs Thatcher this length of time to realise that the purpose of Irish nationalism is not to help the British but to exploit every opportunity to worst them, is a sad reflection on her understanding of the politics of the Republic.

The elements revealed during the courts and extradition imbroglio were to be repeated throughout the deterioration of Anglo-Irish relations in the first six months of 1988. Suspicion, hostility and atavistic bitterness, the living spirit of Irish political inferiority, encountered the hypocrisy, evasiveness and self-interest of the British establishment. On January 25, the British Attorney General, Sir Patrick Mayhew, announced to the House of Commons that no prosecutions were to take place against RUC officers as a consequence of the Stalker and Sampson inquiries into a "shoot-to-kill" policy against terrorists, which, it had been alleged, had been pursued by the police in the early 1980s. The response from Dublin was to link this ruling with the arguments advanced over changes in the Diplock courts. Refusal to prosecute members of the RUC, according to Haughey, had to do with confidence in the administration of justice. The Attorney General's announcement had done "the gravest damage to confidence in the ability and intention of the authorities to uphold the rule of law and to administer justice fairly". It was one more instance of traditional British insensitivity to the Irish people. Haughey intimated a threat of the withdrawal of the Republic's co-operation on cross-border security (such as it is) for, he claimed, it could only be conducted on a basis of mutual trust between the two police forces. This mutual trust had to be founded on the commitment of the British government to pursue political progress by peaceful constitutional means.[27] In other words, nationalists would want something else in return if they could not have the heads of a few senior RUC officers. They were not interested in the technicalities of justice. There had to be either a police sacrifice or a political concession to assuage their sense of alienation.

The British government's position was also morally dubious. If there was evidence of wrongdoing, then legal action ought to have been taken. The Director of Public Prosecutions had implied that there were reasons of "national interest" which argued against such an action, but this was an escape from a much wider responsibility, or rather culpability, on the part of those charged with the protection of the national interest. The national interest is hardly served by the perversion of justice. But in Northern Ireland it might be served by a more intelligent security policy. The measures which have had to be adopted by the police to combat terrorism have been related to the overall character of the security policy which has been determined by London. And London has been concerned, above all, to pursue a policy which has thrust the Royal Ulster Constabulary into the front line of fighting a terrorist war. And its attempt to treat members of the IRA as criminals rather than political insurgents has been a disaster. It may have saved the lives of British soldiers, but it has had a catastrophic effect upon the prisons, police and courts. It has also contributed significantly to the deterioration in community relations. It is the civil servants responsible for thinking up the criminalisation policy and the government ministers who have been prepared to follow it unquestioningly, who must share whatever guilt falls on the shoulders of individual members of the RUC.

Dublin's recriminations concerning the Stalker and Sampson inquiries into the RUC were shortly followed by an outburst of anger when the Appeal Court judges in London upheld the original trial verdict against the six men convicted of the IRA pub bombings in Birmingham in November 1974. The Home Secretary, Douglas Hurd, who had negotiated the Agreement to achieve peace, stability and reconciliation in Ireland, refused to exercise the Royal Prerogative of Mercy to appease the wrath of the Irish government. The decision in the Birmingham Six appeal on January 28 was one more blow to Irish expectations that the British government would concede each and every demand it might have. There must still be doubts about the guilt of the Birmingham Six, and there is still legitimate cause for concern about the conduct of the original trial, but that is not really the issue at stake in the course of Anglo-Irish relations. The charge against the judgement of the Appeal Court was not just a case of Dublin believing it to be unjust. It appeared that the Irish government expected the "right" decision because it had a prior agreement with the British government. Such an expectation of linkage has nothing whatever to do with notions of justice. As Ian Gow correctly put it to the House of Commons, "the Anglo-Irish Agreement could not be about the administration of justice in one part or any part of the United Kingdom as the judicial system is totally independent of the Government." The government of the Republic of Ireland has no right "to say what sort of verdict a court of law should make".[28] Clearly the political class in Dublin had indeed thought that the Agreement was a political achievement which transcended such limitations. Its anger reflected that belief.

Irish sense of outrage on the one hand was matched by British self-righteousness and annoyance on the other. London had no desire to witness its whole legal order being pilloried for not providing justice to Irish people which, stripped of its particulars, was the Republic's claim. For, given the large numbers of Irish citizens living and working in Great Britain, this was a baseless and spurious charge. Nor did the government like its integrity being attacked by a state with which it had hoped to settle the Ulster crisis quietly. The Anglo-Irish Agreement was designed not to embarrass the British government but to rid it of the embarrassment of Northern Ireland. If Dublin felt the British had failed to deliver what had been secretly arranged before Hillsborough, London equally felt that the Irish were not playing the game in confining their attention exclusively to the six counties. In the end, neither side was prepared to allow the crisis to deflect from the common purpose of stitching up the unionists. However, Haughey was well aware of the opportunity which the furore over British justice in Ulster and Great Britain had provided. He could now work the Agreement quietly without having to tone down his traditional republicanism. The Irish Prime Minister had been released from the ideological constraints of the Hillsborough settlement without having to deny the immediate value of its provisions. This was proved during his five-day tour of the United States in April 1988 when he attacked British policy in Northern Ireland and called for Irish unity following an all-party constitutional conference (a policy remarkably similar to that advocated by Sinn Fein). On his return to Ireland, Haughey could deny any weakening of support for the Agreement. The cringing response of Sir Geoffrey Howe, the Foreign Secretary, revealed that the Foreign Office at least was prepared to allow Haughey to have his cake and eat it; that there were no lengths to which it was not prepared to go to appease the "patriotism" of Irish nationalists. That acceptance by the Foreign Office completely undermined the original justification for the Agreement, namely that it would encourage a new responsibility on the part of Irish nationalism by giving it some limited institutionalised form. Howe had conveniently forgotten that premise.

The consequences of such a pusillanimous attitude on the part of the Foreign Office and the open return of the old-style anti-British animus in Dublin were clearly revealed at the time of the Inquest in Gibraltar on three IRA members killed there by a special unit of the British Army, and in the affair surrounding the attempted extradition of the ex-priest accused of terrorist crimes, Patrick Ryan. Indeed the Ryan Affair was significant in a number of ways. Not only did Patrick Ryan seek refuge in that state which was supposed to be intimately involved with the British Government in combating terrorism; but, revealingly, the Irish political establishment also found no difficulty in exploiting all those sentiments of nationalist grievance which have contributed to the persistence of IRA violence. It could do that and still profess respect for the spirit of the Anglo-Irish Agreement simply because that Agreement has become a political absurdity and the Conference the stage on which that absurdity is played out.

The SDLP talks to Sinn Fein

On 12 January 1988, at the instigation of a clerical third party, John Hume, the leader of constitutional nationalism in Northern Ireland, met Gerry Adams, the leader of Sinn Fein, the political wing of the IRA. This was a remarkable piece of politics by Hume. One reason why the British and Irish governments had signed the Agreement was to help Hume head off the electoral threat of Sinn Fein. The SDLP had not been able to do this directly, because apart from the reworked clichés of the defunct Nationalist Party, it is a party without ideas. Those in catholic politics with ideas had either left it, like Paddy Devlin, or were in the Workers' Party. Even Sinn Fein addressed itself to issues of social and economic disadvantage which the SDLP had relied on others (American Funds, the European Community, Anglo-Irish Agreement) to solve for it. Therefore, it was not out of character for Hume to look to Dublin and London to help him win elections against Sinn Fein. It had not worked. Sinn Fein was practically engaged in the articulation of community grievances, especially in West Belfast, in a way in which the SDLP had never been. It had skilfully woven these grievances into support for its own militant republicanism. The Anglo-Irish Agreement made the SDLP appear even more detached from the realities of Ulster life. Its politics were suspended in the ether of inter-state relations and bottled up in the Conference or locked away in the Secretariat at Maryfield. It now seemed that having been unable to circumvent the Sinn Fein electoral challenge by means of the Agreement, Hume was now prepared to get around its challenge by some sort of understanding. The SDLP had run out of political bolt-holes. In these circumstances there was nothing else it could do but rally around its leader. Seamus Mallon argued that "support is comprehensive, not just within the SDLP but the nationalist community."[29] Others were prepared to give him their backing because, as one put it, "they trust John and his leadership."[30]

On the Sinn Fein side, there was also suspicion. But Adams is no moderate and he has come up through the tough school of IRA militancy. The IRA recognises that he will continue to use the ballot box as a tactic and the Armalite as a strategy. Like Hume, he has the trust of his supporters. Again, like Hume, he had an interest in getting together for talks. Sinn Fein could still boast 80,000 votes in Northern Ireland. But it had performed disastrously in the February elections in the Republic, a campaign on which Adams had staked much of his political reputation. In November the whole IRA campaign had been shaken by the response to the Enniskillen atrocity. It damaged the credibility of the "freedom" struggle, and for a time it even looked as if internment might be re-imposed. Therefore Adams had a direct interest in salvaging the fortunes of Sinn Fein, and what better way to do it than by formal discussions with the man of pious politics, hailed as the great peace-maker in Ulster – John Hume? Apart from these calculations of self-interest, what were the talks intended to achieve?

Sinn Fein had set out its position for "a permanent cessation of hostilities" in a discussion paper called *A Scenario for Peace*. The central aspects of this scenario were a declaration of intent by a British government to withdraw within its lifetime and the disarming of the RUC and the UDR. (Only when it has left Ireland will Sinn Fein willingly accept British interference. It will continue to expect the British to subsidise Ulster financially in the manner to which it has become accustomed). There seemed to be a great gulf between the purity of this Sinn Fein position on British withdrawal and that of the SDLP. For instance, Adams argued that no Irish politician "should, intentionally or otherwise, give any credence or respectability to the British claim to ownership of six Irish counties. If Margaret Thatcher wants to maintain the partition of Ireland she should have to do so without our help. International opinion should be focused – not diverted as through the Hillsborough treaty – on the illegitimacy of the British claim." That statement was a direct attack on Hume's strategy, which Adams summed up as "SDLP sponsorship of various British experiments to internalise the partitionist set-up" in Northern Ireland.[31] Adams is astute enough to know that it was the IRA campaign which had delivered the Anglo-Irish Agreement to the

SDLP. He is also astute enough to understand that the scenario for peace is unlikely to be realised in the near future. If Sinn Fein is to maintain the non-negotiability of its demands, then it must be prepared to countenance a protracted war stretching into the next century. Thus there might be mileage in taking some short cut with the help of Hume. It might be possible to devise some pan-nationalist formula which would synthesise the ballot box and the Armalite.

Hume's position is that, in principle, the Anglo-Irish Agreement already embodies a declaration of intent on the part of the British government to withdraw from Ireland. This is a construction which unionists put on the Agreement as well. With suitable encourage-ment – for example, an IRA ceasefire – the British will be only too happy to leave. With the renunciation of violence Sinn Fein would guarantee itself a seat at a new constitutional conference which London and Dublin would be prepared to sponsor. The task of this conference would be to settle the arrangements for the accommodation of the protestant interest in a new Ireland. In that scenario it was of no conse-quence if unionists were outraged. There would be enough pressure from the two governments, from world opinion and crucially from within unionist ranks to ensure an agreement which would give nation-alists all they want. In other words, Hume had been intimating that killing protestants was now dysfunctional to the goal of unity which both the SDLP and the IRA share.[32] Significantly, talk of a new consti-tutional conference to determine the relationships between the people of Ireland links together the statements of Haughey on his American tour, the latest addition to the "healing process" outlined by Hume and the proposition of *A Scenario for Peace*. That is why the politics of a ceasefire had become so crucial to the SDLP.

Thus another of the ironies of contemporary Ulster politics is revealed. For years the SDLP line has been that there can be no security solution to the Northern Ireland crisis. There must be a political (read: nationalist) solution. Now that Hume can see the British government moving in his direction, it is opportune to change the rules. The framework provided by Hillsborough enables nation-alism to define the true problem as a security problem, and there is enough war-weariness within certain sections of unionism to allow this redefinition to take place. Protestant church leaders, unlike the catholic clergy, are not very good at politics. For a long time they have subscribed to the security and peace thesis, thinking that this would be within the United Kingdom. They have not observed the subtle rede-finition which has taken place since November 1985. A security solution is now being mooted within the "totality of relationships" in Ireland. Equally there are certain well-meaning but naive unionists who have made the same error. The Enniskillen atrocity was an indication that the IRA believed that the protestants of Ulster had come to accept any sectarian outrage perpetrated against them; and that the British government would do nothing to protect its own citizens. Despite all the ink which was spilled condemning Enniskillen, and despite all the speeches of sympathy, the IRA is probably right. The massacre has been of great use to Irish nationalism. It helped divert attention away from the constitutional right of unionists to remain citizens of the United Kingdom to a pious search for an end to violence.

This was helped by the attitude of some prominent political figures. For instance, Raymond Ferguson argued that the problem facing unionists was nothing less than how to survive in the long term. They had to find out which constitutional arrangements they should support which would best protect their persons and property.[33] If that is the case, then the IRA has already provided Ferguson with his answer. It will keep on killing until there is a united Ireland or until such time as unionists are prepared to trade security for such a dramatic quali-fication of the Union that unity could not be far off. John Hume's position is that that time has now come. If the IRA were to stop the violence, and the unionists were brought to the negotiating table, they would be easy meat. If security, survival and the protestant interest (whatever that is) are all that remains of unionism then, the game is indeed up. For if it were possible for Hume to bring off an IRA cessation of hostilities, unionist politicians would very quickly find their position undermined.

As it turned out, Hume's manoeuvres, his *pas de deux* with Adams, did not produce the immediate hoped-for results. But for someone who, later that year, was to denounce the IRA as "fascists" the substance of the talks revealed that the SDLP leader happened to share much nationalist common ground with those same "fascists". What Hume had failed to convince the Sinn Fein leadership of was the role of the British Government in the present crisis. For him the British Government is now "neutral" on the question of Ulster's consti-tutional future. A ceasefire would be the key to transform that neutra-lity into active diplomatic and political pressure for Irish unity. That interpretation Adams was unable to accept. For the Provisionals Britain can never be neutral: it *is* the problem. The pan-nationalist political agitation which both Hume and the IRA want can not, according to this analysis, be a substitute for the armed struggle. It must be a complement to it. On this point the talks stalled and collapsed. However, the idea of a pan-nationalist front, with or without the "armed struggle", has become a part of the anti-Union agenda.

Where does this leave unionist politics as the Anglo-Irish Agreement grinds on into its second three-year period of operation? First, it reveals clearly the glaring weakness of the analysis of the advocates of regional autonomy, a spectrum of opinion running from the Charter Group through the Campaign for a Devolved Parliament to the Task Force. There is no hope whatever of the SDLP agreeing to accept some Ulster "identity" or a new Northern Ireland based on a system of devolved, cross-community government. By the Spring of 1988 the word had gone out that the SDLP had no "ideological commitment" to devolution. Of course it never did have. Devolution, which was to be for unionists an end in itself, was always for the SDLP a means to a united Ireland. The Agreement has so raised nationalist expectations that even devolution within the Agreement is hardly likely to satisfy it. And as long as Haughey remains in office and his influence permeates the policy of Fianna Fail, the SDLP have no reason to accommodate the *unionist* tradition. It is merely prepared to speak of the *protestant* tradition. Unionists can only expect "full-blooded" devolution to be up for negotiation as part of a wider settlement in Ireland and a new relationship between London and Dublin. Even then, there is a strong possibility that the SDLP would collapse any arrangement after a few years in order to push for greater unity. There is little evidence that unionist politicians would have the ability to prevent them from doing so.

Secondly, unionists must resist being rushed into some fancy franchise. There is no obligation on them to participate in the attenuation of the Union despite all the rhetoric blowing from Whitehall, journalists and academic analysts urging them to do so. Unionists must continue to make the case for the Union and avoid the reduction of their position to religion, identity or security. This is not an easy task and requires an intelligent advocacy at a number of different levels. Such an observation returns us to the theme of the opening Chapter. The tactics of resistance to the claims of Irish nationalism are pointless without a strategy to gain what some have called the "moral high ground", but what is better termed the ideological initiative. It now seems clear that this will not be achieved on the basis of the old identity and that the idea of the Union must be saved from unionist politics. Indeed the only real advances which have been made in defence of the idea of the Union, of an inclusive, liberal notion of the state have been made not by unionist politicians but by those advancing the cause of equal citizenship. Despite the emergence of differences of emphasis and personality, those advocating the extension of British party politics to Northern Ireland – CEC, Institute of Representative Government, Campaign for Conservative Representation, the Campaign for Labour Representation, local Social Democrats – have done more to construct a positive, non-sectarian alternative to the violent diviseness of political life than anyone else.

NOTES

1. E.Junger, *On the Marble Cliffs* (London: Penguin Books, 1983), pp. 68–70.
2. *Belfast Telegraph*, 5 March 1987.
3. *News Letter*, 28 May 1987.
4. Ibid., 14 May 1987.
5. *Fortnight*, July/August 1987.
6. Ibid.
7. *News Letter*, 22 June 1987.
8. Joint Unionist Task Force, *An End to Drift*, 16 June 1987.
9. *Fortnight*, Sept. 1987.
10. *News Letter*, 9 July 1987.
11. Ibid., 1 Aug. 1987.
12. *Belfast Telegraph*, 26 June 1987.
13. Ibid., 15 July 1987.
14. *News Letter*, 9 July 1987.
15. *Fortnight*, Sept. 1987.
16. *News Letter*, 10 Aug. 1987.
17. *News Letter*, 24 Nov. 1987.
18. *Ulster*, April 1988.
19. *News Letter*, 5 Dec. 1987.
20. Ibid., 2 Oct. 1985.
21. *Belfast Telegraph*, 18 Dec. 1987.
22. *Irish Times*, 27 April 1987.
23. See Campaign for a Devolved Parliament, *A Better Deal Together*, March 1988.
24. *News Letter*, 28 Sept. 1987.
25. *Irish Times*, 28 Sept. 1987.
26. *Belfast Telegraph*, 2 Nov. 1987.
27. *Irish Times*, 29 Jan. 1988.
28. *News Letter*, 30 Jan. 1988.
29. *News Letter*, 13 Jan. 1988.
30. *Fortnight*, May 1988.
31. Ibid., Jan. 1988.
32. Ibid., May. 1988.
33. *News Letter*, 23 April 1988.

7

CONCLUSION

This very brief conclusion stays comfortably within the bounds of a suitably reflective and summary concern. It tries to draw out some consequences of the theoretical understanding outlined in Chapter 1, the assumptions of which have been a consistent thread in the argument of this book. The argument in Chapter 1 was that the character of unionism was not to be understood in terms of "nationality assumptions"; that it had little to do with the idea of the nation, and everything to do with the idea of the state. The idea of the Union is a very pure political doctrine in the sense that it is concerned, almost exclusively, with issues of right and citizenship. *Unionism* has its large share of bigots and sectarians and religious fundamentalists. But to imply that the *idea* of the Union is subordinate to the "supremacy" of loyalists or that it is just the political superstructure of evangelical protestantism is to indulge in analytical inversion. Rather, to support the Union is to embrace a political allegiance the nature of which is to allow one to express whatever cultural values or identity one wishes. This is precisely the sort of ideal which nationalism has tried to appropriate but simply cannot realise. The engines of nationalist propaganda, which find their echoes in the political establishment in London, have tried to convince the world that the idea of the Union is a lost cause. However, as T.S. Eliot was fond of arguing, there is no such thing as a lost cause for there is no such thing as a gained cause. Part of the purpose of this book has been to convince those who are susceptible to being convinced that there is some life in the Union yet.

The idea of the Union is properly one which transcends such outdated concepts as nationalism. As Parekh has put it, modern states are "by their very nature composed of different races, religions and cultures, and necessarily multi-national. Nationhood is not at all a practicable ideal for them. Nor is it a desirable ideal, for the glory of the modern state consists in creating a non-natural or non-biological basis of unity and uniting people with nothing in common save the state itself." The principle of the modern British state, fully and democratically applied in Northern Ireland, is therefore appropriate to an amelioration of the current crisis, for it in no way aspires to attain the "regressive and inherently impracticable goal of nationhood".[1] Far from nationalist "struggles" in Ulster being compatible with the experience of "black Britons" or any other minority; far from nationalism being the suitably progressive cause for the *bien pensants* to rally

behind, it is the idea of the state which is imbedded obscurely but nonetheless deeply within unionism which addresses the common problem
of equality of rights and citizenship within a just political order. It has
also been the purpose of this book to try to draw out some of the consequences of that idea.

Irish nationalism is fully exercised by the issue of identity, with
degrees of nationhood defined in cultural as well as political terms. It
is not concerned with the autonomous principles of the modern state
but with the absolute justice of claims made on the basis of ethnic
community, "an Irish imagined community" complex, rich and
emotional, celebrated in art, language and religion. The Irish
Republic embodies this notion of identity in state form and has
constructed a political order around those principles. Before the Anglo-
Irish Agreement was signed, the Republican state made some pretence
to embrace all the people of the island of Ireland within its exclusive
definition of identity. (This has often been dignified with the title of
"Ireland's unfinished business", a nationalist notion which again
finds its echoes in the whispering galleries of Whitehall. But insofar as
that "unfinished business" happens to concern flesh and blood,
inconveniently human and resistant Ulster folk who refuse to be
"finished"; and insofar as that "unfinished business" is of the same
nasty cloth as the virulent fanaticism of inter-war Europe, then it
would be better left "unfinished".) After the Agreement, the claim of
"unfinished business" cannot be made seriously or honestly. As we
argued in Chapter 3, the Agreement establishes the particularity of
Irish nationalism as a *political ideology*. As a political expression, it has
defined itself as being only concerned with the satisfaction of catholic
demands and interests in Northern Ireland in particular and Ireland in
general. It has been convicted of such exclusiveness by its own authoritative and respectable advocates – the SDLP in Ulster and the vast
majority of the political establishment in Dublin. That modern
admission of the incorrigible sectarianism of Irish nationalism
contradicts flatly all the musings about pluralistic Irelands so prevalent
at the time of the Forum Report, so common in the moralisations of the
leader columns of the *Irish Times*. Those who support the Union should
give at least two cheers for Hillsborough for revealing that clearly as
never before. Sinn Fein and some Fianna Fail members – to the
credit, one supposes, of their own ideological purity and
consistency – have refused to acknowledge the legitimacy of the
Agreement on a principled basis (unlike those unprincipled advocates
of the Agreement in the media, academia and public life who want the
best of both worlds). But then no one could ever accuse the IRA or their
fellow-travellers of being interested in the unionist "ethos" or of
having the slightest regard for liberal sensitivities.

If one wishes to salvage some rational purpose (and self-esteem in London and Dublin) from the experience of the period since November 1985, then one must start by acknowledging the dramatic failure of the Agreement to achieve its stated objectives. The Hillsborough process has been a dead end. It has merely compounded the vicious animosities in Northern Ireland. This fact has been accepted by both protestants and catholics alike. In a poll published in the spring of 1988 in the journal *Fortnight*, 81 per cent of catholics believed that the Anglo-Irish Agreement had done nothing to benefit the "nationalist community", and 94 per cent of protestants believed that it had done nothing to benefit the "unionist community". Only 4 per cent of both religions felt that it gave any hope for the future in Northern Ireland. These are not rogue findings, but have been confirmed in a number of subsequent polls. Insofar as evidence can ever disprove a theory of politics this response would seem perfectly conclusive. Of course the intellectual giants within the SDLP have been trying to use this alienation from their own endeavours to encourage a strengthening and a deepening of the Hillsborough process – despite the survey evidence that less than 25 per cent of Ulster catholics have any interest in a united Ireland.[2] But that is just one more indication of the SDLP's lack of integrity, its ideological decadence.

The signing of the Agreement by the British government represents a policy which Lord Salisbury once described as a "fatal vice", a policy of "buying off the barbarians". In its efforts to defeat the IRA and at the same time to help extricate itself from the responsibility of properly governing Northern Ireland, London attempted to "buy off" the physical force barbarism of Irish nationalism by making constitutional concessions to the claims of Hume and the Dublin political establishment. But this was not an extraordinary action on the part of the British government. Rather it has been in the character of its whole approach to the current crisis. As Salisbury was well aware in his own day, the lack of firm will by the state to assert its sovereignty and act according to right takes "the heart out of defence; it dissolves cohesion; it splits up an organised society into a mob of struggling interests, the idea that the convictions of politicians are never stable, that under adequate pressure every resistance will give way, every political profession will be obsequiously re-cast, is fatal to the existence of either confidence or respect."[3] That has been the London style, and it has had nothing but predictably disastrous consequences for stability in Northern Ireland. It has also diverted attention away from the real and pressing need for Northern Ireland's position within the United Kingdom to be "normalised". That cannot be done by holding out the enticement of "full-blooded" devolution, which only encourages unionist atavism while providing the SDLP with an effective veto on political progress. It can only be done by acknowledging fully the claims of Ulster people to equal citizenship within the United Kingdom – and acting upon that acknowledgement.

The justice of that position is already implied in and intimated by the current practice of protestant politics. The same applies to catholic politics. For instance, the advocacy of increased government financial aid for West Belfast, which is fully justified in terms of what Ralf Dahrendorf has called the "life chances" of modern citizenship, simply stressed the dependence of all Ulster people on the proper management of the economy and the re-distribution of wealth by the British state (even though the SDLP sometimes tries to confuse this with its flirtation with EEC grants and American funds). In other words, Ulster catholics may appreciate that they are members of one Irish nation. But for all practical purposes the majority are willing to accept the reality and the benefit of British citizenship in a formal sense. They are prepared to accept that there are two states on the island of Ireland. And insofar as the idea of the nation is concerned with the cultural identity of a people, their religion, music, sport, language, education and so on, they know that there has never been any serious disability to prevent nationalists from affirming it. Nothing stops Ulster catholics from holding an Irish passport, competing in international sporting events for the Republic, sending their children to a "nationalist" school, watching Irish television or engaging in any number of relevant activities which would reflect their "ethos". The reason is that Ulster catholics live within a state which embraces the spirit of liberal pluralism. The British state can afford to do this precisely because it is not fixated by nationality assumptions. The contrast with the reality, not the image, of the Republic could not be more stark. The Irish state does not want to embrace diversity because diversity is at odds with its very rationale – the construction of a homogeneous, confessional political order. There is no evidence that it wishes to be anything else and no one, certainly not London, will ever convince it that it ought to change. The Republic is right. That is what Irish sovereignty is all about. But it is insupportable that this narrow *political* idea should be invested with the joint authority of deciding the public policy of an integral part of the British state.

In sum, at the level of civil society there is no obstacle in the way of the cultivation of the idea of an Irish nation. This is fully compatible with the acceptance of two states in the island of Ireland, two states which ought to accord to each other full recognition of sovereign authority. That this has not been achieved has been a result of the Irish Republic's historical political immaturity. The contrast between the ideological disposition of Unionist Ulster and Nationalist Ireland between 1920 and 1972 could not be clearer. The Unionist state was concerned to defend the integrity of constitutional arrangements, to achieve an assurance from both London and Dublin that state boundaries would be recognised and respected. Nationalist Ireland made grievance and discontent into its very political essence. It was not interested in political boundaries accepted and agreed by negotiation. It was, and remains, concerned with the ideological boundary of an "imaginary" Irish *Volk*, a boundary miraculously identical with the geographical limits of the island of Ireland. That has been a magnificent obsession but has never been intelligent or practicable. It is a project which does not and cannot include unionists. They are merely an obstacle. And you do not reason with an obstacle. You either circumvent it (as the Agreement tries to do), or you blast it out of the way (as the IRA continues to try to do). Neither has it very much to offer the Ulster catholic beyond the consolation of a common rhetoric. As Dennis Kennedy has revealed, the contribution of Nationalist Ireland to the tragedy of Northern Ireland has been a significant one.[4] The historical refusal of the British state to take seriously its responsibilities to govern Northern Ireland properly has contributed in equal measure to that tragedy.

What is to be done? Paul Bew and Henry Patterson have argued for the conditions in which there could be a "greater expression of the relatively secular and modernising aspects" of unionism, namely through "greater access to mainstream British politics for those who desire it".[5] That would be a start, not just for traditional unionists, but for Ulster catholics as well. As the Provisional IRA and their fellow-travellers in Northern Ireland and in the rest of the United Kingdom try to monopolise the cause of civil rights in Ulster, it is perhaps worthwhile to recall two key slogans of the late 1960s. Civil Rights campaigners marched to the claims of "British Rights for British Citizens" and "One Man, One Vote".

For Catholics, the first was a repudiation of their traditional nationalist political leadership, a leadership which, because it could not have everything (a united Gaelic Ireland), was quite happy to settle for very little within Northern Ireland. All the grievances which arose from this self-imposed political exile were actually functional to its view of the world, namely that catholics could not get justice under British (or surrogate British) rule. The claim for full British rights was a demand to overthrow that demoralising and pathetic policy and to breach the constitutional quarantine which had been placed around Northern Ireland politics by Westminster in 1920. This demand, of course, was double-edged. Positively, it represented a progressive strategy to admit Northern Ireland fully into the life of the British state, and as such had a fund of protestant support. Negatively, it was used by some as a simple tactic to foment unrest within Northern Ireland as a prelude to fulfilling the long-term aim of Hibernia Irredenta. The hijacking of the Civil Rights Movement by the IRA (the term used by Bishop Cahal Daly) does not prove that the latter was always the reality, as Unionist politicians now claim and then acted upon; it merely reveals that an historic opportunity was lost to normalise Ulster's political relationships with the rest of the United Kingdom. It is a lesson which should be taken to heart by the party leaders at Westminster two decades later.

The second demand was more parochial in its scope and, given the minute powers of local government in Northern Ireland today, is of merely historical interest. However the principle behind the slogan is still a live issue. The principle is that casting a vote should have some purpose and some value, for otherwise political alienation is likely to set in and corrode the civilities of public life. The gross disparity between the democratic act of casting a ballot in an election and the outcome of government policy to which one is subjected brings the democratic process itself into disrepute. That clear disparity in Northern Ireland, once confined to catholic politics, now includes all political activity in the Province. It helps explain in large part the virulence and persistence of the Troubles.

Twenty years on, and one might have reason to despair at the sameness of the political landscape. Nationalist politicians still seem more interested in a Gaelic Ireland than in the welfare of their own voters. Having encouraged the British government to sign the Anglo-Irish Agreement as a means to defeat militaristic nationalism, Hume and his constitutionalist nationalists sat down to talk with the political wing of the IRA about the best means of getting the British out of Ireland. An interesting revelation from those talks was the general understanding that economic and welfare issues were to be a useful tactic for nationalist politics but clearly subordinated to the goal of ''self-determination'' for the Irish people. As anyone with even the most elementary grasp of economics can appreciate, British ''disengagement'' would simply mean that everyone, protestant and catholic, northerner and southerner, would be much worse off. Twenty years on and the futility of voting is plain to all with eyes to see. A vote for a unionist Party has no impact at all on the Northern Ireland Office, and a nationalist vote is hardly of significance to Mr. Haughey. The slogan for the end of the 1980s ought to be ''No Person, No Vote''.

Beneath this dismal landscape, the contours of which have a grim familiarity and even comfort for British ministers (after all, they have helped to shape it), seismic movements may be detected. They are movements fed by the same idealism and vision of opportunity as those which motivated the honest campaigners twenty years ago. A recent opinion poll confirms dissident trends detected across the sterile political fault lines. The poll indicates the way forward which can make a reality of the claims to "British Rights for British Citizens" and "One Man, One Vote". The largest percentage of those surveyed – 35 per cent of catholics and protestants – wants integration with the rest of the United Kingdom on an equal basis. To give meaning to that integration, 57 per cent of respondents want to have the possibility, at present denied to them, to join and vote for the main British political parties. In other words, they want to exercise their right of citizenship to have a say in and an influence over the policies of state which affect their everyday lives.[6]

Here is the real opportunity which must not be missed as it was missed in 1968. The political parties in the mainland United Kingdom must not shirk their responsibility to the electors of Northern Ireland. The party hacks, the Tadpoles and Tapers, have not only a moral duty to fulfil. Happily there are votes and seats to be had (one-third of the poll). Nor would such a political opportunity deny anyone's "ethos" (whatever Hume may mean by that term). But it would allow the citizens of Ulster the chance to choose between the programmes held out to them by nationalist and unionist parties and the alternatives of Left, Right and Centre, which determine their material welfare. From that electoral relationship both the mainland parties and the electors of Northern Ireland have something to gain. Equal citizenship in the sphere of party membership must correspond with equal citizenship in terms of economic and social opportunity. This would not constitute an attempt to kill nationalism by kindness. Kindness, like compassion, is not an attribute of states. What is at issue here is right, not largesse or benevolence. Catholics have a right to equal opportunities within Northern Ireland – whatever their political views or national ethos – and both Ulster catholics and protestants have a right to equality of opportunity within the United Kingdom. In making that claim, they link up with the demands of other regions of the state. Such developments would signal, for once, the seriousness of British purpose in Ulster.

But the greatest step towards peace, stability and reconciliation in Ireland would be a reconsideration by the Republican state of its attitude to Irish unity. If the political class in the Republic were fully to acknowledge the distinctive statehood of Northern Ireland as a part of the United Kingdom it would go a long way towards dispelling "neanderthal" unionist attitudes, undermining support for the IRA, and creating the conditions for proper inter-state co-operation between the United Kingdom and the Republic in the island of Ireland. This could be done without in any way denying Irish nationalism as a cultural idea. That would be the basis of a real historic compromise.

NOTES

1. B.Parekh, "The New Right and the Politics of Nationhood" in G.Cohen *et al.*, op. cit., p. 40.
2. *Fortnight*, April 1988.
3. Quoted in P.Smith (ed.), *Lord Salisbury on Politics* (Cambridge: Cambridge University Press, 1972), p. 361.
4. Dennis Kennedy, *The Widening Gulf* (Belfast: Blackstaff Press, 1988).
5. P.Bew and H.Patterson, in P.Teague (ed.), op. cit., p. 56.
6. "What Ulster Thinks", *Belfast Telegraph*, 5 and 6 October 1988.

INDEX